Ultimate Guide to the
MATH ACT®

Created by
Richard F. Corn

√mpb

Math Prep Books
A Wyatt-MacKenzie Imprint

Ultimate Guide to the MATH ACT®
Created by Richard F. Corn

FIRST EDITION

ISBN: 978-1-936214-60-0

Library of Congress Control Number: 2012946338

Errata for this book may be found at
http://www.mathprepbooks.com/errata.html

Published by Math Prep Books, A Wyatt-MacKenzie Imprint
www.wyattmackenzie.com

Math Prep Books
A Wyatt-MacKenzie Imprint

TABLE OF CONTENTS

PART 2: HOW TO TAKE THE MATH ACT®

1. HOW TO PREPARE FOR THE MATH ACT®

This first part of this book helps you review that math that you need for the ACT®, and the second part of this book shows you how to practice and take the math portion of the ACT®.

If you have more than five weeks to prepare for the ACT® then do as many sections of the Part 1 math review as possible. You should concentrate on the math topics where your knowledge is weakest and/or concentrate on the math topics that appear most often (see Appendix 1 for a list of these). For each math topic, read the lesson, do the homework problems, and study the solutions to the problems that you got wrong or that you could not solve.

If you have less than five weeks to prepare for the ACT® then you should go directly to Part 2 of this book and begin a series of practice tests, following the instructions given in Part 2.

The material in this book has been used by more than 5,000 students and has been field tested over and over again. It is the product of many hours of helping students prepare for the math portion of the ACT®. The lessons and problems in this book are real, in that my students have used them, asked questions about them, and pointed out improvements to be made.

Calculator Tips

Calculator tips appear at various places throughout the book. They are based on the graphing calculators from Texas Instruments, specifically the TI-83 and TI-84. Note that the TI-89 and the TI-Nspire calculators with CAS (computer algebra system) are not permitted on the ACT®.

Feedback and Errata

I am always interested in receiving feedback on this book, in order to make it better for the next group of students who use it. Please send feedback, including any errors you may have discovered, to mathprepbooks@gmail.com.

Errata for this book may be found at http://www.mathprepbooks.com/errata.html. Errors will be posted promptly, as they are discovered and verified.

ACT is a registered trademark of ACT, Inc. which was not involved in the production of, and does not endorse, this book.

PART 1: MATH REVIEW

We now begin a review of the math that is in the syllabus for the ACT® starting with middle school math.

2. PRE-ALGEBRA

This book begins by covering the math that you were supposed to have mastered in middle school. Do not skip this chapter even though you think this is "easy math" because

- You may not have mastered the material at the time you were in middle school
- You saw this so many years ago that you forgot some of it
- It takes practice to get used to the way this material is presented on standardized tests.

Just about every student needs a refresher on pre-algebra, for any combination of the reasons above.

Unit 2.1 Integers, primes and digits

For the purposes of the test, you can think of an integer as any number with all zeros to the right of the decimal. Below are examples:

3 is an integer because it can be written as 3.0000000000

-2 is an integer because it can be written as -2.000000000

0 is an integer because it can be written as 0.0000000000

$1/2$ is not an integer because it can be written as 0.500000000

$\sqrt{2}$ is not an integer because it can be written as 1.4142135.

π is not an integer because it can be written as 3.1415926.

Formally, we can write the set of integers as $\{...,-3,-2,-1,0,1,2,3,...\}$.

Substitution rules

Substitution is a technique that is commonly used to solve problems on standardized tests. When certain words or phrases appear in a problem, it is often helpful to substitute specific values in order to solve the problem. Below is a table of popular phrases and the values that should be substituted.

Phrase	Substitute
Integer	0
Positive integer	1
Negative integer	-1
Even integer	0
Odd integer	1
Consecutive integers	0, 1, 2, etc.
Consecutive even integers	0, 2, 4, etc.
Consecutive odd integers	1, 3, 5, etc.

There will also be problems on the test where substitution is not appropriate, and where algebra is needed. In those problems, you will use algebraic expressions for the phrases below.

Phrase	Substitute
Integer	n
Even integer	2n
Odd integer	2n+1
Consecutive integers	n, n+1, n+2, etc.
Consecutive even integers	n, n+2, n+4, etc. or 2n, 2n+2, 2n+4, etc.
Consecutive odd integers	n, n+2, n+4, etc. or 2n+1, 2n+3, 2n+5

Primes

A prime number is a positive integer that is divisible by itself and 1. Note that 1 is **not** a prime number. The smallest prime number is 2 and all the other prime numbers are odd. Two is the smallest prime and the only even prime number.

The prime numbers are: {2, 3, 5, 7, 11, 13, 17, 19, 23, ...}

Note that 9 is not prime (it is divisible by 3), 15 is not prime (it is divisible by 3 and 5), and 21 is not prime (it is divisible by 3 and 7). A good exercise is to write down the first 20 or so prime numbers.

Problems on the test will use phrases that involve the word "prime." When you see these phrases, it is often helpful to substitute specific values in order to solve the problem. Below is a table of some popular phrases and the values to be substituted.

Phrase	Substitute
Prime number	2
Even prime	2
Odd prime	3
Consecutive primes	2, 3, 5, etc.

A concept related to prime numbers is called prime factorization. The idea is that any integer (that is not itself a prime) can be expressed as the product of primes. It can be very useful to construct a factor tree for any given number. Below is the factor tree for 210.

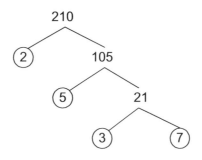

Notice that 210 is an even number. So we divide by two and get 105. The two is circled because two is prime. We notice that 105 is divisible by 5. So we divide by five and get 21. Five is circled because it is prime. The number 21 is divisible by three and seven, which are circled because they are prime.

The prime factorization of 210 is $210 = 2 \cdot 3 \cdot 5 \cdot 7$. The number 210 can be expressed as a product of primes because 210 is not itself prime.

Prime factorization comes in handy later, when adding or subtracting fractions (unit 2.2), finding the common factor (unit 3.4), and factoring polynomials (unit 3.5).

Digits and place value

You may be wondering what this topic is doing in here. Well, the SAT® syllabus has digits and the ACT® syllabus has place value, that's why. Questions on this topic do occur.

Consider the number

$$2345.907$$

It consists of seven digits, ranging from zero through 9. In fact, the set of all possible values for any particular digit appearing in any position is $\{0,1,2,3,4,5,6,7,8,9\}$. The place values are:

2 = the thousands digit

3 = the hundreds digit

4 = the tens digit

5 = the ones or unit digit

9 = the tenths digit

0 = the hundredths digit

7 = the thousandths digit

A common mistake is to choose 3 for hundredths digit instead of 0, or choose 9 for the tens digit instead of 4. This is simple stuff, but it is easy to make a mistake.

Problems on integers, primes and digits (unit 2.1)

1. The sum of the prime factors of 231 is

    (A)   3

    (B)   7

    (C)   11

    (D)   21

    (E)   231

2. How many prime factors are there of the number 15,246 ?

    (A)   2

    (B)   3

    (C)   4

    (D)   5

    (E)   6

3. Which of the following numbers is prime?

    (A)   1

    (B)   55

    (C)   71

    (D)   1617

    (E)   3334

4. The number 509 is prime. What is the next largest prime?

    (A)   510

    (B)   511

    (C)   515

    (D)   519

    (E)   521

5. Including 1 and 50, the number of factors of 50 is:

    (A)   two

    (B)   three

    (C)   four

    (D)   five

    (E)   six

6. If n is an odd integer and $n \neq -1$, then $n+1$ cannot be:

    (A)   positive

    (B)   negative

    (C)   prime

    (D)   zero

    (E)   even

7. If x is a positive integer, what is the smallest possible value of $\dfrac{x+7}{4}$?

    (A)   0

    (B)   1

    (C)   2

    (D)   3

    (E)   4

8. If the sum of three consecutive odd integers is 171, what is the value of the largest integer?

    (A)   27

    (B)   31

    (C)   55

    (D)   59

    (E)   171

9. If the median of five consecutive even integers is 20, what is the value of the smallest integer?

    (A)   16

    (B)   18

    (C)   20

    (D)   22

    (E)   24

10. For the number 4768.325, what is the sum of the tens digit and the tenths digit?

(A)   8

(B)   9

(C)   10

(D)   11

(E)   12

11. If the sum of two prime numbers is odd, one of the numbers must be:

(A)   0

(B)   1

(C)   2

(D)   3

(E)   4

12. The sum of two even integers must always be divisible by

(A)   0

(B)   2

(C)   3

(D)   4

(E)   5

13. If m is an odd integer then $2m+1$ must be:

(A)   odd

(B)   even

(C)   zero

(D)   prime

(E)   none of the above

14. If m is an even integer and n is an odd integer, which expression must be odd?

(A) $2m+n-1$

(B) $m \cdot n$

(C) $m+2n$

(D) $m-n$

(E) $m+2$

15. The sum of seven consecutive integers is zero. What is the value of the smallest integer?

(A)   -3

(B)   -2

(C)   -1

(D)   0

(E)   3

16. If the sum of three integers is odd, which of the statements below must be false?

I.   All three integers are odd.

II.   Only two integers are odd.

III.   Only one integer is odd.

(A)   I only

(B)   II only

(C)   III only

(D)   I and III only

(E)   I, II, and III

17. If the average of four consecutive odd integers is 20, what is the largest integer?

(A)   8

(B)   19

(C)   20

(D)   21

(E)   23

18. If the sum of 105 consecutive integers is 0, what is their median?

(A)   -52

(B)   -1

(C)   0

(D)   1

(E)   52

19. An expression for the product of an even integer and an odd integer is:

(A) n^2

(B) $4n^2 - 1$

(C) $4n^2 + 1$

(D) $4n^2 + 2n$

(E) $4n^2 + 4n + 1$

Solutions to problems on integers, primes and digits (unit 2.1)

1. (D)

$$3 \cdot 7 \cdot 11 = 231$$
$$3 + 7 + 11 = 21$$

2. (C)

The factor tree is:

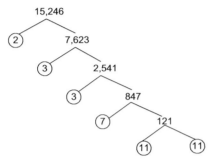

The prime factorization is $2 \cdot 3^2 \cdot 7 \cdot 11^2 = 15,246$

3. (C)

$55 = 5 \cdot 11$, $1617 = 3 \cdot 7^2 \cdot 11$, $3334 = 2 \cdot 1667$

4. (E)

Iterate from 509, skipping the even numbers. $511/7 = 73$, $513/3 = 171$, $515/5 = 103$, $517/11 = 47$, $519/3 = 173$). However 521 is prime.

5. (E)

$50 = 1 \cdot 50, \; 50 = 2 \cdot 25, \; 50 = 5 \cdot 10$

So there are six factors: 1, 2, 5, 10, 25 and 50.

6. (D)

$n + 1$ could be positive if n is positive, negative if n is negative, prime if n=1, always even, but never zero.

7. (C)

The smallest positive integer is 1. So the smallest value of $\dfrac{x+7}{4}$ is $\dfrac{1+7}{4} = 2$.

8. (D)

Set up the equation $n + (n+2) + (n+4) = 171$.

Simplifying gives $3n + 6 = 171$, or $n = 55$. The largest integer is $n + 4 = 55 + 4 = 59$

9. (A)

If the median is 20, then the numbers look like this: 16, 18, 20, 22, 24.

10. (B)

The tens digit is six and the tenths digit is three, 6+3=9.

11. (C)

For the sum to be odd, one of the primes must be even, and the only even prime is 2.

12. (B)

The sum of two evens is even.

13. (A)

Set $m = 1$ and substitute. But be careful because although 3 is prime ($m = 1$), 15 is not ($m = 7$).

14. (D)

Set $m = 0$ and $n = 1$. Then $m - n = -1$, which is odd. The other answer choices produce even results.

15. (A)

$$n + (n+1) + (n+2) + (n+3) + (n+4) + (n+5) + (n+6) = 0$$

Simplifying gives $7n + 21 = 0$, or $n = -3$.

16. (B)

Statement I may be true because 1+1+1=3.
Statement III may be true because 1+0+0=1.
However statement II must be false.

17. (E)

$$n + (n+2) + (n+4) + (n+6) = 80$$
$$4n + 12 = 80, \; n = 17, \; n + 6 = 23$$

18. (C)

If the sum is zero, there must be as many negatives as there are positives. In fact there would be 52 negatives, a zero in the middle, then 52 positives.

19. (D)

An even multiplied by an odd is even. The only answer choice that must be even is (D). Or you could use $2n \cdot (2n+1) = 4n^2 + 2n$

Unit 2.2 Fractions

This unit covers operations on fractions, with some special twists favored on the standardized tests.

Adding and Subtracting

Please remember that **fractions cannot be added or subtracted unless they have the same denominator**, called the common denominator.

Consider a simple case: $\dfrac{1}{2}+\dfrac{2}{7}$. Hopefully you are not thinking that the answer is $\dfrac{1}{2}+\dfrac{2}{7}=\dfrac{1+2}{2+7}=\dfrac{3}{9}=\dfrac{1}{3}$!!!!!
That would be breaking just about every rule in math. (Believe it or not I have seen students do exactly that.) Remember to first convert each fraction so that both fractions have the same denominator, then add or subtract:

$$\frac{1}{2}+\frac{2}{7}=\left(\frac{1}{2}\right)\left(\frac{7}{7}\right)+\left(\frac{2}{7}\right)\left(\frac{2}{2}\right)=\frac{7}{14}+\frac{4}{14}=\frac{7+4}{14}=\frac{11}{14}$$

In this example the common denominator is 14. Although the product of the denominators can always be used, your work will be a bit simpler if you use the least common denominator (LCD). Consider the example of $\dfrac{7}{15}-\dfrac{2}{20}$
You could use 300 as the common denominator:

$$\frac{7}{15}-\frac{3}{20}=\left(\frac{7}{15}\right)\left(\frac{20}{20}\right)-\left(\frac{3}{20}\right)\left(\frac{15}{15}\right)=\frac{140}{300}-\frac{45}{300}=\frac{140-45}{300}=\frac{95}{300}=\frac{19}{60}$$

The drawback to this approach is that you are working with larger numbers, and you have to do some simplification at the end. On the other hand, with the graphing calculator, simplifying fractions is easy using the Math-Frac keys. The key sequence is: $95, \div, 300,$ *math, fract, enter.* So if finding the LCD drives you crazy, you can use this approach together with the calculator.

It is a little easier if you can find the LCD and use that instead. To find the LCD, calculate the prime factorization (see unit 2.1) of each denominator: $15=3\cdot5$ and $20=2^2\cdot5$. Next, make a list of all of the prime factors found in either denominator, and then raise each prime factor to its largest power:

$$LCD=2^2\cdot3^1\cdot5^1=60 .$$

Believe it or not, this technique for finding the LCD always works. But if you only have two fractions to deal with, it is much easier to use Math-Num-lcm keys on the graphing calculator. The key sequence is $math-num-lcm-enter-15-,-60-)-enter$. Now that we found the LCD is 60, we proceed with the subtraction:

$$\frac{7}{15}-\frac{3}{20}=\left(\frac{7}{15}\right)\left(\frac{4}{4}\right)-\left(\frac{3}{20}\right)\left(\frac{3}{3}\right)=\frac{28}{60}-\frac{9}{60}=\frac{19}{60} .$$

You may be wondering if this LCD stuff is worth all the effort. When you are only dealing with two fractions, it may not be. When you are dealing with several fractions it is far better. There are some problems like that at the end of the unit.

It is also necessary to add and subtract fractions involving variables. A simple example would be $\dfrac{3}{x} + \dfrac{y}{2}$. The common denominator would be 2x, and this yields

$$\frac{3}{x} + \frac{y}{2} = \left(\frac{3}{x}\right)\left(\frac{2}{2}\right) + \left(\frac{y}{2}\right)\left(\frac{x}{x}\right) = \frac{6}{2x} + \frac{yx}{2x} = \frac{xy+6}{2x} \ .$$

Multiplying

When multiplying fractions, multiply the numerators together to form the new numerator, and multiply the denominators together to form the new denominator. For example,

$$\left(\frac{2}{3}\right)\left(\frac{5}{7}\right) = \frac{2 \cdot 5}{3 \cdot 7} = \frac{10}{21}$$

The same rule applies to fractions with variables:

$$\left(\frac{x}{3y}\right)\left(\frac{4}{z}\right) = \frac{4x}{3yz}$$

Dividing

When two fractions are to be divided, multiply the fraction in the numerator by the reciprocal of the fraction in the denominator. For example,

$$\left(\frac{2}{3}\right) \div \left(\frac{5}{7}\right) = \left(\frac{2}{3}\right)\left(\frac{7}{5}\right) = \frac{14}{15}$$

The same rule applies to fractions with variables:

$$\left(\frac{x}{3y}\right) \div \left(\frac{4}{z}\right) = \left(\frac{x}{3y}\right)\left(\frac{z}{4}\right) = \frac{xz}{12y}$$

Problems on fractions (unit 2.2)

1. What is the value of $\dfrac{7}{10} - \dfrac{5}{12}$?

   (A)   -1
   (B)   7/24
   (C)   12/22
   (D)   17/60
   (E)   35/120

2. What is the value of $\dfrac{7}{10} + \dfrac{5}{12} - \dfrac{11}{42}$?

   (A)   359/420
   (B)   193/140
   (C)   -1/20
   (D)   11/144
   (E)   118/525

3. What is the value of $\left(\dfrac{3}{5}\right)\cdot\left(\dfrac{-5}{12}\right)$?

   (A)   -2/17
   (B)   -1/4
   (C)   -36/25
   (D)   -15/17
   (E)   3/173.

4. What is the value of $\left(\dfrac{-2}{3}\right)\cdot\left(\dfrac{6}{-11}\right)\cdot\left(\dfrac{3}{2}\right)$?

   (A)   -7/6
   (B)   6/11
   (C)   36/55
   (D)   7/6
   (E)   11/6.

5. What is the value of $\left(\dfrac{3}{5}\right)\div\left(\dfrac{-5}{12}\right)$?

   (A)   -1/4
   (B)   -36/25
   (C)   -4/1
   (D)   -15/60
   (E)   -2/17

6. Simplify $\dfrac{2}{5x^2} - \dfrac{3}{25xy}$

   (A) $7/5x^2y$
   (B) $-1/(5x(x-5y))$
   (C) $(10y-3x)/5x^2y$
   (D) $(10y-3x)/25x^2y$
   (E) $7/(x-5y)$

7. Simplify $\dfrac{x}{1-x} - \dfrac{y}{1-y} = ?$

   (A) $(x+y)/(y-x)$
   (B) $(x-y)/(x^2-2xy+y^2)$
   (C) $(x+y-2xy)/(2-x-y)$
   (D) $(y-x)/(x-y)$
   (E) $(x-y)/(xy-x-y+1)$

8. Simplify $\left(\dfrac{5x^2}{3y}\right)\cdot\left(\dfrac{6y^2}{8x}\right)$

   (A) $5x/4y$
   (B) $20xy/9$
   (C) $4y/5x$
   (D) $20x^3/9y^3$
   (E) $5xy/4$

9. Simplify $\left(\dfrac{5x^2}{3y}\right)\div\left(\dfrac{6y^2}{8x}\right)$

   (A) $5xy/4$
   (B) $20xy/9$
   (C) $4/5xy$
   (D) $20x^3/9y^3$
   (E) $5x/4y$

10. Simplify $\dfrac{y}{x} - \dfrac{x}{y} + \dfrac{3}{xy}$

(A) $\dfrac{y-x+3}{x+y+xy}$

(B) $\dfrac{3}{xy}$

(C) $\dfrac{xy}{3}$

(D) $\dfrac{y-x-3}{xy}$

(E) $\dfrac{y^2-x^2+3}{xy}$

11. Simplify $\left(\dfrac{x}{y}\right) \cdot \left(\dfrac{xz}{y}\right) \cdot \left(\dfrac{yz}{x}\right)$

(A) $\dfrac{x+z(x+y)}{x+2y}$

(B) $\dfrac{z}{xy^2}$

(C) $\left(\dfrac{xz}{y}\right)^2$

(D) $\dfrac{xz^2}{y}$

(E) $\dfrac{xz}{y}$

12. Without a calculator, simplify $\dfrac{3}{\dfrac{5}{2}}$

(A) $6/5$

(B) $5/6$

(C) $15/2$

(D) $2/15$

(E) $6/15$

13. Simplify $\dfrac{x^2-9}{x+1} \div \dfrac{x+3}{x^2-1}$

(A) $\dfrac{x-3}{x-1}$

(B) $\dfrac{x-1}{x-3}$

(C) $\dfrac{(x^2-9)(x+3)}{(x+1)(x^2-1)}$

(D) x^2-4x+3

(E) x^2+2x-3

14. Simplify $\dfrac{x}{x-1} - \dfrac{x}{x+1}$

(A) $\dfrac{2x}{x+1}$

(B) $\dfrac{2x}{x^2-1}$

(C) 0

(D) $\dfrac{-2x}{x^2-1}$

(E) $\dfrac{-2x}{x-1}$

15. The football team had a pretty good season this year, with 2/3 of the games won and 1/9 of the games tied. What was their fraction of losses?

(A) $\dfrac{1}{9}$

(B) $\dfrac{2}{9}$

(C) $\dfrac{3}{9}$

(D) $\dfrac{4}{9}$

(E) $\dfrac{5}{9}$

Solutions to problems on fractions (unit 2.2)

1. (D)

$10 = 2 \cdot 5$ and $12 = 2^2 \cdot 3$. So the LCD is $2^2 \cdot 3 \cdot 5 = 60$. $\quad \dfrac{7}{10} - \dfrac{5}{12} = \dfrac{42}{60} - \dfrac{25}{60} = \dfrac{17}{60}$

2. (A)

$10 = 2 \cdot 5$ and $12 = 2^2 \cdot 3$ and $42 = 2 \cdot 3 \cdot 7$. So the LCD is $2^2 \cdot 3 \cdot 5 \cdot 7 = 420$.

$\dfrac{7}{10} + \dfrac{5}{12} - \dfrac{11}{42} = \dfrac{7 \cdot 42}{420} + \dfrac{5 \cdot 35}{420} - \dfrac{11 \cdot 10}{420} = \dfrac{359}{420}$

3. (B)

$\left(\dfrac{3}{5}\right)\left(\dfrac{-5}{12}\right) = \left(\dfrac{3}{1}\right)\left(\dfrac{-1}{12}\right) = \left(\dfrac{1}{1}\right)\left(\dfrac{-1}{4}\right) = \dfrac{-1}{4}$

4. (B)

$\left(\dfrac{-2}{3}\right) \cdot \left(\dfrac{6}{-11}\right) \cdot \left(\dfrac{3}{2}\right) = \dfrac{-36}{-66} = \dfrac{6}{11}$

5. (B)

$\left(\dfrac{3}{5}\right) \div \left(\dfrac{-5}{12}\right) = \left(\dfrac{3}{5}\right)\left(\dfrac{12}{-5}\right) = \dfrac{36}{-25} = -\dfrac{36}{25}$

6. (D)

$\dfrac{2}{5x^2} - \dfrac{3}{25xy} = \dfrac{2(5y)}{25x^2 y} - \dfrac{3x}{25x^2 y} = \dfrac{10y - 3x}{25x^2 y}$

7. (E)

$\dfrac{x}{1-x} - \dfrac{y}{1-y} = \dfrac{x(1-y) - y(1-x)}{(1-x)(1-y)} = \dfrac{x-y}{xy - x - y + 1}$

8. (E)

$\left(\dfrac{5x^2}{3y}\right)\left(\dfrac{6y^2}{8x}\right) = \dfrac{5 \cdot 6x^2 y^2}{3 \cdot 8xy} = \dfrac{30x^2 y^2}{24xy} = \dfrac{5xy}{4}$

9. (D)

$\left(\dfrac{5x^2}{3y}\right) \div \left(\dfrac{6y^2}{8x}\right) = \left(\dfrac{5x^2}{3y}\right)\left(\dfrac{8x}{6y^2}\right) = \dfrac{40x^3}{18y^3} = \dfrac{20x^3}{9y^3}$

10. (E)

$\dfrac{y}{x} - \dfrac{x}{y} + \dfrac{3}{xy} = \left(\dfrac{y}{x}\right)\left(\dfrac{y}{y}\right) - \left(\dfrac{x}{y}\right)\left(\dfrac{x}{x}\right) + \dfrac{3}{xy} = \dfrac{y^2 - x^2 + 3}{xy}$

11. (D)

$\left(\dfrac{x}{y}\right) \cdot \left(\dfrac{xz}{y}\right) \cdot \left(\dfrac{yz}{x}\right) = \dfrac{x^2 yz^2}{xy^2} = \dfrac{xz^2}{y}$

12. (A)

$\dfrac{\dfrac{3}{5}}{\dfrac{2}{2}} = \left(\dfrac{\dfrac{3}{1}}{\dfrac{5}{2}}\right)\left(\dfrac{\dfrac{2}{5}}{\dfrac{2}{5}}\right) = \dfrac{\dfrac{6}{5}}{1} = \dfrac{6}{5}$

13. (D)

$\dfrac{x^2 - 9}{x+1} \div \dfrac{x+3}{x^2 - 1} = \dfrac{(x+3)(x-3)}{x+1} \cdot \dfrac{(x+1)(x-1)}{x+3}$

$\qquad = (x-3)(x-1) = x^2 - 4x + 3$

14. (B)

$\dfrac{x}{x-1} - \dfrac{x}{x+1} = \left(\dfrac{x}{x-1}\right)\left(\dfrac{x+1}{x+1}\right) - \left(\dfrac{x}{x+1}\right)\left(\dfrac{x-1}{x-1}\right)$

$\qquad = \dfrac{x^2 + x - (x^2 - x)}{(x-1)(x+1)} = \dfrac{2x}{x^2 - 1}$

15. (B)

$\dfrac{2}{3} + \dfrac{1}{9} + x = 1$

$\dfrac{6}{9} + \dfrac{1}{9} + x = 1$

$x = \dfrac{2}{9}$

Unit 2.3 Mixed numbers and remainders

The standardized tests take a different view of mixed numbers than the view taken in most middle schools.

The skill that is most likely to be tested is converting between improper fractions and mixed numbers, with an emphasis on finding the remainder.

Converting improper fractions to mixed numbers

An improper fraction is a fraction where the numerator is larger than the denominator, for example $\dfrac{7}{4}$. The improper fraction is converted to a mixed number by dividing to get a quotient and a remainder.

$$\frac{7}{4} = \frac{4+3}{4} = \frac{4}{4} + \frac{3}{4} = 1 + \frac{3}{4} = 1\frac{3}{4}$$

In this example, the quotient is 1 (the whole number part) and the remainder is 3 (the numerator of the fraction part of the mixed number).

In the real world, you would not do conversions in this way. You would use a calculator. First, divide 4 into 7

$$7 \div 4 = 1.75$$

So now we know that the whole number is 1. To get the remainder,

$$\text{remainder} = 7\text{-}(1 \cdot 4) = 7 - 4 = 3 \, .$$

This gives

$$\frac{7}{4} = 1\frac{3}{4} \, .$$

Try this calculator technique with a more difficult example, say $\dfrac{386}{28}$

$$386 \div 28 = 13.7857$$

So now we know that the whole number is 13. To get the remainder,

$$\text{remainder} = 386\text{-}(13 \cdot 28) = 386 - 364 = 22$$

This gives

$$\frac{386}{28} = 13\frac{22}{28} \, .$$

Terminology: When the remainder is zero, the numerator is said to be divisible by the denominator. For example,

$$\frac{8}{4} = \frac{8+0}{4} = \frac{8}{4} + \frac{0}{4} = 2\frac{0}{4} = 2$$

In the example above, 8 is divisible by 4 because when 8 is divided by 4 the remainder is zero.

Converting mixed numbers to improper fractions

Of course you are also expected to be able to convert a mixed number to an improper fraction.

$$2\frac{5}{8} = 2 + \frac{5}{8} = \frac{16}{8} + \frac{5}{8} = \frac{16+5}{8} = \frac{21}{8}$$

Another way to think of this is

$$2\frac{5}{8} = \frac{(2 \cdot 8) + 5}{8} = \frac{16+5}{8} = \frac{21}{8}$$

This is a better way to convert a mixed number to an improper fraction (it is faster and makes better use of the calculator). Take the whole number, multiply it by the denominator, then add the product to the numerator.

Word problems involving remainders

There is a class of problems on standardized tests that I call "remainder problems" because they are based on converting an improper fraction to a mixed number. Although there are several problems of this type in unit 6.3, it is worth taking a look at them now. A good example is:

Sarah wanted to make jump ropes for herself and her friends, so she went to a store and purchased 100 feet of rope. If each jump rope is 7 feet long, how many jump ropes could Sarah make and how many feet of rope will she have left over?

Begin by dividing the 100 total feet of rope by each of the 7 foot lengths. Using the calculator, this gives

$$\frac{100}{7} = 14.2857$$

So now we know that there will be 14 jump ropes. To get the amount of rope left over:

$$\text{rope left over} = 100 - (14 \cdot 7) = 100 - 98 = 2$$

Mathematically what we just did was

$$\frac{100}{7} = 14\frac{2}{7} \ .$$

Two is the remainder, which in this problem represents the amount of rope left over.

Problems on mixed numbers and remainders (unit 2.3)

1. What is the remainder when 287 is divided by 5?

    (A)   2

    (B)   4

    (C)   20

    (D)   57

    (E)   285

2. What is the remainder when 980 is divided by 28?

    (A)   0

    (B)   1

    (C)   2

    (D)   3

    (E)   35

3. The mixed number $16\frac{7}{8}$ is equivalent to:

    (A)   23/8

    (B)   31/8

    (C)   112/8

    (D)   128/8

    (E)   135/8

4. If a cage can hold 8 chickens, how many cages will be needed to hold 300 chickens?

    (A)   36

    (B)   37

    (C)   38

    (D)   39

    (E)   2400

5. If n is an integer greater than 100, what is the smallest value that n could be if n is divisible by 4?

    (A)   100

    (B)   101

    (C)   102

    (D)   103

    (E)   104

6. If n is a two digit integer that is divisible by 3, then the units digit of n cannot be:

    (A)   0

    (B)   1

    (C)   2

    (D)   3

    (E)   None of the above

7. If an integer is divisible by 5 then

    I.   It must equal a power of 5.

    II.   One of its prime factors must be 5.

    III.   Its units digit must be 0 or 5.

    (A)   I only

    (B)   II only

    (C)   III only

    (D)   II and III only

    (E)   I, II, and III

8. When an integer is divided by 7 its remainder is 3. The value of that integer could be:

    (A)   13

    (B)   17

    (C)   23

    (D)   27

    (E)   33

9. When an integer is divided by 6 its remainder is 3. The value of that integer cannot be

    (A)   3

    (B)   27

    (C)   39

    (D)   47

    (E)   57

10. The night before Halloween, Kyle sorted 1,000 pieces of candy into bags, with each bag containing 12 pieces of candy. If Kyle is allowed to eat any candy left over, how many pieces could he eat?

(A)   0

(B)   4

(C)   8

(D)   16

(E)   83

11. Mary has $25 to make copies of her flyer. If each copy costs 8 cents, how many copies can she make?

(A)   3

(B)   4

(C)   5

(D)   31

(E)   312

12. To get a discount, Bill has to buy at least $50 of newspapers. If each newspaper costs 75 cents, how many newspapers must he buy to get the discount?

(A)   37

(B)   38

(C)   66

(D)   67

(E)   667

13. Emily's Mom sends her into the store with $10, telling her to buy as many apples as possible. If each apple costs 80 cents, how much change (in cents) will Emily receive?

(A)   2

(B)   4

(C)   40

(D)   50

(E)   80

14. When an integer is divided by 8, the remainder is 3. The value of that integer cannot be

(A)   3

(B)   19

(C)   24

(D)   67

(E)   99

15. At a summer camp, 50 campers are assigned to red, white or blue teams, in that order. To which team is the last camper assigned?

(A)   red

(B)   white

(C)   blue

(D)   red or white

(E)   red or blue

16. A certain clock strikes once every 20 minutes. If the clock struck 20 more times after it had struck at midnight, what time is it now?

(A)   5:20 AM

(B)   6:00 AM

(C)   6:20 AM

(D)   6:40 AM

(E)   8:00 PM

17. A certain sequence is

A, B, D, C, A ,B, D, C, A, B, D, C, etc.

What is the 90th term in the sequence?

(A)   A

(B)   B

(C)   C

(D)   D

(E)   Cannot be determined

Solutions to problems on mixed numbers and remainders (unit 2.3)

1. (A)

Use your calculator to find $287/5 = 57.4$. Now we know that the whole number is 57. Next find the remainder $287 - (57 \cdot 5) = 287 - 285 = 2$.

2. (A)

Use your calculator to find $980/28 = 35.0$. The remainder is zero.

3. (E)

$$16\frac{7}{8} = \frac{(16 \cdot 8) + 7}{8} = \frac{128 + 7}{8} = \frac{135}{8}$$

4. (C)

$300/8 = 37.5$ cages. With only 37 cages, 4 chickens would be running loose, and we can't have that!

5. (E)

Although 100 is divisible by 4, you cannot use it because the integer must be <u>greater than</u> 100. The next one is 104 because $104/4 = 26$.

6. (E)

(A) is no good because $30/3=10$. (B) is no good because $21/3=7$. (C) is no good because $42/3=14$. (D) is no good because $33/3=11$.

7. (D)

I. is false because 10 is divisible by 5 but it is not a power of 5. II is true because 5 itself is prime. III is true because all multiples of 5 end in 0 or 5.

8. (B)

13 has a remainder of 6, 23 has a remainder of 2, 27 has a remainder of 6, and 33 has a remainder of 5.

9. (D)

$\frac{47}{6} = 7\frac{5}{6}$, a remainder of 5. All the rest have remainders of 3.

10. (B)

$$\frac{1000}{12} = 83\frac{4}{12}$$

Kyle makes 83 bags and eats 4 pieces of candy.

11. (E)

$$\frac{25.0}{0.08} = 312\frac{4}{8}$$

Mary can make 312 copies and she will have 4 cents left over.

12. (D)

$$\frac{50}{0.75} = 66\frac{2}{3} \ .$$

To exceed $50, Bill must buy 67 newspapers.

13. (C)

$$\frac{10.0}{0.8} = 12\frac{1}{2} \ .$$

Emily will buy 12 apples and pay $9.60. She will receive 40 cents change.

14. (C)

$\frac{24}{8} = 3\frac{0}{8}$. The remainder is zero.

15. (B)

Number each of the campers 1-50. When the camper's number is divided by 3, all campers assigned to the red team will have a remainder of 1, all campers on the white team will have a remainder of 2, and all campers on the blue team will have a remainder of 0. $50/3$ has a remainder of 2, so the 50th camper will be on the white team.

16. (D)

The clock strikes three times per hour. So after 20 strikes, $\frac{20}{3} = 6\frac{2}{3}$. This means that after 6:00 AM it struck two more times. Current time is 6:40 AM.

17 (B)

The sequence repeats every four terms. $\frac{90}{4} = 22\frac{2}{4}$ so the remainder is 2. A remainder of 1 gives A, a 2 gives B, a 3 gives D and a 0 gives C.

Unit 2.4 Order of operations and Scientific Notation

Order of Operations

Order of operations is a fairly important topic in its own right, but it is especially important for students who rely on the calculator. The graphing calculator will always follow the order of operations no matter what, even if that is not what you intended it to do.

The order of operations is best remembered by the acronym, PEMDAS:

P = parenthesis. Always perform operations inside parentheses first

E = exponents. Next, raise terms to their powers (exponents)

M = multiplication . Multiplication and division go together.

D = division. Multiply and divide terms, from left to right.

A = addition. Addition and subtraction go together.

S = subtraction. Last, add and subtract terms, left to right.

Like many things in math, examples are the best way to learn PEMDAS. Start with

$$5 \cdot \left(8 + 2^2\right) \div 4 - 3^2$$

The first step is to simplify the expression within the parenthesis, giving us

$$5 \cdot (12) \div 4 - 3^2$$

Next, we clear the exponents

$$5 \cdot (12) \div 4 - 9$$

Next, we multiply and divide, left to right

$$60 \div 4 - 9$$
$$15 - 9$$

The last step is addition and subtraction, yielding an answer of 6.

PEMDAS does not only apply to numbers, it also applies to variables. Consider

$$2x + \left(2x + x\right)^2 - 6x^2 \div 2x - x$$

First simplify expressions inside parentheses

$$2x + \left(3x\right)^2 - 6x^2 \div 2x - x$$

Next we clear out the exponents

$$2x + 9x^2 - 6x^2 \div 2x - x$$

Next divide

$$2x + 9x^2 - 3x - x$$

The last step is to add and subtract (combine like terms)

$$9x^2 - 2x$$

Calculator tips

On calculators PEMDAS errors often involve negative numbers. First of all, please remember that there is a negative key (labeled as "(-)" on the calculator) and a subtraction key (labeled as "-" on the calculator). These keys are different. The negative key is used to set the sign of a number, whereas the subtraction key is used to subtract one number from another (either number could be positive or negative).

Suppose you want to subtract negative 3 from 5

$$5 - -3 = 8.$$

The key sequence is 5, -, (-), 3, Enter. This gives you the correct result of 8. The calculator is following PEMDAS. It first multiplies -1 by 3. Then it subtracts -3 from 5.

Suppose you wanted to calculate the square of negative 2. Rather than get the correct answer of positive 4 $(-2)^2 = (-2) \cdot (-2) = 4$, many students will get -4. This is because the calculator followed PEMDAS but the student did not. If you enter (-), 2, x^2 the calculator will return -4

$$-2^2 = -2 \cdot 2 = -4.$$

This is due to PEMDAS. The calculator deals with the <u>exponent first</u>, raising 2 to the second power, giving 4. Then it multiplies 4 by -1. To get the correct result of positive 4 you must use parentheses. The correct key sequence is (, (-), 2,), x^2, enter.

$$(-2)^2 = 4.$$

Scientific Notation

Scientific notation involves writing a number in the form of $a \ x \ 10^n$, where $1 \le a < 10$. That sounds pretty complicated but it is not once you've seen some examples.

Number in decimal	Number in scientific notation
1,230,000	1.23 x 10^6
0.0098723	9.8723 x 10^{-3}
12,300,000,000	1.23 x 10^{10}
0.000009123	9.123 x 10^{-6}

In addition to converting between decimal and scientific notation, you must also be able to perform operations on numbers in scientific notation. The approach to follow is: perform operations on the decimal portions of the problem first, next perform operations on the ten-to-a-power portions, and then re-adjust into scientific notation. For example:

$$\frac{1.2 x 10^6}{9.6 x 10^3} = \left(\frac{1.2}{9.6}\right)\left(\frac{10^6}{10^3}\right) = (0.125)(10^3) = 1.25 x 10^2$$

Problems on order of operations and scientific notation (unit 2.4)

1. The expression $\dfrac{2-12\div 2}{-(-2)^2}$ is equal to

  (A) $-\dfrac{5}{4}$

  (B) -1

  (C)   -0.5

  (D)   1

  (E) $\dfrac{5}{4}$

2. The expression $5-2^2+3(1+2)^2$ is equal to:

  (A)   10

  (B)   28

  (C)   30

  (D)   36

  (E)   145

3. The expression $\dfrac{-4}{2}-(-2)^3+1$ is equal to:

  (A) -9

  (B) -7

  (C)   -5

  (D)   7

  (E)   11

4. The expression $3^2+\dfrac{2^3+1}{(1-2)^3}$ is equal to:

  (A) -18

  (B) -9

  (C)   0

  (D)   9

  (E)   18

5. The expression $\dfrac{8+(6-3)^2}{2^2-3^2-12}$ is **closest** to:

  (A) -2

  (B) -1

  (C)   0

  (D)   1

  (E)   2

6. The expression $\dfrac{(3x)^3-x^3}{x^3}$ is equal to:

  (A)   0

  (B)   2

  (C)   8

  (D)   26

  (E)   27

7. The expression $-x^2-(-2x)^2-x+(-3)^3$ is equivalent to:

  (A) $3x^2-x+9$

  (B) $3x^2-x-27$

  (C) $7x^2-x+-27$

  (D) $-6x^2-27$

  (E) $-5x^2-x-27$

8. <u>Extra Credit:</u> The expression $\dfrac{(x^2)^2+2x^2-6x\div 2x}{x\cdot x\cdot x-x\cdot x+x+x+x-3}$ is equivalent to:

  (A) $x+1$

  (B) x^2+3

  (C) $x-1$

  (D) x^2-3

  (E)   None of the above.

9. When expressed in scientific notation 150,000 is:

(A) 1.5×10^{-5}

(B) 1.5×10^{5}

(C) 0.15×10^{-5}

(D) 15×10^{4}

(E) 0.15×10^{6}

10. When expressed in scientific notation 0.000506 is:

(A) 506×10^{-3}

(B) 506×10^{3}

(C) 5.06×10^{4}

(D) 5.06×10^{-4}

(E) 50.6×10^{-5}

11. What is the product of 1,350,000 and 2,300,000?

(A) 3.105×10^{12}

(B) 3.105×10^{-12}

(C) 3.65×10^{5}

(D) 3.65×10^{-5}

(E)   27/46

12. When expressed in decimal, 6.2×10^{9} is

(A)   0.0000000062

(B)   0.00000000062

(C) $6,200,000,000$

(D)   6.2000000000

(E) $6,200,000$

13. When expressed in decimal, 3.2×10^{-8} is

(A) $32,000,000$

(B)   0.0000000032

(C)   32.000000

(D)   .000000032

(E)   328

14. What is the product of $5,330,000$ and 0.22×10^{-10}?

(A)   11.726

(B) $1,172,600$

(C) 1.1726×10^{-4}

(D) 1.1726×10^{-5}

(E) 1.1726×10^{-6}

15. Simplify $\left(1.2 \times 10^{-3}\right) \div \left(3.2 \times 10^{2}\right)$

(A)   0.0375

(B)   0.375

(C) 3.75×10^{-4}

(D) 3.75×10^{-5}

(E) 3.75×10^{-6}

16. The quantity $\left(9.1 \times 10^{10}\right)^{5}$ is equivalent to:

(A)   6.24

(B) $62,403$

(C) 6.24×10^{46}

(D) 6.24×10^{50}

(E) 6.24×10^{54}

Solutions to problems on order of operations (unit 2.4)

1. (D)

$$\frac{2-12\div2}{-(-2)^2}=\frac{2-6}{-4}=\frac{-4}{-4}=1$$

2. (B)

$$5-2^2+3(1+2)^2=5-2^2+3\cdot3^2$$
$$=5-4+3\cdot9=5-4+27=28$$

3. (D)

$$\frac{-4}{2}-(-2)^3+1=-2-(-8)+1=-2+8+1=7$$

4. (C)

$$3^2+\frac{2^3+1}{(1-2)^3}=9+\frac{8+1}{-1}=9-9=0$$

5. (B)

$$\frac{8+(6-3)^2}{2^2-3^2-12}=\frac{8+3^2}{2^2-3^2-12}=\frac{8+9}{4-9-12}=\frac{17}{-17}=-1$$

6. (D)

$$\frac{(3x)^3-x^3}{x^3}=\frac{27x^3-x^3}{x^3}=\frac{26x^3}{x^3}=26$$

7. (E)

$$-x^2-(-2x)^2-x+(-3)^3=-x^2-4x^2-x-27$$
$$=-5x^2-x-27$$

8. (A)

$$\frac{(x^2)^2+2x^2-6x\div2x}{x\cdot x\cdot x-x\cdot x+x+x+x-3}=\frac{x^4+2x^2-3}{x^3-x^2+3x-3}$$
$$=\frac{(x^2+3)(x^2-1)}{x^2(x-1)+3(x-1)}$$
$$=\frac{(x^2+3)(x+1)(x-1)}{(x^2+3)(x-1)}$$
$$=x+1$$

Congratulations if you got this one right!

9. (B)

Although (D) and (E) are correct mathematically, the value of the number portion must be between 1 and 10.

10. (D)

Although (E) is correct mathematically, the value of the number portion must be between 1 and 10.

11. (A)

Convert each to scientific notation, then multiply.

$$(1.35)(10^6)(2.3)(10^6)=3.105 \text{ x } 10^{12}$$

12. (C)

13 (D)

14. (C) .

$$(5.33)(10^6)(2.2)(10^{-11})=11.726 \text{ x } 10^{-5}=1.1726 \text{ x } 10^{-4}$$

15. (E)

$$\frac{(1.2)(10^{-3})}{(3.2)(10^2)}=(0.375)(10^{-5})=3.75 \text{ x } 10^{-6}$$

16. (E)

$$(9.1 \text{ x } 10^{10})^5=(9.1)^5 \text{ x } 10^{50}=62,403 \text{ x } 10^{50}=6.24 \text{ x } 10^{54}$$

Unit 2.5 Percentages

Percentages are a favorite topic for standardized tests, and they can come in several forms. Let's start with a good drill: How many ways can we write five percent? Three ways are possible:

$$5\%, .05 \text{ and } \frac{5}{100}.$$

The last way, as a fraction, is the most important to remember.

How many ways can we write x percent? Two ways are possible:

$$x\% \text{ and } \frac{x}{100}.$$

The last way, as a fraction, is the only useful way to write x percent. It is critical to remember that because in word problems the phrase "what percent" is substituted by $\frac{x}{100}$ when we set up an equation. Consider:

What percent of 86 is 18?

This is not difficult if you substitute correctly. The equation becomes:

$$\left(\frac{x}{100}\right)86 = 18, \quad 86x = 1800, \quad x = \frac{1800}{86}, \quad x = 20.93$$

Consider another simple word problem:

28 is 16 percent of what number?

When written as an equation we have:

$$28 = \left(\frac{16}{100}\right)x, \quad 2800 = 16x, \quad \frac{2800}{16} = x, \quad 175 = x$$

It is faster (and better) to approach this problem directly, using decimals:

$$28 = 0.16x, \quad \frac{28}{.16} = x, \quad 175 = x$$

Lastly we consider an even simpler word problem

What is 5% of 185?

If we were to set up an equation, we would have:

$$\left(\frac{5}{100}\right)185 = \frac{925}{100} = 9.25$$

It is faster (and better) to solve using decimal notation:

$$(.05)185 = 9.25$$

With practice, you will gain insight into when it is better to use the decimal or fraction representations of percentage amounts. You should begin by using the fraction and then start using the decimal amounts to speed up calculations.

Percentage Increase

Just as there are two forms to remember for percentages (as decimals and fractions), there are two forms to remember for percentage increase, and both forms are useful. First, we consider:

$$\text{percentage increase} = \left(\frac{new - old}{old}\right)100$$

If a store raises its price for a shirt from \$80 to \$90, the percentage increase is

$$\left(\frac{90 - 80}{80}\right)100 = \left(\frac{10}{80}\right)100 = \frac{1000}{80} = 12.5$$

Another useful form of percentage increase is that to:

$$\text{inflate y by x\%} = \left(1 + \frac{x}{100}\right)y$$

If a store decides to raise all of its prices by 5%, then a shirt that originally costs \$80 will now cost

$$\left(1 + \frac{5}{100}\right)80 = (1.05)80 = 84 .$$

Percentage Decrease

The equations for percentage decrease are similar to the ones above for percentage increase. The first is:

$$\text{percentage decrease} = \left(\frac{old - new}{old}\right)100$$

If a store marks its price for a shirt from \$90 to \$80, the percentage decrease is

$$\left(\frac{90 - 80}{90}\right)100 = \left(\frac{10}{90}\right)100 = \frac{1000}{90} = 11.1$$

The other useful form of percentage is that to:

$$\text{deflate y by x\%} = \left(1 - \frac{x}{100}\right)y$$

If a store decides to reduce all of its prices by 5%, then a shirt that originally costs \$80 will now cost

$$\left(1 - \frac{5}{100}\right)80 = (0.95)80 = 76 .$$

Problems on percentages (unit 2.5)

1. What is 28% of 600?

    (A)   0.47

    (B)   21.42

    (C)   168

    (D)   2,142

    (E)   16,800

2. 15 is what percent of 500?

    (A)   0.03

    (B)   3

    (C)   33

    (D)   75

    (E)   7,500

3. 65 is 20 percent of what number?

    (A)   0.31

    (B)   3.25

    (C)   13

    (D)   325

    (E)   1,300

4. 300 is what percent of 15?

    (A)   4.5

    (B)   20

    (C)   45

    (D)   450

    (E)   2000

5. Some time ago, the price of a pound of sugar was 25 cents. It is now $3. How much has the price changed?

    (A)   0.9%

    (B)   11%

    (C)   91.6%

    (D)   1100%

    (E)   1200%

6. Diana chose a new pair of shoes marked $120, and the store is having a sale of 20% off everything. How much will she pay for the shoes (excluding sales tax)?

    (A) $24

    (B) $96

    (C) $114

    (D) $144

    (E) $240

7. Two years ago the average rainfall was 30 inches. If it has increased by 15% per year since then, what is the average annual rainfall now?

    (A)   30.0

    (B)   34.5

    (C)   39.0

    (D)   39.7

    (E)   67.5

8. 98% of Mr. Corn's students increase their math SAT score. Of those, 50% increase their score by at least 100 points. Overall, what percent of students increase their math SAT score by at least 100 points?

    (A)   49

    (B)   50

    (C)   51

    (D)   98

    (E)   148

9. In order to stay in business, Madeline must make a 35% profit on everything she sells. If her supplier charged her $60 for a pair of shoes, what should her price tag on the shoes be?

    (A)   21

    (B)   39

    (C)   60

    (D)   81

    (E)   102

10. The difference between a certain number and 12 is equal to 85% of that number. What is the number?

(A)   6.49

(B)   12.85

(C)   14.11

(D)   15

(E)   80

11. 115% of what number is equal to 26.25?

(A)   3.9

(B)   22.3

(C)   22.8

(D)   30.2

(E)   175.0

12. The price of oil this year is $4.10 per gallon. If that represents a 30% increase over last year, what was the price of oil last year?

(A)   1.23

(B)   2.87

(C)   3.15

(D)   5.33

(E)   5.86

13. A store clerk was instructed to mark everything up by 15%. Instead he marked everything down by 15%. If a pair of shoes was originally marked $80, what is difference between the correct price and the incorrect price marked by the clerk?

(A) $8

(B) $12

(C) $24

(D) $68

(E) $92

14. Goeff bought a hat with a price tag of $15.50. Due to a sale, the store charged $11 for the hat. What percentage off was the sale price?

(A)   13.25%

(B)   26%

(C)   29%

(D)   36%

(E)   41%

15. You have traveled to a state where they charge 10% sales tax. A store window announces that everything is 10% off today. If you go into that store to buy a pair of shoes marked $65, how much will you pay, including sales tax?

(A) $7.15

(B) $58.50

(C) $64.35

(D) $65.00

(E) $71.50

16. The hockey team has been great! In 2008, they won 20% more games than in 2007. In 2009 they won 50% more games than in 2008. What was their overall percentage increase from 2007 through 2009?

(A)   20

(B)   70

(C)   80

(D)   90

(E)   170

17. Danny has a baseball collection, and 15% of his balls are from games he attended. Of those, 15% are balls that he actually caught during a game. How many balls could Danny have in his collection?

(A)   150

(B)   225

(C)   300

(D)   400

(E)   450

Solutions to problems on percentages (unit 2.5)

1. (C)

$$\left(\frac{28}{100}\right)600 = \frac{16800}{100} = 168$$

2. (B)

$$15 = \left(\frac{x}{100}\right)500, \quad 1500 = 500x, \quad 3 = x$$

3. (D)

$$65 = \left(\frac{20}{100}\right)x, \quad 6500 = 20x, \quad \frac{6500}{20} = x, \quad 325 = x$$

4. (E)

$$300 = \left(\frac{x}{100}\right)15, \quad 30,000 = 15x, \quad 2,000 = x$$

5. (D)

$$\left(\frac{3.0-0.25}{0.25}\right)100 = \left(\frac{2.75}{0.25}\right)100 = (11)100 = 1,100\%$$

6. (B)

$$\left(1 - \frac{20}{100}\right)120 = (.80)120 = 96$$

7. (D)

$$\left(1 + \frac{15}{100}\right)30 = (1.15)30 = 34.5 \text{ after one year.}$$

$$\left(1 + \frac{15}{100}\right)34.5 = (1.15)34.5 = 39.7 \text{ after two years.}$$

8. (A)

$$(0.98)(0.50) = 0.49$$

9. (D)

$$60 \cdot \left(1 + \frac{35}{100}\right) = 81$$

10. (E)

$$n - 12 = 0.85n, \quad 0.15n = 12, \quad n = 80$$

11. (C)

$$1.15n = 26.25, \quad n = 26.25 / 1.15 = 22.8$$

12. (C)

The easy way is $4.10 = 1.3x$, $x = 3.15$ or use

$$.30 = \frac{4.10 - x}{x}, \quad .3x = 4.10 - x, \quad 1.3x = 4.1$$

13. (C)

The price should have been $80\left(1 + \dfrac{15}{100}\right) = 92$.

Instead the customer was charged

$$80\left(1 - \frac{15}{100}\right) = 80(.85) = 68.$$

So the store lost 92-68=24 dollars.

14. (C)

$$\left(\frac{15.5-11}{15.5}\right)100 = \left(\frac{4.5}{15.5}\right)100 = 29\% \text{ off}$$

15. (C)

First calculate the price with the discount

$$\left(1 - \frac{10}{100}\right)65 = (.90)65 = 58.5. \text{ Next calculate}$$

how much you pay including sales tax

$$58.5\left(1 + \frac{10}{100}\right) = 58.5(1.1) = 64.35. \text{ Notice that}$$

you will not pay the original price of \$65, but
something slightly less.

16. (C)

Suppose they won 100 games in 2007. Then they
won (1.2)(100)=120 games in 2008. Then they won
(1.5)(120)=180 games in 2009.

17. (D)

The quick way to do this is to see that

$(.15)(.15) = .0225 = 9/400$. The long way is to
take 2.25% and multiply by each answer choice.

Unit 2.6 Averages

Like many so-called simple things, the standardized tests can take something simple like an average and stand it on its head. We all know that

$$average = \frac{sum}{count} \ .$$

The average of 5 and 8 is $\frac{5+8}{2} = \frac{13}{2} = 6.5$ and the average of x and y would be $\frac{x+y}{2}$.

In general, when you see the word "average" on a standardized test, you should think about the sum. Many word problems involving averages are really about sums, and the following form of the equation for an average is <u>essential</u> to keep in mind:

$$sum = (average) \cdot (count)$$

Consider this word problem:

> Two people are on an elevator, and their average weight is 200 pounds. The elevator has a capacity of 500 pounds. The elevator comes to stop and a third person wants to get in. What is the maximum amount that the third person can weigh?

The solution comes from thinking in terms of sums. If the two people on the elevator have an average weight of 200 pounds, the sum of their weights must be 400 pounds. They could each weigh 200 pounds, or one could weigh 50 pounds while the other weighs 350 pounds. It does not matter what either weighs. What matters is that together they weigh 400 pounds. As the elevator has a capacity of 500 pounds, the third would-be passenger cannot weigh more than 100 pounds.

Average change

Sometimes you will be asked to calculate an average change. The formula for this is

$$average\ change = \frac{ending\ value\ -\ starting\ value}{number\ of\ time\ periods}$$

For example, suppose the price of lettuce went from \$1.50 to \$2.50 over a period of four years. The average increase per year was

$$\frac{2.50-1.50}{4} = 0.25$$

In words, the price of lettuce increased an average of 25 cents per year.

Please take careful note that this is not the overall increase or overall percentage increase that was covered in the previous unit. The overall increase over the period of four years is

$$2.50-1.50 = 1.00 \ .$$

In words, the price of lettuce increased one dollar over a four year period.

The overall percentage increase over the period of four years is

$$\left(\frac{2.50 - 1.50}{1.50}\right)100 = 67\%$$

In words, the price of lettuce increased by 67% over this four year period.

In the overall increase or the overall percentage increase, the number of years is irrelevant. In the average increase, the overall increase is divided by the number of years.

Averages and sequences

There is more on sequences in unit 5.1, but arithmetic sequences have special properties related to the average. An arithmetic sequence is one which is evenly spread, where the difference between any two adjacent terms is always the same. This is called the common difference. An example of an arithmetic sequence is

$$8, 12, 16, 20, 24.$$

The common difference is 4.

It turns out that the median of an arithmetic sequence is the average. In the example above, the median is 16 and so is the average. You can check by adding up the numbers on your calculator and dividing by 5. If the average is 16 then the sum must be $16 \cdot 5 = 90$. For an arithmetic sequence, we can find the average and sum quickly, even without a calculator.

A special case of the arithmetic sequence (and a favorite for standardized tests) is where the median is zero

$$-15, -10, -5, 0, 5, 10, 15$$

The average is zero and the sum is zero. Keep a sharp lookout for these.

Problems on averages (unit 2.6)

1. If the average of x, y and z is 15, what is their sum?

   (A)   5

   (B)   15

   (C)   30

   (D)   45

   (E)   60

2. If the average of x and y is 11 and the average of x, y and z is 5, what is the value of z?

   (A)   -17

   (B)   -7

   (C)   -6

   (D)   6

   (E)   7

3. An expression for the average of x, 2x, and 3y is

   (A) $3x + 3y$

   (B) $\dfrac{x + y}{2}$

   (C) $\dfrac{x + y}{3}$

   (D) $x + y$

   (E) $\dfrac{3}{2}(x + y)$

4. If the average of x^2 and x is ten, what is the value of x?

   (A)   -5.0

   (B)   -3.7

   (C)   -2.7

   (D)   3.3

   (E)   30.0

5. If the average of x and y is 12 and z=6, what is the average of x, y, and z?.

   (A)   6

   (B)   10

   (C)   15

   (D)   24

   (E)   30

6. Twelve students took a test and their average score was 85. However, Bob was sick that day. After Bob took the test, the average score dropped to 82. What was Bob's score on the test?

   (A)   3

   (B)   36

   (C)   46

   (D)   56

   (E)   83.5

7. On a recent math test, the boys averaged 81 and the girls averaged 90. If there are twice as many boys in the class as girls, what was the overall average for the class?

   (A)   84

   (B)   84.5

   (C)   85

   (D)   85.5

   (E)   86

8. What is the sum of 5, 7, 9, 11, 13, 15 and 17 (do not use a calculator)?

   (A)   5

   (B)   11

   (C)   17

   (D)   66

   (E)   77

9. If the average of nine consecutive integers is zero, what is the largest integer?

(A)   0

(B)   1

(C)   2

(D)   3

(E)   4

10. If the average of 120 numbers is -20, what is their sum?

(A)   -0.17

(B)   -6

(C)   -24

(D)   -2400

(E)   Cannot be determined

11. The average of 11 consecutive odd integers is -3. What is the smallest integer?

(A)   -15

(B)   -13

(C)   -11

(D)   -8

(E)   2

The table below pertains to problems 12-14. It shows hypothetical sales numbers for Mr. Corn's book.

Year	Books Sold
2006	1,250
2007	2,350
2008	3,500
2009	4,750

12. In the table above, what was the average annual sales during the period of 2006 through 2008?

(A)   2,366

(B)   2,962

(C)   3,950

(D)   4,033

(E)   4,212

13. In the table above, by what percent did sales increase from 2007 to 2009?

(A)   -17

(B)   -34

(C)   102

(D)   280

(E)   800

14. In the table above, what was the average annual increase from 2006 through 2009?

(A)   -280

(B)   -290

(C)   -750

(D)   875

(E)   1167

This pertains to problems 15 and 16.

The price of XYZ stock fluctuates widely. In January it closed at $3.50 but in February it closed at $2.25. However at the end of March it shot back up to $5.00.

15. What was the average monthly change in the price of XYZ stock from January through March?

(A) $0.50

(B) $0.75

(C) $1.00

(D) $1.30

(E) $1.50

16. What was the change in the stock price from January through March?

(A)   14%

(B)   30%

(C)   42%

(D)   63%

(E)   150%$

Solutions to problems on averages (unit 2.6)

1. (D)

If $\dfrac{x+y+z}{3}=15,$ then $x+y+z=45$

2. (B)

$x+y=22$

$x+y+z=15$

So $z=15-22=-7$

3. (D)

The average is

$$\frac{x+2x+3y}{3}=\frac{3x+3y}{3}=x+y$$

4. (A)

$$\frac{x^2+x}{2}=10,\ x^2+x-20=0,\ (x+5)(x-4)=0$$

$x=4$ or $x=-5$

5. (B)

If the average of x and y is 12, then the sum of x and y is 24. The sum of x, y and z is 24+6=30. The average of x, y, and z is 30/3 = 10.

6. (C)

Before Bob took the test, the class sum was $85\cdot12=1020$. After Bob took the test, the class sum was $82\cdot13=1066$. Therefore Bob's score on the test was $1066-1020=46$. Bob didn't do very well.

7. (A)

Let g be the number of girls in the class. Then the sum for the girls is $90g$ and the sum for the boys is $81(2g)=162g$. So the sum for the entire class is 252g. There are a total of 3g students in the class so the class average is 252g/3g = 84.

8. (E)

The median is 11 so the average must be 11 because this is an arithmetic sequence with a common difference of 2. There are 7 numbers so their sum must be $7\cdot11=77$.

9. (E)

Consecutive integers form an arithmetic sequence with a common difference of 1. If their average is zero then their median must be zero. So the sequence must be -4, -3, -2, -1, 0, 1, 2, 3, 4. The largest integer is 4.

10. (D)

If the average of 120 numbers is -20 then their sum must be $120(-20)=-2400$.

11. (B)

This constitutes an arithmetic sequence with a common difference of 2, so the average is the median is -3. Therefore there are five numbers to either side of -3. The sequence is -13, -11, -9, -7, -5, -3, -1, 1, 3, 5, 7. The smallest term -13.

12. (A)

$$\frac{1250+2350+3500}{3}=2366$$

13. (C)

$$\left(\frac{4750-2350}{2350}\right)100=102.1$$

14. (D)

$$\frac{4750-1250}{4}=875$$

15. (A)

$$\frac{5.00-3.50}{3}=0.50$$

16. (C)

$$\left(\frac{5.00-3.50}{3.50}\right)100=42.8\%$$

3. ALGEBRA 1

Congratulations, you have now graduated from middle school! Seriously though, that early math can be tricky. Now you are ready for some algebra.

Unit 3.1 Solving equations and inequalities

Algebra is mostly about solving equations. Sometimes this is called balancing equations rather than solving equations, because whatever you do to one side of an equation must also be done to the other side of the equation.

The first technique to be learned is combining like terms. This means moving terms from one side of the equation to the other so that they can be combined. Start with a simple equation such as

$$x - 3 = 12$$ original equation

$$x - 3 + 3 = 12 + 3$$ add 3 to both sides (combine constant terms)

$$x = 15$$ simplify

A somewhat more complicated example of combining like terms:

$$x + 19 = 4x - 2$$ original equation

$$x + 19 - x = 4x - 2 - x$$ subtract x from both sides (combine x-terms)

$$19 = 3x - 2$$ simplify by combining like terms

$$19 + 2 = 3x - 2 + 2$$ add 2 to both sides (combine constant terms)

$$21 = 3x$$ simplify by combining like terms

$$\frac{21}{3} = \frac{3x}{3}$$ divide both sides by 3

$$7 = x$$ simplify

The other technique to be learned is opposites. This was used in the example just above. We use opposites to isolate the variable to be solved. In the equation $21 = 3x$ the variable x is being multiplied by 3. The opposite of multiplication is division, so we isolate the variable by dividing both sides of the equation by 3, yielding $7 = x$. In the equation $\frac{x}{5} = 3$ the variable is being divided by 5. The opposite of division is multiplication, so we isolate the variable by multiplying both sides of the equation by 5, yielding $x = 15$.

In an inequality, expressions are not necessarily equal to each other. Instead of an equals sign (=), any of the following signs may be used:

$<$	less than
$\leq$	less than or equal to
$>$	greater than
$\geq$	greater than or equal to

The same two techniques are used to solve inequalities: combining like terms and opposites. The only difference is that when opposites involve a negative quantity, you must remember to change the direction of the inequality. In other words, multiplying or dividing an inequality by a negative number causes the direction of the inequality to change.

Consider the inequality:

$$-2(x-8) \leq 4 \qquad \text{original equation}$$

$$-2x + 16 \leq 4 \qquad \text{distribute the -2}$$

$$-2x \leq -12 \qquad \text{combine like terms (add 16 to both sides)}$$

$$x \geq 6 \qquad \text{isolate the variable (divide both sides by -2, change direction)}$$

The last step uses opposites to isolate the variable. Because both sides of the equation are divided by negative two, the direction of the inequality is changed.

Sometimes you are required to write the solution using interval notation or identify the graph of the solution on a number line. The "trick" here is to use a closed endpoint if the $\leq$ or $\geq$ sign is present. Use an open endpoint if the $<$ or $>$ sign is present. The examples below are helpful.

Inequality	Interval	Number Line
$x \geq 1$	$[1, \infty)$	
$x < -2$	$(-\infty, -2)$	
$-3 \leq x < 3$	$[-3, 3)$	

Some students find it helpful to remember their brackets this way: when the bracket is square, it reaches out and includes the endpoint; whereas a rounded bracket pushes back and excludes the endpoint.

When using interval notation and positive infinity or negative infinity is an endpoint, the interval is always open because infinity can never be reached. A bracket can never get its arms around infinity or negative infinity.

Problems on solving equations and inequalities (unit 3.1)

1. The solution to the equation

$$4(x+2) = 3(5-x) \text{ is:}$$

(A) $\quad x = 7/15$

(B) $\quad x = 1$

(C) $\quad x = 13/7$

(D) $\quad x = 7$

(E) $\quad x = 15$

2. The solution to the equation

$$\frac{3(x-6)}{5} = x \text{ is:}$$

(A) $\quad x = -9$

(B) $\quad x = -3$

(C) $\quad x = -9/4$

(D) $\quad x = 9/4$

(E) $\quad x = 9$

3. The solution to the equation

$$\frac{4x}{3} = 2(x+9) \text{ is:}$$

(A) $\quad x = -54$

(B) $\quad x = -27$

(C) $\quad x = -6.75$

(D) $\quad x = -4.5$

(E) $\quad x = 27$

4. The solution to the inequality

$$2x + 7 < -11 \text{ is}$$

(A) $\quad x > 2$

(B) $\quad x > 9$

(C) $\quad x < -2$

(D) $\quad x < -9$

(E) $\quad$ None of the above

Problems 5-8 below pertain to this number line:

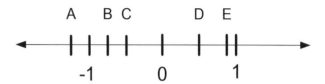

5. Which point most closely approximates the product of A and B ?

(A) $\quad$ A

(B) $\quad$ B

(C) $\quad$ C

(D) $\quad$ D

(E) $\quad$ E

6. Which point most closely approximates the product of B and E ?

(A) $\quad$ A

(B) $\quad$ B

(C) $\quad$ C

(D) $\quad$ D

(E) $\quad$ E

7. Which point most closely approximates the difference of B and A, that is $(B-A)$?

(A) $\quad$ A

(B) $\quad$ B

(C) $\quad$ C

(D) $\quad$ D

(E) $\quad$ E

8. Which of the following statements is <u>false</u>?

(A) $\quad A < B$

(B) $\quad B > A$

(C) $\quad B > C$

(D) $\quad A < D$

(E) $\quad E > A$

Problems 9-11 below pertain to this number line. The middle of the number line has been divided into **five equal segments**.

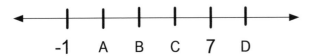

9. What is the coordinate of Point A?

(A) $-1/2$

(B)   0

(C) $1/2$

(D)   1

(E) $3/2$

10. Which of the following statements are true?

I. $B - A = A - 1$

II. $A + C = 6$

III. $A + B + C = 8$

(A)   I only

(B)   II only

(C)   III only

(D)   I and II only

(E)   II and III only

11. If $\sqrt{x}$ is equal to the coordinate of Point D in the diagram above, then x is equal to:

(A)   3

(B)   9

(C)   16

(D)   25

(E)   81

12. John must save at least $25.50 to buy a hat. If he saves 80 cents per day, how many days will it take him to save enough?

(A)   3

(B)   4

(C)   30

(D)   31

(E)   32

13. The solution to the inequality $5 - \dfrac{x}{2} \le 4$ is:

(A) $[2, \infty]$

(B) $(2, \infty)$

(C) $[2, \infty)$

(D) $(-\infty, 1]$

(E) $[-\infty, 1]$

14. The solution to the inequality $2 \le 2x + 1 < 3$ is:

(A) $(-0.5, 1]$

(B) $[-0.5, 1)$

(C) $[-0.5, 2)$

(D) $(0.5, 1]$

(E) $[0.5, 1)$

15. The solution to the inequality $6x - 3 < -9$ is

(A) $x < 1$

(B) $x > 1$

(C) $x < -1$

(D) $x > -1$

(E) $x < -2$

16. All together, Michael and his two friends have exactly $30 to spend on lunch. Hot dogs cost $3.50 and drinks cost $1.50. If they each get two hot dogs, how many drinks can they buy?

(A)   4

(B)   6

(C)   7

(D)   8

(E)   13

17. Mary and Sarah want to get on a ride at the amusement park that can hold no more than 100 pounds. If Mary weighs more than 35 pounds, what is the most that Sarah can weigh?

(A)   64 pounds

(B)   64.9 pounds

(C)   65 pounds

(D)   65.1 pounds

(E)   65.9 pounds

Solutions to problems on solving equations and inequalities (unit 3.1)

1. (B).

$$4(x+2)=3(5-x)$$
$$4x+8=15-3x$$
$$7x=15-8=7$$
$$x=1$$

2. (A)

$$\frac{3(x-6)}{5}=x$$
$$3(x-6)=5x$$
$$3x-18=5x$$
$$-18=2x$$
$$-9=x$$

3. (B)

$$\frac{4x}{3}=2(x+9)$$
$$4x=6(x+9)$$
$$4x=6x+54$$
$$-2x=54$$
$$x=-27$$

4. (D)

$$2x+7<-11$$
$$2x<-18$$
$$x<-9$$

5. – 8. Set values for each of the points. Let A=-1.25, B=-0.75, C=-0.5, D=0.5 and E=0.9. Values do not need to be precise.

    5. (E)

$$A\cdot B\approx-1.25(-.75)=0.9375$$

    6. (C)

$$B\cdot E\approx-.75(0.9)=-0.68$$

    7. (D)

$$B-A\approx-.75--1.25=0.5$$

    8. (C)

9-11. There are four segments between -1 and 7. Therefore each segment must represent a distance of $\dfrac{7--1}{4}=2$ units each. That makes A=1, B=3, C=5 and D=9.

    9. (D)

    10. (B)

        B-A=3-1=2. A-1=0. False

        A+C=1+5=6 True

        A+B+C=1+3+5=9 False

    11. (E)

$$\sqrt{x}=9,\ \left(\sqrt{x}\right)^2=9^2,\ x=81$$

12. (E)

$$.80d\geq25.5$$
$$d\geq31.875$$

John will not have enough money until the 32nd day.

13. (C)

$$5-\frac{x}{2}\leq4$$
$$-\frac{x}{2}\leq-1$$
$$x\geq2\text{ or }[2,\infty)$$

14. (E)

$$2\leq2x+1\ \text{ and }\ 2x+1<3$$
$$1\leq2x\ \text{ and }\ 2x<2$$
$$0.5\leq x\ \text{ and }\ x<1,\text{ the interval is }[0.5,1)$$

15. (C)

$$6x-3<-9$$
$$6x<-6$$
$$x<-1$$

16. (B)

After they pay $21 for hot dogs, they will have $9 left.

Drinks cost $1.50 each, so they can buy six drinks.

17. (C)

$$x+35\leq100$$
$$x\leq65$$

Unit 3.2 Square roots (radicals)

Remember that the square root symbol $\sqrt{}$ means the positive square root. There is an invisible + sign in front of the radical. Although it is invisible, it is very important. For example, $\sqrt{9}$ is positive 3, not negative 3. In words, this would be "the positive square root of nine is positive three, not negative three."

When we mean to indicate the negative square root, we write $-\sqrt{9} = -3$. In words, this would be "the negative square root of nine is negative three." When we mean to indicate the positive **and** negative square roots, we write $\pm\sqrt{9} = \pm 3$. In words, this would be "the positive and negative square roots of nine are positive and negative three."

Positive and negative square roots are used mostly for solving equations, such as

$$x^2 = 64$$
$$x = \pm\sqrt{64}$$
$$x = \pm 8$$

In words, this would be "the solutions to the equation $x^2 = 64$ are $x = 8$ and $x = -8$". Remember that the $\pm$ symbol means positive AND negative. So the symbol $\pm\sqrt{}$ means the positive and negative square root, while the symbol ± 8 means positive 8 AND negative 8.

Check these:

$$\sqrt{25} = 5 \text{ only}$$
$$-\sqrt{25} = -5 \text{ only}$$
$$\pm\sqrt{25} = 5 \text{ and -5 (you could also write } \pm 5)$$

Remember:

$$\pm \text{ means positive AND negative}$$
$$\sqrt{} \text{ means positive square root}$$

General radicals

There is more material on radicals in unit 5.3. But for now, just be aware that the positive square root symbol has another invisible element: there is an invisible two. The symbol $\sqrt{}$ is actually $+\sqrt[2]{}$. Please note the invisible positive sign and the invisible two.

In general, the positive nth root is symbolized by $\sqrt[n]{}$, where n is a positive integer.

For example to find the cube root of 8, we write $\sqrt[3]{8} = x$ if $x \cdot x \cdot x = 8$.

Nth roots of numbers can be found easily on the calculator using fractional exponents because of the identity:

$$\sqrt[n]{x} = x^{\frac{1}{n}}$$

To find the 5th root of 7776, simply enter 7776, ^, (, 1, ÷, 5,) into your calculator and then press enter. Your display should look like:

$$7776\wedge(1/5)$$

$$6$$

In other words $\sqrt[5]{7776} = 6$ or $7776 = 6^5$.

Laws of radicals

There are two laws of radicals to be covered here. The rest are covered in Chapter 5. These laws are typically used to simplify radicals. They are:

$$\sqrt[n]{xy} = \sqrt[n]{x} \cdot \sqrt[n]{y}$$

$$\sqrt[n]{\frac{x}{y}} = \frac{\sqrt[n]{x}}{\sqrt[n]{y}}$$

Some examples of the multiplication law are:

$$\sqrt{50} = \sqrt{50 \cdot 2} = \sqrt{25} \cdot \sqrt{2} = 5\sqrt{2}$$

$$\sqrt[3]{192} = \sqrt[3]{64 \cdot 3} = \sqrt[3]{64} \cdot \sqrt[3]{3} = 4\sqrt[3]{3}$$

An example of the division law:

$$\sqrt{\frac{5}{12}} = \frac{\sqrt{5}}{\sqrt{12}} = \frac{\sqrt{5}}{\sqrt{4 \cdot 3}} = \frac{\sqrt{5}}{\sqrt{4} \cdot \sqrt{3}} = \frac{\sqrt{5}}{2\sqrt{3}}$$

In general, we do not like to have a radical in a denominator, so this should be further simplified as follows:

$$\frac{\sqrt{5}}{2\sqrt{3}} = \left(\frac{\sqrt{5}}{2\sqrt{3}}\right)\left(\frac{\sqrt{3}}{\sqrt{3}}\right) = \frac{\sqrt{15}}{2 \cdot 3} = \frac{\sqrt{15}}{6}$$

Problems on radicals (unit 3.2)

1. $\sqrt{49}$ is equivalent to:

   (A)   7 only

   (B)   -7 only

   (C)   -7 or 7

   (D)   -7 and 7

   (E)   all of the above

2. $\sqrt[3]{-27}$ is equivalent to:

   (A)   3 only

   (B)   -3 only

   (C)   -3 or 3

   (D)   -3 and 3

   (E)   all of the above

3. Which of the following is the solution to the equation $x^2 - 5 = 20$?

   (A)   5 only

   (B)   -5 only

   (C)   -5 and 5

   (D) $\sqrt{15}$

   (E) $\pm\sqrt{15}$

4. $\sqrt{72}$ is equivalent to:

   I. $6\sqrt{2}$

   II. $3\sqrt{8}$

   III. $2\sqrt{18}$

   (A)   I only

   (B)   II only

   (C)   III only

   (D)   I and III only

   (E)   I, II and III

5. $\sqrt[3]{-384}$ is equivalent to:

   (A) $8\sqrt{6}$

   (B) $-8\sqrt{6}$

   (C) $4\sqrt{24}$

   (D) $4\sqrt[3]{6}$

   (E) $-4\sqrt[3]{6}$

6. The solution to the equation

   $8 + \sqrt{2x} = 16$ is:

   (A) $x = 4$

   (B) $x = 8$

   (C) $x = 16$

   (D) $x = 32$

   (E) $x = 64$

7. The solution to the equation

   $1 - \sqrt{x} = \dfrac{-7}{2}$ is:

   (A) $x = 1.5$

   (B) $x = 2$

   (C) $x = 4$

   (D) $x = 16$

   (E) $x = 20.25$

8. 497 is ten less than three times the square of a number. The value of that number is:

   I. -13

   II.   13

   III. 12.74

   (A)   I only

   (B)   II only

   (C)   III only

   (D)   I and II only

   (E)   None of the above

9. If $\sqrt{x} = 25$ then x is equal to:

(A) 5

(B) 25

(C) 125

(D) 500

(E) 625

10. The expression $\left(3+\sqrt{x}\right)^2$ is equal to:

(A) $9+x$

(B) $9+x^2$

(C) $9+3\sqrt{x}+x^2$

(D) $9+6\sqrt{x}+x$

(E) $9+6x+x^2$

11. The quantity $\dfrac{\sqrt{15}}{\sqrt{20}}$ reduces to:

(A) $\dfrac{\sqrt{3}}{4}$

(B) $\dfrac{\sqrt{3}}{2}$

(C) $\sqrt{3}$

(D) $2\sqrt{3}$

(E) $10\sqrt{3}$

12. The expression $\dfrac{\sqrt{x}+\sqrt{x}}{\sqrt{2x}}$ reduces to:

(A) 1

(B) $\sqrt{2}$

(C) 2

(D) $\dfrac{\sqrt{2}}{2}$

(E) $x\sqrt{x}$

13. The quantity $\sqrt{\dfrac{52}{27}}$ reduces to:

(A) $\dfrac{2\sqrt{13}}{3}$

(B) $\dfrac{4\sqrt{13}}{3}$

(C) $\dfrac{2\sqrt{39}}{3}$

(D) $\dfrac{4\sqrt{39}}{3}$

(E) $\dfrac{2\sqrt{39}}{9}$

14. If $x^2 = -\left(x-10\right)\left(x+10\right)$ then one possible value of x could be:

(A) $2\sqrt{5}$

(B) $5\sqrt{2}$

(C) 5

(D) 10

(E) 25

15. If the cube root of a integer is equal to the square of that integer divided by 243, then the integer is:

(A) 0

(B) 2

(C) 3

(D) 8

(E) 27

Solutions to practice problems on radicals (unit 3.2)

1. (A)

$\sqrt{49} = +7$

2. (B)

$\sqrt[3]{-27} = -3$ because $(-3)(-3)(-3) = -27$

3. (C)

$x^2 - 5 = 20$, $x^2 = 25$, $x = \pm 5$

4. (E)

Start by dividing perfect squares into 72

$\sqrt{72} = \sqrt{36 \cdot 2} = \sqrt{36} \cdot \sqrt{2} = 6\sqrt{2}$

$\sqrt{72} = \sqrt{9 \cdot 8} = \sqrt{9} \cdot \sqrt{8} = 3\sqrt{8}$

$\sqrt{72} = \sqrt{4 \cdot 18} = \sqrt{4} \cdot \sqrt{18} = 2\sqrt{18}$

5. (E)

Start by dividing perfect cubes into 384

$\sqrt[3]{-384} = \sqrt[3]{-64 \cdot 6} = \sqrt[3]{-64} \cdot \sqrt[3]{6} = -4\sqrt[3]{6}$

6. (D)

$8 + \sqrt{2x} = 16$, $\sqrt{2x} = 8$, $\left(\sqrt{2x}\right)^2 = 8^2$, $2x = 64$, $x = 32$

7. (E)

$1 - \sqrt{x} = \dfrac{-7}{2}$, $\sqrt{x} = \dfrac{9}{2}$, $x = \dfrac{81}{4} = 20.25$

8. (D)

$3x^2 - 10 = 497$, $3x^2 = 507$

$x^2 = 169$, $x = \pm 13$

9. (E)

$\sqrt{x} = 25$, $x = 25^2 = 625$

10. (D)

$\left(3 + \sqrt{x}\right)^2 = \left(3 + \sqrt{x}\right)\left(3 + \sqrt{x}\right)$

$= 9 + 3\sqrt{x} + 3\sqrt{x} + x$

11. (B)

$\dfrac{\sqrt{15}}{\sqrt{20}} = \dfrac{\sqrt{15}}{2\sqrt{5}} = \left(\dfrac{1}{2}\right)\left(\sqrt{\dfrac{15}{5}}\right) = \dfrac{\sqrt{3}}{2}$

12. (B)

$\dfrac{\sqrt{x} + \sqrt{x}}{\sqrt{2x}} = \dfrac{2\sqrt{x}}{\left(\sqrt{2}\right)\left(\sqrt{x}\right)} = \dfrac{2}{\sqrt{2}} = \sqrt{2}$

13. (E)

$\sqrt{\dfrac{52}{27}} = \dfrac{\sqrt{52}}{\sqrt{27}} = \dfrac{2\sqrt{13}}{3\sqrt{3}} = \dfrac{2\sqrt{13}}{3\sqrt{3}}\left(\dfrac{\sqrt{3}}{\sqrt{3}}\right) = \dfrac{2\sqrt{39}}{9}$

14. (B)

$x^2 = -(x - 10)(x + 10) = -(x^2 - 100)$

$2x^2 = 100$, $x^2 = 50$, $x = \pm\sqrt{50} = \pm 5\sqrt{2}$

15. (E)

Plug the answer choices into $\sqrt[3]{n} = \dfrac{n^2}{243}$. You will

find that $\sqrt[3]{27} = \dfrac{27^2}{243}$

Unit 3.3 Solving pairs of equations

Unit 3.1 dealt with solving one equation with one variable. But how do you handle two equations with two variables? There are two techniques to know: substitution and linear combination.

Substitution

Substitution is a very simple way to do the job. When given a pair of equations, re-write one of the equations to isolate one of the variables. Then substitute that variable into the second equation. For example, consider the pair of equations:

$$x + 2y = 10$$
$$2x + 3y = 500$$

Substitution for this pair of equations is simple because the first equation can be re-written as $x = 10 - 2y$. Next replace x with $10 - 2y$ in the second equation:

$$2x + 3y = 500$$
$$2(10 - 2y) + 3y = 500$$
$$20 - 4y + 3y = 500$$
$$y = -480$$

Finish the problem by finding the value of x:

$$x = 10 - 2y = 10 - 2(-480) = 10 + 960 = 970$$

Elimination

The other method of solving a pair of equations is elimination. First, one or both equations are multiplied by constants. Next, the equations are added to one another or subtracted from one another. In our example above, we could have first multiplied the top equation by two, yielding:

$$2x + 4y = 20$$
$$2x + 3y = 500$$

Next we can subtract the second equation from the first equation, giving

$$2x - 2x + 4y - 3y = 20 - 500$$
$$y = -480$$

In general, elimination is faster than substitution, but more prone to error.

Sometimes it is necessary to multiply both equations by constants, as you can see in the next example.

$$3x + 2y = 255$$
$$2x + 5y = 500$$

Multiply the top equation by two and the bottom equation by three. This yields

$$6x + 4y = 510$$
$$6x + 15y = 1500$$

Subtracting the bottom equation gives

$$4y - 15y = 510 - 1500$$
$$-11y = -990, \quad y = 90$$

Substituting 90 for y in the first equation gives

$$3x + 2 \cdot 90 = 255, \quad 3x = 75, \quad x = 25.$$

<u>Calculator Tip:</u> Pairs of equations may also be solved on the calculator. First, on paper, you must put each equation into y= format, isolating the y variable. Then enter each equation into the equation editor (the Y= button). Now press the graph key. Each equation is represented by a line on the graph. The intersection of the lines represents the solution. Once the two lines appear on the graph, the point of intersection may be found by using 2nd-calc-intersect.

Triples

Sometimes you will see a system of three equations with three variables. Do not let this bother you. Simply combine equations to create a new system of two equations with two variables. Then solve the reduced pair. For example

$$x + y - z = 40$$
$$2x - y + z = 80$$
$$2x + y + z = 100$$

Combining the top two equations gives $3x = 120$, whereas combining the bottom two equations gives $-2y = -20$. These are solved easily.

Important Tip: When a problem on the test contains two or more equations, always stack the equations vertically so that the variables are aligned. That way, you can see what technique will be best.

Problems on solving pairs of equations (unit 3.3)

1. If $x+y=3$ and $3x+5y=13$, then $x-y$ is equal to:

    (A)   -2

    (B)   -1

    (C)   1

    (D)   2

    (E)   3

2. Tickets to a show cost \$3 for students and \$7 for adults. If 250 tickets were sold and ticket sales totaled \$1102, how many adult tickets were sold?

    (A)   35

    (B)   88

    (C)   111

    (D)   162

    (E)   352

3. If $3x+5y=13$ and $6x+7y=20$, find the value of $\dfrac{y}{x}$.

    (A)   0.5

    (B)   1

    (C)   1.5

    (D)   2

    (E)   2.5

4. If $5x+2y=8$ and $3x-7y=13$, find the value of $x-y$.

    (A)   -2

    (B)   -1

    (C)   1

    (D)   2

    (E)   3

5. Solve for x:

$$x+2y+z=3$$
$$2x-y-z=-5$$
$$3x-y+z=-2$$

    (A)   -2

    (B)   -1

    (C)   0

    (D)   1

    (E)   2

6. Find the average of x, y, and z:

$$x+2y-z=-8$$
$$2x+y+2z=19$$
$$2x+2y+4z=34$$

    (A)   0

    (B)   1

    (C)   3

    (D)   9

    (E)   45

7. Joanna saves nickels and quarters in a jar. If she saved five times as many nickels as quarters, and her coin collection is worth \$390, how many quarters has she saved?

    (A)   195

    (B)   300

    (C)   780

    (D)   1500

    (E)   7500

8. Lizzy's cell phone plan charges 5 cents per message for in-network text messages and 10 cents per message for out-of-network text messages. If she sent a total of 1500 messages and her bill was \$80, how many out-of-network messages did she send?

    (A)   50

    (B)   55

    (C)   60

    (D)   100

    (E)   1400

Solutions to problems on solving pairs of equations (unit 3.3)

1 (B)

Use substitution:

$3x + 5y = 13$

$3(3 - y) + 5y = 13$

$9 - 3y + 5y = 13, \; y = 2, \; x = 3 - 2 = 1$

$x - y = 1 - 2 = -1$

2. (B)

Use substitution:

$S + A = 250$

$3S + 7A = 1102$

$3(250 - A) + 7A = 1102$

$750 + 4A = 1102, \; A = 88$

3. (D)

Multiply the top equation by 2, then subtract:

$3x + 5y = 13$

$6x + 7y = 20$

$10y - 7y = 26 - 20, \; 3y = 6, \; y = 2$

$3x + 5(2) = 13, \; x = 1, \; y/x = 2/1 = 2$

4. (E)

Multiply top by 3, bottom by 5, then subtract:

$5x + 2y = 8$

$3x - 7y = 13$

$15x + 6y = 24$

$15x - 35y = 65$

$6y + 35y = 24 - 65, \; 41y = -41, \; y = -1, \; x = 2$

$\qquad x - y = 2 - -1 = 3$

5. (B)

Reduce to two equations by eliminating z, then solve. First add the top two then add the bottom two.

$$x + 2y + z = 3$$
$$2x - y - z = -5$$
$$3x - y + z = -2$$

$$3x + y = -2$$
$$5x - 2y = -7$$

Next multiply the top equation by 2, then add:

$$6x + 5x = -4 - 7, \; 11x = -11, \; x = -1$$

6. (C)

Add all of the equations together to find the sum. Then divide by three to find the average.

$5x + 5y + 5z = -8 + 19 + 34$

$5x + 5y + 5z = 45$

$x + y + z = 9$

$\dfrac{x + y + z}{3} = \dfrac{9}{3} = 3$

7. (C)

$5Q = N$

$.25Q + .05N = 390$

$.25Q + .05(5Q) = 390$

$.50Q = 390, \; Q = 780$

8. (D)

$5x + 10y = 8000$

$x + y = 1500, \; x = 1500 - y$

$5(1500 - y) + 10y = 8000$

$7500 - 5y + 10y = 8000$

$5y = 500, \; y = 100$

Unit 3.4 Distributing and common factors

Distribution involves multiplying a quantity across parentheses. For example:

$$3(2x-3y)=(3\cdot 2x)-(3\cdot 3y)=6x-9y$$

Distribution problems can involve a combination of constants and variables. For example:

$$6xy(2x+3y)=(6xy\cdot 2x)+(6xy\cdot 3y)=12x^2y+18xy^2$$

Factoring

Once the art of distributing is mastered, you are ready for factoring. Factoring is the opposite of distributing.

Suppose we want to factor the expression $6x-9y$. Look for the factors that each term has in common:

$$6x=2\cdot 3\cdot x \qquad 9y=3\cdot 3\cdot y$$

The only factor in common to $6x$ and $9y$ is 3. So now we take out the common factor:

$$6x-9y=3(2x-3y).$$

Consider the expression $12x^2y+18xy^2z$. Break each term into its factors and look for the factors that are common to both:

$$12x^2y=2^2\cdot 3\cdot x\cdot x\cdot y \qquad 18xy^2z=2\cdot 3^2\cdot x\cdot y\cdot y\cdot z$$

The common factors are $2\cdot 3\cdot x\cdot y$. We take these common factors out of the terms and get

$$12x^2y+18xy^2z=2\cdot 3\cdot xy(2x+3yz)=6xy(2x+3yz).$$

Greatest Common Factor (GCF)

In the example above, the constant terms we were dealing with were 12 and 18. We could have factored out 2, leaving 6 and 9. But 6 and 9 have a common factor of 3. We would then have to factor out the 3. It is far better to take out the greatest common factor (GCF) in one step.

Suppose we want to find the greatest common factor for 72 and 756. The greatest common factor can be found by following these steps:

1. Use a factor tree to find the prime factorization for each term (if you forgot how, see unit 2.1).
2. Make a list of the prime factors that appear in every term.
3. Raise each of these factors to the smallest power that is used.

For the example of 72 and 756, we have the following:

1. $72 = 2^3 \cdot 3^2$ and $756 = 2^2 \cdot 3^3 \cdot 7$.
2. The common primes are 2 and 3.
3. The smallest power of 2 is 2, and the smallest power of 3 is 2.
4. The GCF is $2^2 \cdot 3^2 = 4 \cdot 9 = 36$.

Calculator Tip: This technique works for finding the GCF for any number of terms. However, if you only need to find the GCF for two terms the "best way" is to use your calculator. To find the GCF of 72 and 756, simply enter the following sequence: *math-num-gcd-72-,-756-)-enter.*

Common Factors in Division

So far we have looked at how to use common factors in multiplication. Using the constants from the GCF example above, we have

$$72xy - 756x = 36x\left(2y - 21\right).$$

But what if we were given a division problem? The process is much the same:

$$\frac{756x}{72xy} = \left(\frac{36x}{36x}\right)\left(\frac{21}{2y}\right) = \frac{21}{2y}$$

Whether multiplying or dividing, we pull out the GCF, which in this case is $36x$.

When doing division, many students find it easier to break the fraction into stacks, sort of how we stacked pairs of equations in the previous unit. Using the same example as before, we break the fraction into a constant stack, an x-stack, and a y-stack. Then we simplify each stack. Then we combine the stacks to make a new fraction.

$$\frac{756x}{72xy} = \left(\frac{756}{72}\right)\left(\frac{x}{x}\right)\left(\frac{1}{y}\right) = \left(\frac{21}{2}\right)\left(\frac{1}{1}\right)\left(\frac{1}{y}\right) = \frac{21}{2y}$$

Problems on distributing and factoring (unit 3.4)

1. The expression $3xy\left(2x^2 + xy\right)$ is equivalent to:

(A) $\qquad 7x^2y$

(B) $\qquad 7x^3y$

(C) $\qquad 9x^2y$

(D) $\qquad 6x^3y + xy$

(E) $\qquad 6x^3y + 3x^2y^2$

2. The expression $3xy^2 - 18x^3y^3$ is equivalent to:

(A) $\qquad 3xy^2\left(1 - 6x^2y\right)$

(B) $\qquad 3xy(1 - 6xy)$

(C) $\qquad 3x^2y^2(1 - 6xy)$

(D) $\qquad xy(3y - 18xy)$

(E) $\qquad$ None of the above

3. The expression $648x^3y^6 - 162xyz$ is equivalent to:

(A) $\qquad 81xy(8x^2y^5 - z)$

(B) $\qquad 81xyz(8x^2y^5 - 1)$

(C) $\qquad 162xy(4x^2y^5 - z)$

(D) $\qquad 162xyz(4x^2y^5 - 1)$

(E) $\qquad$ None of the above

4. The simplest form of the expression

$360x^8y^5z^2 - 480x^3y^2z^3 + 540x^5y^7z^8$ is:

(A) $15x^3y^2z\left(24x^5y^3z - 32z^2 + 36x^2y^5z^5\right)$

(B) $60x^3y^2z\left(6x^5y^3z - 8z^2 + 9x^2y^5z^5\right)$

(C) $15x^3y^2z^2\left(24x^5y^3 - 32z + 36x^2y^5z^6\right)$

(D) $60x^3y^2z^2\left(6x^5y^3 - 8z + 9x^2y^5z^6\right)$

(E) None of the above

5. The expression $5xy$ is equivalent to:

(A) $\qquad \dfrac{50x^2y^2}{5xy}$

(B) $\qquad \dfrac{30x^2y}{6x}$

(C) $\qquad \dfrac{12x^3y}{60x^2}$

(D) $\qquad \dfrac{15x^3y^8}{3x^4y^7}$

(E) $\qquad$ None of the above

6. The expression $\dfrac{120x^3y^2 - 136x^2z}{8x^2}$ can be simplified to:

(A) $\qquad 15xy^2 - 17z$

(B) $\qquad 15y^2 - 17z$

(C) $\qquad -2xyz$

(D) $\qquad -2(xy^2 - 17)$

(E) $\qquad \dfrac{15y^2}{x} - \dfrac{17z}{x^2}$

7. The expression $\dfrac{96xy^2z^3 - 36x^2yz^2}{12x^3yz^6}$ can be simplified to:

(A) $\qquad \dfrac{8yz - 3x}{xz^2}$

(B) $\qquad 8yz - 3x$

(C) $\qquad \dfrac{8y}{x^2} - \dfrac{3}{xz^4}$

(D) $\qquad \dfrac{8yz - 3x}{x^2z^4}$

(E) $\qquad \dfrac{8}{x^2} - \dfrac{3}{xz^4}$

Solutions to problems on distributing and factoring (unit 3.4)

1. (E)

$$3xy\left(2x^2+xy\right)=3xy\cdot 2x^2+3xy\cdot xy=6x^3y+3x^2y^2$$

2. (A)

$$3xy^2-18x^3y^3=3xy^2\left(1-6x^2y\right)$$

3. (C)

Find GCF of 648 and 162:

$$648=2^3\cdot 3^4\quad\text{and}\quad 162=2\cdot 3^4\quad\text{so GCF}=2\cdot 3^4=162$$
$$648x^3y^6-162xyz=162xy\left(4x^2y^5-z\right)$$

4. (D)

Use factor trees to find the GCF of 360 480 and 540

$$360=2^3\cdot 3^2\cdot 5\quad 480=2^5\cdot 3\cdot 5\quad 540=2^2\cdot 3^3\cdot 5$$
$$\text{so GCF}=2^2\cdot 3\cdot 5=60$$

$$360x^8y^5z^2-480x^3y^2z^3+540x^5y^7z^8=$$
$$60x^3y^2z^2\left(6x^5y^3-8z+9x^2y^5z^6\right)$$

5. (B)

$$\frac{30x^2y}{6x}=\frac{6x\left(5xy\right)}{6x}=5xy$$

6. (A)

Use your calculator or factor trees to find GCF of 120 and 136

$$120=2^3\cdot 3\cdot 5\quad\text{and}\quad 136=2^3\cdot 17\ \text{ so GCF}=2^3=8$$

$$\frac{120x^3y^2-136x^2z}{8x^2}=\frac{8x^2\left(15xy^2-17z\right)}{8x^2}=15xy^2-17z$$

7. (D)

Use factor trees or calculator for the GCF of 96 and 36

$$96=2^5\cdot 3\quad\text{and}\quad 36=2^2\cdot 3^2\quad\text{so GCF}=2^2\cdot 3=12$$

$$\frac{96xy^2z^3-36x^2yz^2}{12x^3yz^6}=\frac{12xyz^2\left(8yz-3x\right)}{12x^3yz^6}=\frac{8yz-3x}{x^2z^4}$$

Unit 3.5 FOILing and factoring

The acronym FOIL reminds us how to multiply terms that look like

$$(a+b)(c+d) = a(c+d) + b(c+d) = ac + ad + bc + bd$$

The acronym comes from

F	= first (the first terms are a and c)
O	= outer (the outer terms are a and d)
I	= inner (the inner terms are b and c)
L	= last (the last terms are b and d)

That's all there is to it! For example

$$(2x+3)(x-y) = 2x^2 - 2xy + 3x - 3y$$

First $\quad 2x \cdot x = 2x^2$

Outer $\quad 2x(-y) = -2xy$

Inner $\quad 3 \cdot x = 3x$

Last $\quad 3(-y) = -3y$

Factoring

Factoring is just FOILing in reverse. In fact, one of my students used to call factoring "reverse FOILing." The general problem is that we want to factor the expression

$$ax^2 + bx + c .$$

There are two cases to consider. The easy case is where a=1, so let's start there.

Factoring when $a = 1$

When a=1, the equation looks like

$$x^2 + bx + c$$

There are three steps to factoring this:

1. Begin with the setup of $(x \quad)(x \quad)$.

2. Find all of the pairs of factors of c. Then find a pair for which the sum or difference equals b. Enter that pair into the setup.
3. Adjust the signs.

Consider the following example:

$$x^2 - 9x - 10$$

1. Begin with the setup $(x \quad)(x \quad)$.
2. The factors of 10 are 2x5 and 1x10. 2 and 5 will not work because 2+5=7 and 5-2=3. We are looking for 9, not 7 or 3. Next try 1 and 10. 1+10=11 but 10-1=9. So we know to use 1 and 10. We fill the setup as follows: $(x \quad 1)(x \quad 10)$.
3. We know we need a plus sign and a negative sign because 10 is negative. The negative must go with the 10 and not the 1 because the 9 is negative, so

$$x^2 - 9x - 10 = (x+1)(x-10).$$

<u>Always confirm your answer by FOILING</u>:

$$(x+1)(x-10) = x^2 - 10x + x - 10 = x^2 - 9x - 10.$$

Factoring when $a \neq 1$

Now consider the more difficult case of

$$ax^2 + bx + c.$$

The steps are:

1. Create a setup for each pair of factors of a.
2. For each setup follow steps 1-3 above.

Consider factoring the following:

$$4x^2 + 5x - 6$$

Two setups will be needed, one for 2 and 2; and another for 4 and 1. The setup for 2 and 2 looks like $(2x \quad)(2x \quad)$. For this setup we can try factors of 6, namely 6 and 1; and 2 and 3. The combination of 6 and 1 does not work because 12 and 2 neither add or subtract to give 5. The combination of 2 and 3 does not work because 4 and 6 neither add or subtract to give 5. How annoying! So next we try the setup for 4 and 1, which looks like $(4x \quad)(x \quad)$. Now we try factors of 6, starting with 6 and 1. That combination does not work because neither 24 and 1, nor 4 and 6 will give us the 5 that we need. The combination of 2 and 3 can work because 8-3 equals 5. So the answer is

$$4x^2 + 5x - 6 = (4x-3)(x+2).$$

$$(4x-3)(x+2) = 4x^2 - 3x + 8x - 6 = 4x^2 + 5x - 6$$

Factoring is not difficult but it can be a nuisance and it does require practice.

Special cases (perfect squares)

There are three patterns of factoring and FOILing that you must memorize and be able to recognize on the test. These pertain to perfect squares:

$$(x+y)^2 = x^2 + 2xy + y^2$$
$$(x-y)^2 = x^2 - 2xy + y^2$$
$$(x+y)(x-y) = x^2 - y^2$$

It is not good enough to be able to FOIL or factor these from scratch when you encounter them on the test. This sample problem illustrates why.

Suppose $(x+y)^2 = 100,\ x^2 = 20,\ $ and $y^2 = 30$. Find the value of xy. If you do not recognize the pattern you will not know what to do. However recognizing the pattern enables the problem to be solved easily.

$$(x+y)^2 = x^2 + 2xy + y^2$$
$$100 = 20 + 2xy + 30$$
$$50 = 2xy$$
$$25 = xy$$

Factoring in Division

Factoring is often used to simplify an expression that is being divided. This is illustrated below:

$$\frac{x^2 - 9}{x^2 + 5x + 6} = \frac{(x+3)(x-3)}{(x+3)((x+2)} = \left(\frac{x+3}{x+3}\right)\left(\frac{x-3}{x+2}\right) = \frac{x-3}{x+2}$$

First the factor $(x+3)$ is isolated in the numerator and the denominator. Then they cancel out.

Problems on FOILing and factoring (unit 3.5)

1. The expression $(2x-3)(5x+7)$ is equivalent to:

   (A) $7x+4$

   (B) $-3x-10$

   (C) $10x^2+14$

   (D) $10x^2-x-21$

   (E) $10x^2+29-21$

2. The expression $(x+8)^2$ is equivalent to:

   (A) $2x+16$

   (B) $x^2+8x+64$

   (C) x^2+64

   (D) x^2-64

   (E) $x^2+16x+64$

3. The expression x^2-6x+8 is equivalent to:

   (A) $(x+8)(x-1)$

   (B) $(x-8)(x+1)$

   (C) $(x+4)(x+2)$

   (D) $(x+4)(x-2)$

   (E) None of the above

4. The expression $x^2-5xy-176y^2$ is equivalent to:

   (A) $(x-16y)(x+11y)$

   (B) $(x-8y)(x-22y)$

   (C) $(x-8y)(x+22y)$

   (D) $(x+8y)(x-22y)$

   (E) $(x+8y)(x+22y)$

5. The expression $3x^2-19x+20$ is equivalent to:

   (A) $(3x-5)(x-4)$

   (B) $(3x-5)(x+40)$

   (C) $(3x-4)(x-5)$

   (D) $(3x-4)(x+5)$

   (E) None of the above

6. The expression $20x^2-36xy+16y^2$ is equivalent to:

   (A) $(5x+8y)(4x+8y)$

   (B) $(5x-8y)(4x+2y)$

   (C) $(2x+y)(10x-16y)$

   (D) $4(x-y)(5x-4y)$

   (E) $(20x+8y)(x-2y)$

7. The expression $\dfrac{2x^2-6x-8}{x^2-1}$ is equivalent to:

   (A) -8

   (B) $\dfrac{2x-8}{x-1}$

   (C) $\dfrac{2x+8}{x+1}$

   (D) $\dfrac{2x-8}{x+1}$

   (E) None of the above

8. If $x^2-y^2=50$ and $x+y=20$, what is the value of $x-y$?

   (A) 0

   (B) 1

   (C) 2

   (D) 2.5

   (E) Cannot be determined

9. Which of the following are equivalent?

    I. $(x-y)^2$

    II. $(y-x)^2$

    III. $-(x-y)^2$

    (A)   I and II only

    (B)   I and III only

    (C)   II and III only

    (D)   all are equivalent

    (E)   none are equivalent

10. If $(x+y)^2 = 50$ and $x^2 + y^2 = 30$, what is the value of xy?

    (A)   10

    (B)   20

    (C)   30

    (D)   40

    (E)   50

11. The expression $\dfrac{x^2 - 4}{4x}$ is equivalent to:

    (A)   0

    (B)   1

    (C) $x-4$

    (D) $x-1$

    (E) $\dfrac{x}{4} - \dfrac{1}{x}$

12. Simplify $\dfrac{x^2 + x - 6}{2x^2 + 6x} \div \dfrac{x-2}{x}$

    (A) $\dfrac{1}{2}$

    (B)   1

    (C)   2

    (D) $\dfrac{(x-2)^2}{2x^2}$

    (E) $\dfrac{x+3}{x-3}$

13. If the difference between the area of a circle and the circumference of a circle is 35π, how long is the radius of the circle?

    (A)   1

    (B)   2

    (C)   5

    (D)   7

    (E)   35

14. A crate contains cartons, each carton contains boxes and each box contains 18 balls. If there are 540 balls per crate and if there are seven fewer cartons than boxes, how many cartons are there in a crate?

    (A)   3

    (B)   7

    (C)   10

    (D)   18

    (E)   30

15. Mr. Corn needs exactly 600 feet of fencing to enclose his rectangular yard. If the area of his yard is 12,500 square feet, what is the length (in feet) of his yard?

    (A)   75

    (B)   100

    (C)   200

    (D)   250

    (E)   300

Solutions to problems on FOILing and factoring (unit 3.5)

1 (D)

$$\left(2x-3\right)\left(5x+7\right)=10x^2+14x-15x-21$$
$$=10x^2-x-21$$

2. (E)

$$\left(x+8\right)^2=\left(x+8\right)\left(x+8\right)=x^2+8x+8x+64$$
$$=x^2+16x+64$$

3. (E)

$$x^2-6x+8=\left(x-4\right)\left(x-2\right)$$
$$=x^2-4x-2x+8=x^2-6x+8$$

4. (A)

$$x^2-5xy-176y^2=\left(x-16y\right)\left(x+11y\right)$$
$$=x^2-16xy+11xy-176=x^2-5xy-176$$

5. (C)

$$3x^2-19x+20=\left(3x-4\right)\left(x-5\right)$$
$$=3x^2-15x-4x+20=3x^2-19x+20$$

6. (D)

$$20x^2-36xy+16y^2=4(5x^2-9xy+4y^2)$$
$$=4(x-y)(5x-4y)$$

7. (B)

$$\frac{2x^2-6x-8}{x^2-1}=\frac{2\left(x^2-3x-4\right)}{\left(x+1\right)\left(x-1\right)}=\frac{2\left(x+1\right)\left(x-4\right)}{\left(x+1\right)\left(x-1\right)}$$
$$=\frac{2(x-4)}{x-1}=\frac{2x-8}{x-1}$$

8. (D)

$$x^2-y^2=\left(x+y\right)\left(x-y\right)$$
$$50=20\left(x-y\right)$$
$$2.5=x-y$$

9. (A)

$$(x-y)^2=(x-y)(x-y)=x^2-2xy+y^2$$
$$(y-x)^2=(y-x)(y-x)=y^2-2xy+x^2$$
$$-(x-y)^2=-(x-y)(x-y)=-(x^2-2xy+y^2)$$

10. (A)

$$(x+y)^2=x^2+2xy+y^2=50$$
$$2xy+30=50,\ 2xy=20,\ xy=10$$

11. (E)

$$\frac{x^2-4}{4x}=\frac{x^2}{4x}-\frac{4}{4x}=\frac{x}{4}-\frac{1}{x}$$

12. (A)

$$\frac{x^2+x-6}{2x^2+6x}\div\frac{x-2}{x}=\frac{(x+3)(x-2)}{2x(x+3)}\left(\frac{x}{x-2}\right)=\frac{1}{2}$$

13. (D)

$$\pi r^2-2\pi r=35\pi$$
$$r^2-2r-35=0$$
$$(r-7)(r+5)=0,\ r=7$$

14. (A)

Let x be the number of cartons and y be the number of boxes. If there are 540 balls per crate then $18xy=540$, or $xy=30$. If there are seven fewer cartons than boxes then $x=y-7$. Substitute:

$$xy=30,\ (y-7)y=30$$
$$y^2-7y-30=0,\ (y-10)(y+3)=0$$
$$y=10,\ x=y-7=10-7=3\text{ cartons.}$$

15. (D)

If 600 is the perimeter of the yard, then

$$600=2l+2w,\ 300=l+w$$

If the area of the yard is 12,500 then $lw=12,500$.

$$l(300-l)=12,500\quad l^2-300l+12,500=0$$
$$(l-250)(l-50)=0,\quad l=250$$

Unit 3.6 Ratios

Ratios are very useful things to know. But before they can be applied, it is necessary to be able to solve them by cross-multiplying. For example:

$$\frac{3}{5} = \frac{12}{x}$$ original problem

$$3x = 5 \cdot 12$$ cross-multiply

$$3x = 60$$ simplify

$$x = 20$$ solve for x by dividing both sides by 3.

Ratios can be written as fractions (as shown above) or they can be written using the : symbol. For example, the problem above could be written 3:5 as $12:x$. Or a problem might use words, as in "3 is to 5 as 12 is to x."

Constant Rate Problems

A popular problem has a very easy pattern. First the problem establishes a rate, and then asks you to apply that rate. For example: "It takes Paul 12 days to paint 5 toys. At this rate, how long will it take for him to paint 12 toys? This is easily accomplished with ratios. Just setup the ratio, and then solve by cross-multiplying:

$$\frac{12 \text{ days}}{5 \text{ toys}} = \frac{x \text{ days}}{12 \text{ toys}}, \ 5x = 144, \ x = 28.8 \text{ days}$$

The key phrase in these problems is "at this rate." Make sure your units matchup properly.

Unit Conversions

Ratios are especially useful for unit conversions. For example, suppose we want to know how many feet there are in 84 inches. We can find the answer using ratios:

$$\frac{12 \text{ inches}}{1 \text{ foot}} = \frac{84 \text{ inches}}{x \text{ feet}}, \ 12x = 84, \ x = 7 \text{ feet}$$

The first ratio comes from the fact that there are 12 inches in a foot. The second ratio is setup so that the inches amount is in the numerator and the unknown variable for the feet amount is in the denominator. When you setup ratios to do unit conversion, make sure that your units match up -- the same units should be in both numerators and the same units should be in both denominators.

Mixture Problems

There is a type of problem called mixture problems and they frequently show up on standardized tests. At first they look difficult but once you see how to solve them, they are easy. Consider the following:

> You are making pizza dough according to the recipe of 9 parts flour to 2 parts water. You need to make 165 pounds of dough. How many pounds of flour and how many pounds of water should you use?

This seems difficult at first, but the solution is very easy. We just set up the equation

$$9x + 2x = 165$$

What this equation says is that the same multiplier (x) will be applied to the 9 parts of flour and the 2 parts of water, and that they must sum to 165. Solving for x gives us 15. So we must use $9 \cdot 15 = 135$ pounds of flour and $2 \cdot 15 = 30$ pounds of water. Notice that 135 and 30 sum to the 165 pounds of dough required.

Direct and Inverse Variation

This is another type of word problem that seems difficult until you see how to do it. We begin with the definitions:

The variables x and y vary directly if their relationship can be modeled as

$$y = kx$$

where k is a non-zero constant. If we suppose k to be positive, you can see that when the value of x increases, y increases. This is where the name "direct" variation comes from. The variables x and y move in the same direction.

The variables x and y vary inversely if their relationship can be modeled as

$$y = \frac{k}{x}$$

where k is a non-zero constant. If we suppose k to be positive, you can see that when the value of x increases, y decreases. This is where the name "indirect" variation comes from. The variables x and y move in opposite directions.

These problems usually take the same form. They begin by saying whether the relationship is direct or inverse and supply initial values of x and y. This enables you to evaluate k. Then the problem asks for a new value of y when the value of x changes. For example:

X and Y are inversely proportional, and when X=10 Y=20. What is the value of Y when X=5?

The problem is solved as follows:

$$y = \frac{k}{x}$$ given

$$20 = \frac{k}{10}, \quad 200 = k$$ substitute and solve for k

$$y = \frac{200}{x}$$ new partial equation

$$y = \frac{200}{5} = 40$$ substitute for X, solve for Y.

Note that Y increased when X decreased because X and Y are inversely related.

Problems on ratios (unit 3.6)

1. Solve for x $$\frac{5}{6x} = \frac{10}{7}, \ x \neq 0$$

(A) $\dfrac{7}{12}$

(B) $\dfrac{12}{7}$

(C) $\dfrac{25}{21}$

(D) $\dfrac{21}{25}$

(E) Cannot be determined

2. Solve for x: $\dfrac{4}{x} = \dfrac{x}{16}, \ x \neq 0$

I. 1/4

II. 8

III. -8

(A) I only

(B) II only

(C) III only

(D) I and II only

(E) II and III only

3. You sell mixed nuts over the Internet. Your secret recipe is 9 parts peanuts to 3 parts cashews to 1 part pecans. How many pounds of cashews will be needed to fill an order for 195 pounds of mixed nuts?

(A) 15

(B) 38

(C) 45

(D) 49

(E) 135

4. The interior angles of a quadrilateral are in the ratio of 4:3:2:1. What is the size of the largest angle?

(A) 18

(B) 36

(C) 72

(D) 108

(E) 144

5. If there are 16 ounces in a pound, how many pounds are in 80 ounces?

(A) 1/5

(B) 5

(C) 64

(D) 96

(E) 1280

6. A blueprint is drawn to scale, where two inches represents 25 feet. If a room is 70 feet long, how many inches long will it be on the blueprint?

(A) 0.2

(B) 0.7

(C) 1.4

(D) 5.6

(E) 875

7. Y varies directly with X. When X=5, Y=40. What is the value of Y when X increases to 7?

(A) 7/8

(B) 8/7

(C) 15

(D) 25

(E) 56

8. Y varies inversely with X. When X=5, Y=40. What is the value of Y when X increases to 7?

(A) 7/8

(B) 8/7

(C) 25

(D) 200/7

(E) 1600

9. It takes Hayley 14 days to paint two rooms. At this rate, how many days would it take for her to paint five rooms?

(A)   0.7

(B)   1.4

(C)   12.5

(D)   17.5

(E)   35.0

10. If in the figure below $a:b$ as $5:13$, how large is b (in degrees)?

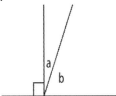

(A)   5

(B)   10

(C)   25

(D)   50

(E)   65

11. A map is drawn to scale so that two inches is 70 miles. If two towns are 5 inches apart on the map, how far apart are they (in miles)?

(A)   7

(B)   35

(C)   150

(D)   175

(E)   350

12. Paul has played 10 lacrosse games and scored 3 goals. At this rate how many goals should he expect to score over the entire season if there are 14 games remaining in the season?

(A)   3

(B)   4

(C)   5

(D)   6

(E)   7

13. In general, grades are directly proportional to amount of time spent studying.. When students spend 2 hours per week studying for the SAT®, their math score increases by 70 points. If Kelsey wants her score to increase by 105 points, how many hours per week should she study?

(A)   2

(B)   3

(C)   4

(D)   5

(E)   6

14. Suppose the strength of gravitational pull is inversely proportional to the square of the distance between two bodies. If the gravitational pull is 50 units when two bodies are 10 units apart, how strong is the pull when the two bodies are 100 units apart?

(A)   0.05

(B)   0.50

(C)   5.00

(D)   50.00

(E)   500.00

15. The matches won, tied and lost by the tennis team have the ratio of 3:2:1. How many matches could the tennis team have played?

(A)   15

(B)   20

(C)   25

(D)   30

(E)   35

16. In problem 15 above, if the tennis team has played 102 matches total, how many have they tied?

(A)   17

(B)   34

(C)   51

(D)   66

(E)   85

Solutions to problems on ratios (unit 3.6)

1. (A)

$$\frac{5}{6x} = \frac{10}{7}, \quad 60x = 35, \quad x = \frac{35}{60} = \frac{7}{12}$$

2. (E)

$$\frac{4}{x} = \frac{x}{16}, \quad x^2 = 64, \quad x = \pm 8$$

3. (C)

$$9x + 3x + x = 195$$
$$13x = 195$$
$$x = 15, \quad 3x = 45 \text{ pounds of cashews}$$

4. (E)

The interior angles of a quadrilateral sum to 360.

$$4x + 3x + 2x + x = 360$$
$$10x = 360$$
$$x = 36, \quad 4x = 144 = \text{the largest angle}$$

5. (B)

$$\frac{16}{1} = \frac{80}{x}, \quad 16x = 80, \ x = 5 \text{ pounds}$$

6 (D)

$$\frac{2}{25} = \frac{x}{70}, \quad 25x = 140, \quad x = 5.6 \text{ inches}$$

7. (E)

$$y = kx$$
$$40 = 5k, \quad k = 8$$
$$y = 8x, \quad y = 8 \cdot 7 = 56$$

8 (D)

$$y = \frac{k}{x}$$
$$40 = \frac{k}{5}, \quad k = 200$$
$$y = \frac{200}{x}, \quad y = \frac{200}{7}$$

9. (E)

$$\frac{14}{2} = \frac{x}{5}, \ 2x = 70, \ x = 35$$

10. (E)

$$5x + 13x = 90, \ 18x = 90, \ x = 5$$
$$13x = 13 \cdot 5 = 65$$

11. (D)

$$\frac{2}{70} = \frac{5}{x}, \ 2x = 350, \ x = 175$$

12. (E)

$$\frac{10}{3} = \frac{24}{x}, \ 10x = 72, \ x = 7.2$$

13. (B)

$$y = kx, \ 70 = 2k, \ k = 35$$
$$y = 35x, \ 105 = 35x, \ 3 = x$$

14. (B)

$$y = \frac{k}{x^2}, \ 50 = \frac{k}{10^2}, \ k = 5{,}000$$
$$y = \frac{5{,}000}{x^2} = \frac{5{,}000}{100^2} = 0.5$$

15. (D)

The answer must be divisible by 6.

$$3x + 2x + x = 6x = \text{ total matches played}$$

16. (B)

$$3x + 2x + x = 102, \ 6x = 102, \ x = 17$$
$$2x = 2 \cdot 17 = 34$$

Geometry uses different circuitry in your brain from that used by algebra. If you have not done geometry in a while you will probably need to get those wheels turning again.

Unit 4.1 Angles and lines

There are three types of angles to know:

$$0° < \text{acute angle} < 90°$$

$$\text{right angle} = 90°$$

$$90 < \text{obtuse angle} < 180°$$

Supplementary angles comprise a straight angle (they sum to 180 degrees); whereas complementary angles comprise a right angle (they sum to 90 degrees).

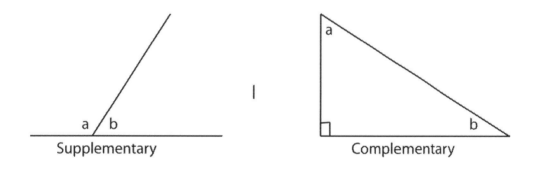

Remember that vertical angles are congruent (they have the same measure).

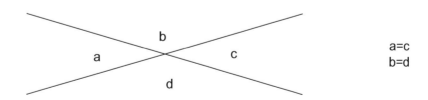

The bulk of what you need to remember about angles and lines has to do with parallel lines with a transversal line. The picture looks like this:

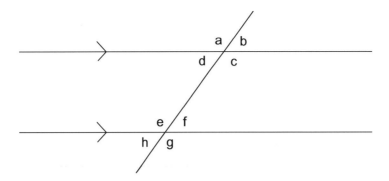

There is a bit of terminology to be mastered with this. The interior angles are those angles that lie inside the parallel lines, namely c, d, e and f. The exterior angles are those that lie outside the parallel lines, namely a, b, h and g.

There are several sets of congruent pairs to remember, as you can see in the table below.

Vertical angles	a=c
	b=d
	e=g
	f=h
Alternate interior angles	c=e
	d=f
Corresponding angles	a=e
	d=h
	b=f
	c=g
Alternate exterior angles	a=g
	b=h

Problems on angles and lines (unit 4.1)

Questions 1 and 2 refer to the diagram below.

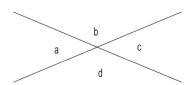

1. Which of the following statements must be true?

    I.   a=c

    II. a=d

    III. a+b=c+d

  (A)   I only

  (B)   II only

  (C)   III only

  (D)   I and II only

  (E)   I and III only

2. Which of the following may not be supplementary?

  (A)   a and b

  (B)   a and c

  (C)   a and d

  (D)   b and c

  (E)   c and d

Questions 3 and 4 refer to the diagram below.

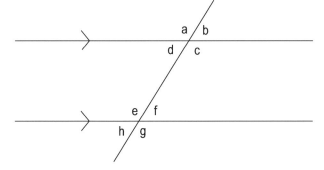

3. Which of the following statements must be true?

    I.   a=c

    II. a=h

    III. a+c=e+g

  (A)   I only

  (B)   II only

  (C)   III only

  (D)   I and II only

  (E)   I and III only

4. Which of the following statements is not necessarily true?

    I.   a=g

    II. b=e

    III. d=h

  (A)   I only

  (B)   II only

  (C)   III only

  (D)   I and II only

  (E)   II and III only

5. If A and B are complementary angles and the measure of A is 20 degrees, what is the measure of B?

  (A)   70 degrees

  (B)   90 degrees

  (C)   160 degrees

  (D)   180 degrees

  (E)   340 degrees

6 If a and b are supplementary angles, and a and c are complementary angles, then which of the following must be true?:

  (A)   a+b+c = 270 degrees

  (B)   b - a = 90 degrees

  (C)   b −c = 90 degrees

  (D)   a+b-c = 90 degrees

  (E)   b + c = 180 degrees

Solutions to problems on angles and lines (unit 4.1)

1 (E)

I is true (a and c are vertical angles). II is not necessarily true. III is true (a+b=180=c+d).

2. (B)

A and C are congruent because they are vertical angles; however they are not necessarily supplementary. The only way they could be supplementary would be if the lines were perpendicular.

3. (E)

I is true because a and c are vertical. II is false because a and h are not alternate exterior. III is true because a=c and e=g (vertical) <u>and</u> c=e (alternate interior). Therefore a=c=e=g and a+c=e+g.

4. (B)

I is always true because a and g are alternate exterior angles. II may not be true. III is always true because d and h are corresponding angles.

5. (A)

$$A + B = 90, \quad B = 90 - 20 = 70$$

6. (C)

This is a pair of equations:

$$a + b = 180$$
$$a + c = 90$$
$$b - c = 180 - 90 = 90$$

Unit 4.2 Triangles

Triangles are a big part of standardized tests, especially right triangles. But first we begin with information about triangles in general. There are three types of triangles:

	Sides	Angles
Equilateral	All congruent	All 60 degrees
Isosceles	Two congruent	Two congruent
Scalene	None congruent	None congruent

The formulas for the area of a triangle are:

Any triangle	$A = \dfrac{1}{2}bh$
Right triangle	$A = \dfrac{1}{2}leg_1 \cdot leg_2$
Equilateral triangle	$A = \dfrac{s^2\sqrt{3}}{4}$

Triangle Inequality

For reasons that are unclear to me, the standardized tests are fond of the triangle inequality. It simply states that any leg of any triangle is strictly less than the sum of the other two legs. Graphically, it looks like this:

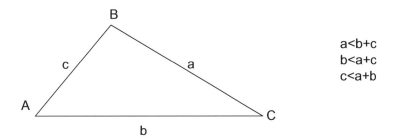

$$a<b+c$$
$$b<a+c$$
$$c<a+b$$

Note that it is only necessary to test whether the longest leg is strictly less than the sum of the other two legs. In the diagram above, it is only necessary to test whether b is less than $a+c$. Using a variety of means, a question may ask whether a particular triplet can form a triangle, for example 1,2,3. That cannot be a triangle because 3=1+2. However 1,2,2 can be a triangle because 2<1+2.

Largest and Smallest Angles and Sides

Along with the triangle inequality, remember that the longest side (b in the diagram) is opposite the largest angle (B in the diagram); whereas the shortest side (c in the diagram) is opposite the smallest angle (C in the diagram). A special case is the right triangle. The hypotenuse of a right triangle is the longest side (and it is opposite the largest angle, the right angle).

Similar Triangles

Most students remember congruent triangles, where corresponding angles are congruent and corresponding sides are congruent (remember SSS, SAS, AAS, and ASA?). However, there is a tendency to forget similar triangles, where corresponding angles are congruent and corresponding sides are proportional. Similar triangles are illustrated below: In the diagram below, $\triangle ABC \sim \triangle DEF$. Take careful note of the corresponding angles and sides. Also note that angles are labeled with capital letters; sides are labeled with lower case letters.

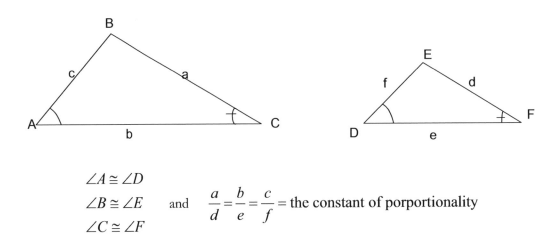

$$\angle A \cong \angle D$$
$$\angle B \cong \angle E \quad \text{and} \quad \frac{a}{d} = \frac{b}{e} = \frac{c}{f} = \text{the constant of porportionality}$$
$$\angle C \cong \angle F$$

A special case of similar triangles is where a line has been drawn through a triangle so that the line is parallel to one of the sides of the triangle, as shown below. The result is two similar triangles, where the larger triangle is similar to the smaller triangle.

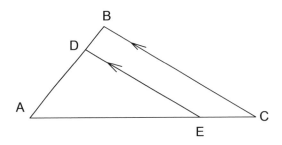

Note that $\angle ADE$ and $\angle ABC$ are congruent because they are corresponding angles. The same is true for $\angle AED$ and $\angle ACB$. Having proved angles to be congruent we can conclude that the triangles are similar (remember AA?). When writing out the similar statement, make sure you get the corresponding sides lined up, $\triangle ABC \sim \triangle ADE$. Do you see how the corresponding sides line up? The proportionality relationships are

$$\frac{AD}{AB} = \frac{AE}{AC} = \frac{DE}{BC}$$

Right Triangles

The most famous theorem in all of math, the Pythagorean Theorem, applies to right triangles,. The theorem states

$$a^2 + b^2 = c^2$$

where c is the length of the hypotenuse, and a and b are the lengths of the legs.

It is absolutely necessary to memorize the relationships of the sides of the two special triangles shown below, even though these are supplied on the SAT®. You must recognize these relationships when they show up on the test, without flipping pages back and forth when a formula is needed.

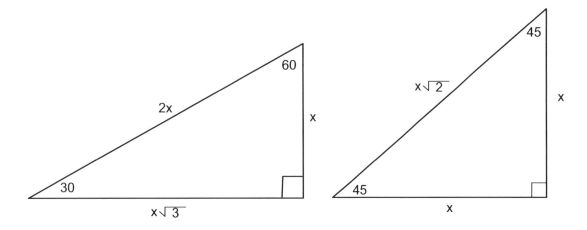

Be on the lookout for these special right triangles because they are very popular on standardized tests. The table below gives some tips on how to spot them.

When you see:	Look out for:
$\sqrt{3}$	30-60-90
A side that is $\dfrac{1}{2}$ the hypotenuse	30-60-90
A hypotenuse that is twice the length of a side	30-60-90
An equilateral triangle	30-60-90
$\sqrt{2}$	45-45-90
The diagonal of a square	45-45-90

A useful exercise is to use the Pythagorean Theorem to prove the relationships of the sides of each of the special right triangles. The proof for the 45-45-90 triangle is shown below as an example, and the 30-60-90 triangle is left as an exercise.

$$x^2 + x^2 = \left(x\sqrt{2}\right)^2$$
$$2x^2 = \sqrt{2} \cdot \sqrt{2} \cdot x \cdot x = 2x^2$$

Practice problems on triangles (unit 4.2)

The diagram below pertains to problems 1-3.

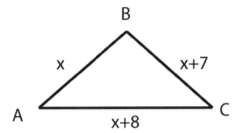

1. What is the perimeter of $\triangle ABC$?

   (A) $3x+15$

   (B) $x+15$

   (C) $x(x+7)(x+8)$

   (D) $x^2+(x+7)^2+(x+8)^2$

   (E) $\sqrt{x^2+(x+7)^2}$

2. If B is a right angle, what is the area of $\triangle ABC$.

   (A) $3x+15$

   (B) $x+15$

   (C) $\dfrac{1}{2}x(x+7)$

   (D) $\dfrac{1}{2}x(x+8)$

   (E) $\dfrac{1}{2}(x+7)(x+8)$

3. If B is a right angle, what is the value of x?

   (A)   3

   (B)   4

   (C)   5

   (D)   12

   (E)   13

4. What is the perimeter of an equilateral triangle whose area is $4\sqrt{3}$?

   (A)   2

   (B)   4

   (C)   8

   (D)   12

   (E)   16

5. What is the side of an equilateral triangle whose altitude is 3?

   (A)   1.5

   (B) $\sqrt{3}$

   (C) $2\sqrt{3}$

   (D)   3

   (E)   6

6. What is the area of a square whose diagonal is 2?

   (A)   -2

   (B)   1

   (C)   2

   (D) $\sqrt{2}$

   (E)   4

7. One leg of a right triangle is 5 and its hypotenuse is 10. What is the size of its smallest angle?

   (A)   15 degrees

   (B)   30 degrees

   (C)   45 degrees

   (D)   60 degrees

   (E)   75 degrees

8. One leg of a right triangle is 7 and the hypotenuse is 10. What is the length of the other leg?

   (A)   6

   (B)   9

   (C) $\sqrt{51}$

   (D)   36

   (E) $\sqrt{149}$

9. One side of a triangle is 7 and another side is 10. Which of the values below could be the third side of the triangle?

I.   2   IV 16
II.   3   V. 17
III. 4   VI. 18

(A)   I and IV only
(B)   II and V only
(C)   III and IV only
(D)   I, II and III only
(E)   IV, V, and VI only

10. In the diagram below, $\triangle ABC \sim \triangle DEF$. What is the value of y-x?

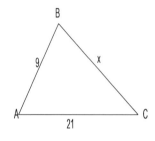

(A)   -53
(B)   -8
(C)   5/3
(D)   7
(E)   -63

11. A six foot tall man stands in the shadow of a 18 foot tall telephone pole. If the man is standing three feet from the base of the telephone pole, what is the length of the telephone pole's shadow?

(A)   3
(B)   3.5
(C)   4
(D)   4.5
(E)   Cannot be determined

12. In the diagram below, if $\overline{AB} \parallel \overline{ED}$, then what is the value of x?

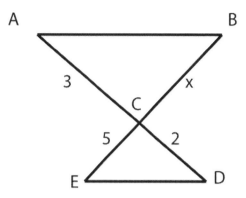

(A)   2.0
(B)   3.0
(C)   3.3
(D)   5.0
(E)   7.5

13. In $\triangle ABC$, side c=3 and side a=7. If $\angle B$ is the largest angle, then side b could be:

(A)   3
(B)   4
(C)   9
(D)   10
(E)   11

14. What is the area of a 30-60-90 triangle whose shortest leg is 2?

(A)   2
(B) $2\sqrt{2}$
(C) $2\sqrt{3}$
(D) $4\sqrt{2}$
(E) $4\sqrt{3}$

(E)   11

Solutions to practice problems on triangles (unit 4.2)

1. (A)

$x + (x+7) + (x+8) = 3x + 15$

2. (C)

$A = \dfrac{1}{2}bh = \dfrac{1}{2}(x)(x+7)$

3. (C)

$x^2 + (x+7)^2 = (x+8)^2$

$x^2 + (x^2 + 14x + 49) = x^2 + 16x + 64$

$x^2 - 2x - 15 = 0, \ (x-5)(x+3) = 0, \ x = 5$

4. (D)

$A = s^2 \dfrac{\sqrt{3}}{4}$

$4\sqrt{3} = \dfrac{s^2\sqrt{3}}{4}, \ s^2 = 16, \ s = 4, \ P = 12$

5. (C)

The altitude of an equilateral triangle forms two 30-60-90 triangles. The altitude is opposite the 60 degree angle, and the side opposite the 30 degree angle is s/2. So if the altitude is 3 then

$3 = \dfrac{s}{2}\sqrt{3}, \quad \dfrac{6}{\sqrt{3}} = s, \quad 2\sqrt{3} = s \cdot$

6. (C)

The diagonal of a square forms two 45-45-90 triangles, with the diagonal being the hypotenuse of each right triangle. So if the diagonal is 2 then

$s^2 + s^2 = 2^2, \ 2s^2 = 4, \ s = \sqrt{2}, \ A = s^2 = 2 \cdot$

7. (B)

This must be a 30-60-90 triangle because the hypotenuse is twice as long as of one of the sides. Therefore the smallest angle is 30 degrees.

8. (C)

$x^2 + 7^2 = 10^2, \ x^2 = 100 - 49 = 51, \ x = \sqrt{51}$

9. (C)

I. False $10 \ not < \ 2+7$

II False $10 \ not < \ 3+7$

III. True $10 < 4+7$

IV True $16 < 7+10$

V. False $17 \ not < \ 7+10$

VI. False $18 \ not < \ 7+10$

10. (B)

$\dfrac{3}{9} = \dfrac{y}{21}, \quad 9y = 63, \quad y = 7$

$\dfrac{3}{9} = \dfrac{5}{x}, \quad 3x = 45, \ \text{x=15}$

$y - x = 7 - 15 = -8$

11. (D)

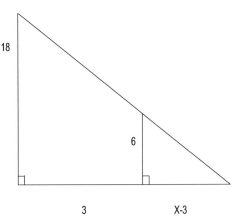

SUN

18

6

3   X-3

There are two similar right triangles, where the base of the large triangle is x and the base of the small triangle is x-3. Use the ratios of little over big to find

$\dfrac{x-3}{x} = \dfrac{6}{18}, \ 18x - 54 = 6x, \ x = 54/12 = 4.5$

12. (E)

$\triangle ABC \sim \triangle DEC$ because of alternate interior angles, $\angle E \cong \angle B$ and $\angle A \cong \angle D$.

$\dfrac{2}{3} = \dfrac{5}{x}, \ 2x = 15, \ x = 7.5$

13. (C)

Side b is the longest side because angle B is the largest angle. Therefore b must be greater than 3 or 7. On the other hand, the triangle inequality requires b to be less than 3+7=10.

14. (C)

$A = \dfrac{1}{2}bh = \left(\dfrac{1}{2}\right)(2)(2\sqrt{3}) = 2\sqrt{3}$

Unit 4.3 Circles

There are just a few things to remember about circles, and most of them are things you probably know already. Everyone remembers that the central angle of an entire circle measures 360 degrees and that the measure of the entire arc of a circle is 360 degrees. But you must also remember the relationship between arcs, central angles, and inscribed angles, as shown below.

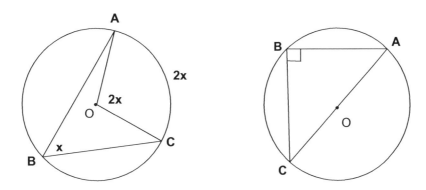

Take a look at circle O on the left. It has a central angle $\angle AOC$ ($\angle AOC$ is a central angle because its vertex is the center of the circle). Note that the measure of central angle $\angle AOC$ is the same as the measure of its inscribed arc, $\overset{\frown}{AC}$. On the other hand, $\angle ABC$ is an inscribed angle, not a central angle (its vertex is not at the center of the circle). Its measure is one-half the measure of its inscribed arc, $\overset{\frown}{AC}$.

Circle O on the right illustrates a special case of an inscribed angle. $\angle ABC$ is inscribed in a semi-circle, where chord $\overline{AC}$ is a diagonal of the circle. Therefore $\overset{\frown}{AC}$ is a semi-circle and must be 180 degrees (half of a 360 degree circle). Because $\angle ABC$ is inscribed in a semi-circle, its measure must be 90 degrees (half of the 180 degree arc in which it is inscribed). For some reason, inscribed right angles are popular questions.

Sectors

Another favorite topic has to do with sectors of circles. Think of these as slices from a pizza pie. You need to memorize formulas for the area of the pizza slice (area of the sector) and the length of the crust of the pizza slice (arc length). These are shown below.

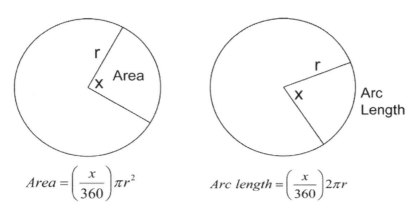

$$Area = \left(\frac{x}{360}\right)\pi r^2 \qquad\qquad Arc\ length = \left(\frac{x}{360}\right)2\pi r$$

In the figures above, notice that the central angle, which is x degrees, is the key to understanding how these formulas work. As x increases, the size of the slice increases. If the slice were half of the pizza, x would be 180 degrees. The formulas simply take the fraction of the whole that the central angle represents and then multiply that fraction by the area of the whole pie (πr^2) or by the circumference of the whole pie ($2\pi r$).

Equation of a Circle

A favorite topic on the ACT is the equation of a circle. If you know the coordinates of the center of the circle (h,k) and you know that the radius is r, then the equation of the circle is:

$$(x-h)^2 + (y-k)^2 = r^2$$

Tangents

Lastly, it is necessary to remember that the tangent to a circle forms a right angle with the radius of a circle at the point where the tangent and radius meet. This is illustrated below.

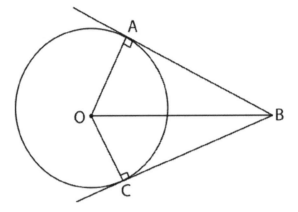

In addition to the right angles that are formed at the points of tangency, notice that we have two congruent right triangles, $\triangle AOB \cong \triangle COB$. Of particular interest is that the external point B is equidistant from the points of tangency, or $\overline{AB} \cong \overline{CB}$.

Circle Graphs (Pie Charts)

Most people rely on computers to construct a circle graph (also known as a pie chart). But sometimes you will see a question that asks you to construct it by hand.. To see how, consider a sock drawer with 10 red socks, 40 white socks and 30 blue socks. To construct a circle graph, just calculate the size of the central angle for each color:

$$red = \left(\frac{10}{80}\right)360 = 45°, \; white = \left(\frac{40}{80}\right)360 = 180°, \; blue = \left(\frac{30}{80}\right)360 = 135°$$

Once the central angles are calculated, it is easy to draw the circle graph. In this case it would look like:

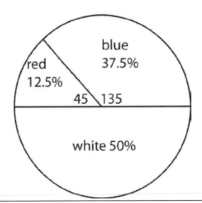

Practice problems on circles (unit 4.3)

1. If circle A has a radius that is twice the length of the radius of circle B, then the following must be true:

       I. The area of circle A is two times the area of circle B.

       II. The circumference of circle A is two times the circumference of circle B.

       III. The area of circle A is four times the area of circle B.

    (A)   I only

    (B)   II only

    (C)   III only

    (D)   I and II only

    (E)   II and III only

2. In the figure below, which of the following must be true?

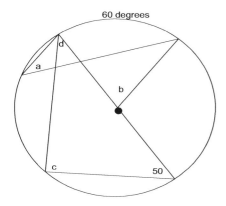

60 degrees

       I. a=60

      II. c-d=50

      III. b=120

    (A)   I only

    (B)   II only

    (C)   III only

    (D)   I and II only

    (E)   None of the above

3. If a circle is divided into eight congruent sectors and each sector has an area of 8π, what is the radius of the circle?

    (A)   4

    (B)   8

    (C)   12

    (D)   18

    (E)   32

4. If a sector has an arc length of π and a radius of 10, what is the size of its central angle (in degrees)?

    (A)   4

    (B)   8

    (C)   12

    (D)   18

    (E)   20

5. Billy ordered a pizza with a crust that is 10π inches long. What is the area of the pizza?

    (A) 5π

    (B) 10π

    (C) 15π

    (D) 20π

    (E) 25π

6. A tangent is drawn to a circle from an external point that is 20 inches from the center of the circle. If the external point is 10 inches from the point of tangency, what is the radius of the circle?

    (A)   10

    (B) $10\sqrt{3}$

    (C) $10\sqrt{5}$

    (D)   20

    (E)   Cannot be determined

7. About 20% of the clothes that Rachel has are from Italy. If she were to construct a circle graph of her clothes, what would be the size (in degrees) of the central angle representing Italy?

(A)   20

(B)   36

(C)   40

(D)   72

(E)   80

8. About 20% of the clothes that Rachel has are from Italy. If she were to construct a circle graph of her clothes using a circle with a radius of 3 inches, what would be the area (in square inches) of the portion of the circle representing Italy?

(A) 0.2π

(B) 0.6π

(C) 1.8π

(D) 2π

(E) 20π

9. About 20% of the clothes that Rachel has are from Italy. If she were to construct a circle graph of her clothes using a circle with a radius of 1 inch, what would be length of the arc of the portion of the circle representing Italy?

(A) 0.2π

(B) 0.4π

(C) π

(D) 2π

(E) 4π

10. If a sector of a circle has an area of π units squared and the measure of its central angle (in degrees) is an integer, then the radius of the circle must be:

(A) π

(B) π^2

(C)   6

(D)   10

(E)   36

11. In the diagram below, find the value of x (in degrees).

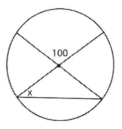

(A)   20

(B)   30

(C)   40

(D)   50

(E)   60

12. A circle graph is to be constructed from the data below. What is the size (in degrees) of the angle representing math majors?

Major	Number of Students
Math	50
Science	150
Business	300
Other	400

(A)   .05

(B)   5

(C)   10

(D)   20

(E)   50

13. If a circle is tangent to the x-axis at x=5 and is tangent to the y-axis at y=-5, what is the equation of the circle?

(A) $x^2 + y^2 = 25$

(B) $(x+5)^2 + (y+5)^2 = 25$

(C) $(x+5)^2 + (y-5)^2 = 25$

(D) $(x-5)^2 + (y+5)^2 = 25$

(E) $(x-5)^2 + (y-5)^2 = 25$

Solutions to practice problems on circles (unit 4.3)

1 (E)

I is false and III is true:

$$\frac{A_A}{A_B} = \frac{\pi r_A^{\,2}}{\pi r_B^{\,2}} = \frac{\left(2r_B\right)^2}{r_B^{\,2}} = 4$$

II is true:

$$\frac{C_A}{C_B} = \frac{2\pi r_A}{2\pi r_B} = \frac{r_A}{r_B} = \frac{2r_B}{r_B} = 2$$

2. (B)

I is false; a=30, inscribed angle

II is true because c=90 and therefore d=40

III is false because b=60, central angle.

3. (B)

$$8\pi = \left(\frac{45}{360}\right)\pi r^2,\ \ 8 = \frac{1}{8}r^2,\ \ 64 = r^2,\ \ 8 = r$$

4. (D)

$$\pi = \left(\frac{x}{360}\right)2\pi \cdot 10,\ 1 = 20\left(\frac{x}{360}\right)$$

$$\frac{1}{20} = \frac{x}{360},\ \ \ x = 18$$

5. (E)

$2\pi r = 10\pi,\ r = 5$

$A = \pi r^2 = 25\pi$

6. (B)

$r^2 + 10^2 = 20^2$

$r^2 = 400 - 100 = 300$

$r = \sqrt{300} = 10\sqrt{3}$

7. (D)

$.20(360) = 72$

8. (C)

$$A = \left(\frac{72}{360}\right)\pi 3^2 = 1.8\pi$$

9. (B)

$$l = \left(\frac{72}{360}\right)2\pi \cdot 1 = 0.4\pi$$

10. (C)

$$\pi = \left(\frac{n}{360}\right)\pi r^2$$

$$1 = \frac{n}{360}r^2$$

$360 = nr^2,\ n = 10 \text{ and } r^2 = 36,\ r = 6$

11. (C)

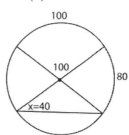

12. (D)

$$\left(\frac{50}{900}\right)360 = 20$$

13. (D)

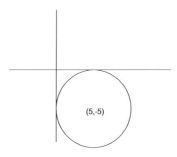

center $= (5,-5)$, radius $= 5$

$\left(x-5\right)^2 + \left(y+5\right)^2 = 5^2$

Unit 4.4 Polygons

A polygon is a closed shape with n straight sides. If n=3 the polygon is a triangle. If n=4 the polygon is a quadrilateral, etc. A **regular polygon** has all sides congruent and all interior angles congruent. There are two formulas to be memorized for polygons

$$\text{sum of interior angles} = (n-2)180$$

$$\text{sum of exterior angles} = 360$$

The derivation of the first formula above is interesting and kind of fun to do. Draw a polygon and then choose a vertex at random. From that vertex draw lines to all of the other vertices in the polygon. You should now have divided the polygon into $(n-2)$ triangles. As each triangle contains angles that sum to 180 degrees, the sum of the interior angles of the polygon is $(n-2)180$.

Quadrilaterals

The most popular polygon is the four-sided polygon or quadrilateral. There are quite a few properties to remember about quadrilaterals, and the easiest way to remember them is to use a "quadrilateral tree," as shown below.

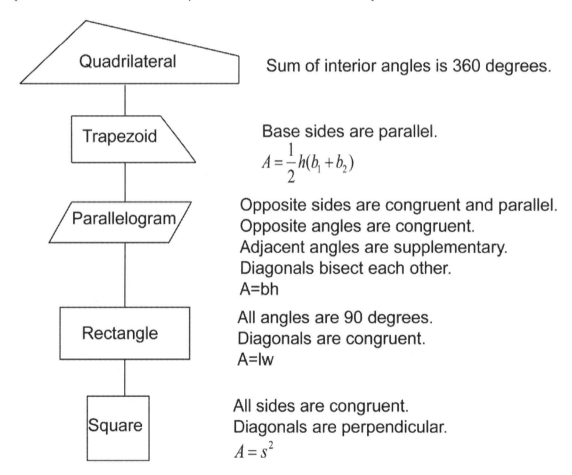

Quadrilateral — Sum of interior angles is 360 degrees.

Trapezoid — Base sides are parallel.
$$A = \frac{1}{2}h(b_1 + b_2)$$

Parallelogram — Opposite sides are congruent and parallel.
Opposite angles are congruent.
Adjacent angles are supplementary.
Diagonals bisect each other.
A=bh

Rectangle — All angles are 90 degrees.
Diagonals are congruent.
A=lw

Square — All sides are congruent.
Diagonals are perpendicular.
$$A = s^2$$

The key to understanding the tree is that properties are inherited by the "children" from the "parents." The parallelogram is a special type of quadrilateral, the rectangle is a special type of parallelogram, and the square is a special type of rectangle. For example, the diagonals of a rectangle bisect each other because that property is inherited from the parallelogram.

Practice problems on polygons (unit 4.4)

1. How large (in degrees) is the interior angle of a regular pentadecagon (all 15 sides are congruent)?

    (A)   40

    (B)   66

    (C)   110

    (D)   125

    (E)   156

2. How large (in degrees) is the exterior angle of a regular dodecagon (all 12 sides are congruent)?

    (A)   15

    (B)   30

    (C)   45

    (D)   60

    (E)   90

3. If sum of the interior angles of a regular polygon(all angels and sides congruent) is 1800 degrees, how many sides does it have?

    (A)   6

    (B)   8

    (C)   10

    (D)   12

    (E)   14

4. In the parallelogram below, what is the measure of z (in degrees)?

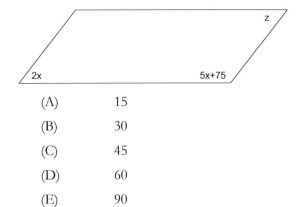

    (A)   15

    (B)   30

    (C)   45

    (D)   60

    (E)   90

5. If a rectangle has an area of 60 units and a width of 5 units, what is the length of its diagonal?

    (A) $\sqrt{61}$

    (B)   12

    (C)   13

    (D) $\sqrt{119}$

    (E)   Cannot be determined

6. In the parallelogram below, what is the measure (in degrees) of z?.

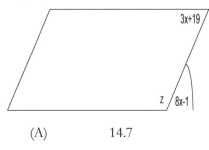

    (A)   14.7

    (B)   31

    (C)   63.2

    (D)   116.8

    (E)   149

7. If the base of a parallelogram is doubled and its height is tripled, the ratio of the area of the new parallelogram to the area of the old parallelogram is:

    (A)   1

    (B)   2

    (C)   3

    (D)   6

    (E)   36

8. If the area of a square is 10 square units, what is the sum of its diagonals?

    (A) $2\sqrt{5}$

    (B) $4\sqrt{5}$

    (C) $2\sqrt{10}$

    (D) $4\sqrt{10}$

    (E)   20

9. If the area of the trapezoid below is 140 square units, what is the height?

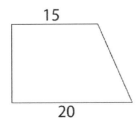

(A)   4

(B)   6

(C)   8

(D)   28

(E)   56

The figure below applies to problems 10 and 11. Point E is the center of square ABCD.

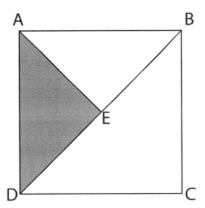

10. If the area of $\triangle ADE$ is 4/3, then the area of square ABCD would be:

(A)   1/3

(B)   9/4

(C)   3/1

(D)   4/1

(E)   16/3

11. If DE is 5 units long, then the area of square ABCD would be:

(A)   5

(B) $5\sqrt{2}$

(C)   10

(D)   25

(E)   50

The figure below applies to problems 12 and 13. Quadrilateral ABCD is a parallelogram and $\triangle ABE$ is equilateral.

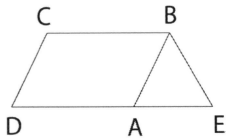

12. If AE is 10 units long, then how long is CD?

(A)   2.5

(B)   5

(C)   10

(D)   15

(E)   20

13. What is the measure (in degrees) of $\angle C$?

(A)   30

(B)   45

(C)   60

(D)   120

(E)   150

---

14. A circle is inscribed in a square, as shown below. If the diagonal of the square is 36 units, then what is the diameter of the circle?

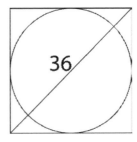

(A) $3\sqrt{2}$

(B) $9\sqrt{2}$

(C) $18\sqrt{2}$

(D) $36\sqrt{2}$

(E) $64\sqrt{2}$

Solutions to practice problems on polygons (unit 4.4)

1. (E)

Interior angles sum to $(15-2)180 = 2340$.

   Each interior angle must be $2340/15 = 156$ degrees.

2. (B)

Each exterior angle must be $360/12 = 30$ degrees.

3. (D)

$$1800 = (n-2)180$$
$$10 = n-2, \quad n = 12 \text{ sides}$$

4. (B)

Because they are supplementary,

$$2x + (5x+75) = 180, \quad x = 15$$
$$z = 2x = 2 \cdot 15 = 30$$

5. (C)

$$5l = 60, \quad l = 12$$
$$5^2 + 12^2 = d^2, \quad 169 = d^2, \quad 13 = d$$

6. (E)

Because of alternate interior angles of parallel lines,

$$3x + 19 = 8x - 1, \; 5x = 20, \; x = 4$$

Angle z and 8x-1 are supplementary, so

$$z + (8x-1) = 180, \quad z + 31 = 180, \quad z = 149$$

7. (D)

$$old = bh$$
$$new = (2b)(3h) = 6bh$$
$$new/old = 6/1$$

8. (B)

$$\left(\sqrt{10}\right)^2 + \left(\sqrt{10}\right)^2 = d^2$$
$$10 + 10 = d^2$$
$$d = \sqrt{20} = 2\sqrt{5}$$
$$d + d = 4\sqrt{5}$$

9. (C)

$$140 = \frac{1}{2}h(20+15), \; 280 = 35h, \; 8 = h$$

10. (E)

The shaded region comprises 1/4 of the square. So the area of the square is four times the area of the shaded region, $A = 4\left(\dfrac{4}{3}\right) = \dfrac{16}{3}$

11. (E)

If DE=5 then AE=5. By Pythagorean Theorem:

$$Area = AD^2 = 5^2 + 5^2 = 50$$

12. (C)

If AE is 10 units long then AB is also 10 units long because triangle ABE is equilateral. If AB is 10 units long then CD is 10 units long because opposite sides of a parallelogram are congruent.

13. (D)

If triangle ABE is equilateral then $\angle BAE$ is 60 degrees. Then $\angle BAD$ is 120 degrees because it is supplemental. Therefore $\angle C$ must also be 120 degrees because opposite angles of a parallelogram are congruent.

14. (C)

The diameter of the circle is equal to the side of the square. By Pythagorean Theorem:

$$s^2 + s^2 = 36^2, \; s^2 = 648, \; s = \sqrt{648} = 18\sqrt{2}$$

Unit 4.5 Solids

Fortunately there are only three solids that are popular on the standardized tests: the rectangular solid, the cube, and the cylinder.

Rectangular solids

Take a look below at a diagram of a rectangular solid. Think of a sandbox filled with sand. It has a certain width and a certain length, which define the base of the sandbox, and it has a certain height. The box has six faces. Each face is a rectangle with a surface area (SA) equal to the area of its respective rectangle. The total surface area of the rectangular solid is the sum of the surface areas of the faces.

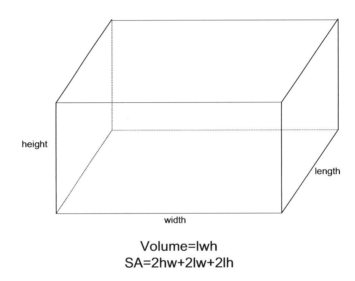

Volume=lwh
SA=2hw+2lw+2lh

Cubes

An important special case of the rectangular solid is the cube. The width, length and height of a cube are all the same, represented by the letter s which stands for side. The volume and surface area of the cube are:

$$Volume = lwh = s \cdot s \cdot s = s^3$$
$$SA = 2hw + 2lw + 2lh = 2s^2 + 2s^2 + 2s^2 = 6s^2$$

Cylinders

When you think of a cylinder, think of a can of soup (or soda or beer, whichever you prefer). The volume of a cylinder is the area of the circular base times the height of the cylinder. The surface area is a bit trickier. It is the sum of the areas of the two circular bases plus the area of the side. To get the area of the side, pretend to have removed both lids of the can. Then cut the can vertically and flatten out the sides. The length of the resulting rectangle will be the circumference of the circular base and the width of the rectangle is the height of the cylinder.

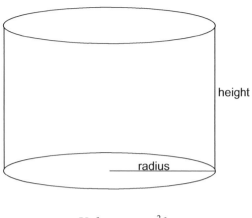

$$Volume = \pi r^2 h$$

$$SA = 2\pi r^2 + 2\pi rh$$

Diagonals of rectangular solids

An important type of question that you might see on a standardized test involves the diagonal of a rectangular solid. When you see a question of this sort, use the Pythagorean Theorem twice. First find the legs of the right triangle formed by the diagonal, then find the diagonal itself.

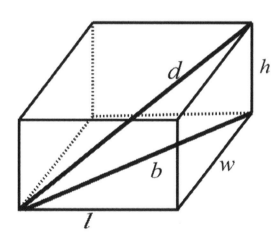

$$First: \quad b^2 = l^2 + w^2$$

$$Second: \quad d^2 = b^2 + h^2$$

How many small things fit in a big thing?

Another important type of problem involving solids is the question of how many small solids can fit in a large solid. To find the answer, calculate the volume of the large solid and then divide by the volume of the small solid. For a fun example, find the number of glasses of beer that can be served from a keg (assuming all glasses are the same and all participants are over 21) by dividing the volume of the keg by the volume of the glass.

IMPORTANT NOTE: This same reasoning can be applied to area. How many tiles are needed to cover a floor? Calculate the area of the floor and divide by the area of each tile.

Practice problems on solids (unit 4.5)

1. What is the width of a rectangular solid that has a volume of 375, a length of 5 and a height of 5?

  (A)   5
  (B)   10
  (C)   15
  (D)   25
  (E)   75

2. How many cubes of length 2 would it take to fill a rectangular solid with a volume of 120?

  (A)   15
  (B)   30
  (C)   45
  (D)   60
  (E)   75

3. What is the height of a cylinder whose volume is 18π and whose radius is 3?

  (A)   2
  (B)   4
  (C)   6
  (D)   8
  (E)   10

4. How long is the edge of a cube whose surface area is 150 square units?

  (A)   2
  (B)   5
  (C) $2.5\sqrt{6}$
  (D) $5\sqrt{6}$
  (E)   25

5. What is the surface area of a cylinder with a radius of π and a height of π?

  (A) $2\pi^2$
  (B) $2\pi^3$
  (C) $4\pi^2$
  (D) $4\pi^3$
  (E) $4\pi^4$

6. What is the length of the diagonal of a cube whose side is 3 units?

  (A) $2\sqrt{2}$
  (B) $2\sqrt{3}$
  (C)   3
  (D) $3\sqrt{2}$
  (E) $3\sqrt{3}$

7. A roll of wallpaper is 3 feet wide and 25 feet long. How many rolls will be needed to cover a cube whose edge is 15 feet?

  (A)   3
  (B)   12
  (C)   16
  (D)   18
  (E)   45

8. What is the length of the diagonal of a rectangular solid with a length of 4 and a width of 3 and a height of 6?

  (A)   5
  (B)   6
  (C)   7.8
  (D)   8.5
  (E)   9

9. If 50 guests are expected at a party, and each guest is expected to drink 3 cylindrical glasses of punch, and each glass has a radius of 5cm and a height of 10 cm, what must be the minimum capacity of the punch bowl (in cubic centimeters)?

  (A) 7500π
  (B) 12500π
  (C) 25000π
  (D) 37500π
  (E) 50000π

Solutions to practice problems on solids (unit 4.5)

1.(C)

$$375 = 5 \cdot 5 \cdot h, \quad 15 = h.$$

2. (A)

$$\frac{120}{2^3} = 15$$

3. (A)

$$18\pi = \pi 3^2 h, \quad 2 = h$$

4. (B)

$$SA = 150 = 6s^2$$
$$25 = s^2, \quad 5 = s$$

5. (D)

$$SA = 2\pi r^2 + 2\pi rh = 2\pi^3 + 2\pi^3 = 4\pi^3$$

6. (E)

Find the diagonal of the base:
$$3^2 + 3^2 = d^2, \quad 3\sqrt{2} = d$$

Find the diagonal of the cube:
$$3^2 + \left(3\sqrt{2}\right)^2 = d^2, \quad 9 + 18 = d^2, \quad 3\sqrt{3} = d$$

7. (D)

Each roll has $3 \cdot 25 = 75$ square feet.

Cube has $15 \cdot 15 \cdot 6 = 1350$ square feet.

$1350/75 = 18$ rolls

8. (C)

Find the diagonal of the base:
$$3^2 + 4^2 = d^2, \quad 5 = d$$

Find the diagonal of the cube:
$$6^2 + 5^2 = d^2, \quad 36 + 25 = d^2, \quad \sqrt{61} = d$$

9. (D)

Glasses are $50 \cdot 3 = 150$

Each glass holds $\pi \cdot 5^2 \cdot 10 = 250\pi$

Capacity must be $150 \cdot 250\pi = 37500\pi$

Unit 4.6 Slope, distance and midpoint

Remember how to find the equation of a line? The general equation is

$$y = mx + b,$$

where m is the slope of the line and b is where the line crosses the y-axis (the y-intercept).

The equation of a line can be determined if you know two of the points through which it travels (two points determine a line). We denote the points as (x_1, y_1) and (x_2, y_2). The first step is to find the slope

$$m = \frac{y_2 - y_1}{x_2 - x_1}.$$

Once we have the slope, we can use one of the points to find the equation of the line. For example, suppose we want the equation of the line that passes through (1,2) and (5, 14). We determine the slope to be

$$m = \frac{14 - 2}{5 - 1} = \frac{12}{4} = 3.$$

Next write the partial equation

$$y = 3x + b.$$

Substitute the values (1,2) in the partial equation and solve for b:

$$2 = 3 \cdot 1 + b, \quad -1 = b.$$

So we know that the equation is: $y = 3x - 1$.

Instead of providing two points, some problems will provide the slope of the line and a single point (the slope and a point determine a line). If a problem gives the slope and a point, simply write the partial equation, plug in the point and solve for b. For example, given a slope of -3 and the point (2,3) we write the partial equation

$$y = -3x + b$$

then plug in (2,3) to solve for b

$$3 = -3(2) + b, \; 9 = b \quad.$$

The equation of the line is $y = -3x + 9$.

Rather than provide the slope directly, sometimes the slope is provided indirectly through information about another line. In order to do this type of problem you must remember that:

- The slopes of parallel lines are the same
- The slopes of perpendicular lines are negative reciprocals of each other.

For example, if a line has a slope of 3 then all lines parallel to it must also have a slope of 3; whereas all lines perpendicular to it must have a slope of $-\dfrac{1}{3}$.

There are two special cases of slope to keep in mind:

- The slope of a horizontal line is zero. For example, the line $y = 3$ has a slope of zero.
- The slope of a vertical line is undefined. For example, the slope of the line $x = 3$ is undefined.

Distance formula

The distance formula is something that you should memorize, or if memorizing does not suit you, remember that it is a simple application of the Pythagorean Theorem. You are given two points and need to find the distance between them.

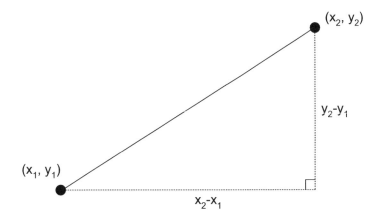

Notice that the vertical distance is just $y_2 - y_1$ and the horizontal distance is just $x_2 - x_1$. Applying the Pythagorean Theorem gives

$$d^2 = \left(y_2 - y_1\right)^2 + \left(x_2 - x_1\right)^2$$
$$d = \sqrt{\left(y_2 - y_1\right)^2 + \left(x_2 - x_1\right)^2}$$

Midpoint formula

The midpoint of the line segment with endpoints $\left(x_1, y_1\right)$ and $\left(x_2, y_2\right)$ has the coordinates:

$$\text{midpoint} = \left(\frac{x_1 + x_2}{2}, \ \frac{y_1 + y_2}{2} \right)$$

Problems on slope, distance and midpoint (unit 4.6)

1. The equation of the line passing through points (5,7) and (-15, 23) is:

    (A) $y = -0.8x + 11$

    (B) $y = -0.8x + 3$

    (C) $y = 0.8x + 12.6$

    (D) $y = 0.8x - 0.6$

    (E) $y = -1.25x + 13.25$

2. What is the length of the line segment whose endpoints are (5,7) and (-15, 23)?

    (A)   4.0

    (B)   25.6

    (C)   31.6

    (D)   36.0

    (E)   900.0

3. Find the equation of the line that passes through (1,3) and is perpendicular to the line with the equation $3x - 2y = 5$.

    (A) $y = 3x$

    (B) $2y = 3x + 3$

    (C) $2y = -3x + 9$

    (D) $3y = 2x + 4$

    (E) $3y = -2x + 11$

4. What is the slope of the line that passes through the points (3, -2) and (3, 2)?

    (A)   0.0

    (B)   0.4

    (C)   0.6

    (D)   0.75

    (E)   Cannot be determined

5. The diameter of a circle has as its endpoints (-1,2) and (9, 24). What are the coordinates of the center?

    (A)   (4, 11)

    (B)   (4, 13)

    (C)   (5, 11)

    (D)   (5, 13)

    (E)   (8, 26)

6. If two vertices of rectangle ABCD are at A=(1,2) and B=(5,8), what is the slope of $\overline{BC}$?

    (A) $-2/3$

    (B) $-3/2$

    (C) $2/3$

    (D)   1

    (E) $3/2$

7. What is the equation of the perpendicular bisector of the line segment whose endpoints are (5,7) and (-5,11)?

    (A) $y = 0.4x + 9$

    (B) $y = -0.4x + 9$

    (C) $y = -0.4x - 9$

    (D) $y = 2.5x + 9$

    (E) $y = 2.5x - 5.5$

8. The line $y = 3$ does <u>not</u> pass through

    I.   (1, 3)

    II.   (3,1)

    III. (3,3)

    (A)   I only

    (B)   II only

    (C)   III only

    (D)   I and III only

    (E)   II and III only

9. If ΔABC has two of its vertices at (0, 0) and (3, 4), which of the following could be the other vertex?

    I.   (-3, 4)

    II.   (3, -1)

    III. (-3, -4)

    (A)   I only

    (B)   II only

    (C)   III only

    (D)   I and II only

    (E)   I, II, and III

10. If a line passes through points (1,5) and (3,8) then it must also pass through points

    I.   (-1, 2)

    II. (3, 2)

    III. (2,3)

(A)   I only

(B)   II only

(C)   III only

(D)   I and II only

(E)   I, II, and III

The diagram below is used in problems 11-13. $\overline{AB}$ is a diameter of the circle and it is 12 units long.

Point M is the midpoint of $\overline{AC}$.

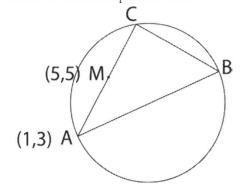

11. What are the coordinates of point C?

(A)   (-3,1)

(B)   (7,9)

(C)   (9,7)

(D)   (11,13)

(E)   (13,11)

12. What is the slope of $\overline{BC}$?

(A)   -2.0

(B)   --1.0

(C)   -0.5

(D)   1.0

(E)   2.0

13. What is the length of $\overline{BC}$?

(A)   4

(B)   8

(C) $2\sqrt{31}$

(D) $2\sqrt{41}$

(E) $2\sqrt{46}$

---

14. If a line passes through points (1,5), (3,8) and (x,-10) then x must be equal to:

(A)   -11

(B)   -9

(C)   9

(D)   11

(E)   23.5

15.

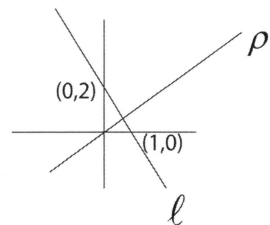

In the diagram above, line ℓ passes through points (0,2) and (1,0). If line ρ is perpendicular to line ℓ, then the two lines intersect at the point:

(A)   (.4, .2)

(B)   (.4, .8)

(C)   (.5, 1)

(D)   (.8, .4)

(E)   (1, .5))

Solutions to problems on slope, distance and midpoint (unit 4.6)

1. (A)

$$m = \frac{23-7}{-15-5} = \frac{-4}{5}, \qquad y = \frac{-4}{5}x + b$$

at $(5,7)$ $\quad 7 = \frac{-4}{5}(5) + b, \quad 11 = b$

$$y = \frac{-4}{5}x + 11$$

2. (B)

$$d = \sqrt{(23-7)^2 + (-15-5)^2} = \sqrt{656}$$

3. (E)

$$3x - 2y = 5, \quad -2y = -3x + 5, \quad y = \frac{3}{2}x - 2.5$$

$$y = \frac{-2}{3}x + b \quad \text{at } (1,3) \quad 3 = \frac{-2}{3}(1) + b, \quad \frac{11}{3} = b$$

$$y = \frac{-2}{3}x + \frac{11}{3} \quad \text{or} \quad 3y = -2x + 11$$

4. (E)

This a vertical line with the equation is $x = 3$. Its slope is undefined.

5. (B)

$$\text{center} = \text{midpoint} = \left(\frac{-1+9}{2}, \frac{2+24}{2}\right) = (4, 13)$$

6. (A)

$$\text{slope of AB} = \frac{8-2}{5-1} = \frac{3}{2}$$

$$\text{slope BC} = \frac{-2}{3}$$

7. (D)

$$\text{original slope} = \frac{11-7}{-5-5} = \frac{4}{-10}$$

desired slope $= 10/4 = 2.5$

$$\text{midpoint} = \left(\frac{5-5}{2}, \frac{11+7}{2}\right) = (0, 9)$$

at $(0, 9)$, equation is $y = 2.5x + 9$

8. (B)

I. is false because the line passes through (1,3)
II is true because the line does not pass through (3,1)
III is false because the line passes through (3,3)

9. (D)

I. could be a triangle with (0,0), (3,4) and -3,4)
II could be a triangle with (0,0), (3,4) and (3,-1)
III could not be a triangle because the points (0,0), (-3,-4) and (3,4) all lie on the straight line with
equation $y = \dfrac{4x}{3}$.

10. (A)

A line has constant slope. The slope must be:

$$m = \frac{y_2 - y_1}{x_2 - x_1} = \frac{8-5}{3-1} = \frac{3}{2}. \text{ Test the other points:}$$

$$\frac{2-5}{-1-1} = \frac{3}{2}, \quad \frac{2-5}{3-1} = \frac{-3}{2}, \quad \frac{3-5}{2-1} = -2$$

11. (C)

$$5 = \frac{1+x}{2}, \ x = 9 \qquad 5 = \frac{y+3}{2}, \ y = 7$$

12. (A)

$$\text{slope } \overline{AC} = \frac{5-3}{5-1} = \frac{1}{2}, \quad \text{slope } \overline{BC} = \text{neg reciprocal} = -2$$

13. (B)

$$AC = 2 \cdot AM = 2\sqrt{(5-3)^2 + (5-1)^2} = 2\sqrt{20} = \sqrt{80}$$

$$CB = \sqrt{12^2 - AC^2} = \sqrt{144 - 80} = \sqrt{64} = 8$$

14. (B)

$$m = \frac{y_2 - y_1}{x_2 - x_1} = \frac{8-5}{3-1} = \frac{3}{2}$$

$$\frac{3}{2} = \frac{-10-5}{x-1}, \quad 3x - 3 = -30, \ x = -9$$

15. (D)

Equation of line ℓ: $y = -2x + 2$

Equation of line ρ: $y = \dfrac{1}{2}x$

At the point of intersection:

$$-2x + 2 = \frac{1}{2}x, \quad -4x + 4 = x,$$

$$-5x = -4, \ x = \frac{4}{5} \text{ and } y = \frac{1}{2}x = \frac{4}{10} = \frac{2}{5}$$

5. ALGEBRA 2

Algebra 2 is a loose collection of topics, and fortunately not all of them are on the ACT®. But there are quite a few things you should know, starting with sequences. Recall that a sequence is a collection of terms, denoted by a_1, a_2, ..., a_n and a series is the sum of consecutive terms of a sequence. There are two types of sequences, arithmetic and geometric.

Arithmetic sequences

Arithmetic sequences have the common difference d, i.e., the difference between adjacent terms is always the same. The expression for the nth term of an arithmetic sequence is

$$a_n = a_1 + (n-1)d$$

The sum of n consecutive terms of an arithmetic sequence is

$$s_n = \frac{n(a_1 + a_n)}{2},$$

where a_1 is the first term to be summed, a_n is the last term to be summed, and n is the number of terms to be summed.. For example, consider the sequence: 3,11,19, ... The sum of the first 100 terms of the sequence would be:

$$s_{100} = \frac{100(a_1 + a_{100})}{2}$$

From $a_{100} = 3 + (100-1)8 = 795$ we get

$$s_{100} = \frac{100(a_1 + a_{100})}{2} = \frac{100(3+795)}{2} = 39,900$$

Geometric sequences

Geometric sequences have the common ratio r, i.e., the ratio of any term to the previous term is always the same. The expression for the nth term of a geometric sequence is

$$a_n = a_1 r^{n-1}$$

The sum of n consecutive terms of a geometric sequence is

$$s_n = \frac{a_1(1-r^n)}{1-r},$$

where a_1 is the first term to be summed and n is the number of terms to be summed. For example, consider the sequence 3,27,243, etc. The sum of the first 5 terms would be:

$$s_5 = \frac{3(1-9^5)}{1-9} = \frac{3(-59,048)}{-8} = 22,143$$

The sums above are called partial sums or finite sums because they involve adding only n consecutive terms in the sequence. For infinite geometric sequences, if $|r| < 1$ then the sum of all the elements of the sequence will converge as n becomes larger and larger. Specifically, the sum will converge to:

$$s_\infty = \frac{a_1}{1-r}, \text{ when } |r| < 1$$

A special case of geometric sequences is especially useful to know, not only for standardized tests but also it is very useful in the real world. The special case is money compounding over time. If A dollars is invested (say in a savings account) and interest is allowed to compound annually at the rate of r per year, after t years the investment will be worth $A(1+r)^t$. In the real world, interest on an investment usually compounds more often than once per year. If the investment compounds n times per year at an annual interest rate of r per year, after t years the investment will be worth $A\left(1+\dfrac{r}{n}\right)^{nt}$.

A simple example will illustrate the power of compound interest. At an annual rate of 5% per year, after 20 years an investment of \$25,000 would be worth $25,000(1+0.05)^{20} = 66,332$ when compounded annually. If that same

\$25,000 investment were to compound monthly, after 20 years it would be worth $25,000\left(1+\dfrac{.05}{12}\right)^{240} = 67,816$.

Problems on sequences (unit 5.1)

The sequence below applies to problems 1 and 2:

$$3, -1, \underline{\hphantom{xx}}, -9$$

1. What is the missing value in this sequence?

   (A)   -6
   (B)   -5
   (C)   -4
   (D)   0
   (E)   4

2. What is the 33rd element of this sequence?

   (A)   -125
   (B)   -128
   (C)   -129
   (D)   -131
   (E)   -132

The sequence below applies to problems 3 and 4:

$$-3, \underline{\hphantom{xx}}, -12, 24$$

3. What is the missing value in this sequence?

   (A)   -6
   (B)   -2
   (C)   0
   (D)   2
   (E)   6

4. What is the 19th element of this sequence?

   (A)   -1,572,864
   (B)   -786,432
   (C)   -262,144
   (D)   786,432
   (E)   -1,572,864

---

5. A study of fish in a pond found that the number of fish doubles every 5 years. If the number of fish is now 10, how many fish will be in the pond 20 years from now?

   (A)   80
   (B)   160
   (C)   320
   (D)   2,621440
   (E)   5,242,880

6. At the end of every year John deposits $1,500 into his savings account. How many years will it take for John's deposits to amount to $19,500?

   (A)   12
   (B)   13
   (C)   14
   (D)   15
   (E)   16

7. The number of carbon particles in the air over a certain city is reduced by 50% every year. If there are 1,499,968 particles now, how many years will it take to reduce the number to 23,437 particles?

   (A)   4
   (B)   5
   (C)   6
   (D)   7
   (E)   8

8. A certain investment pays 7% every year. If $20,000 is invested today, what will that investment be worth 10 years from now?

   (A)   12.600
   (B)   21,400
   (C)   36,769
   (D)   39,343
   (E)   42,097

9. If a car depreciates in value by 20% per year, what percentage of its original value will the car be worth when it reaches its third birthday?

   (A)   0.8%
   (B)   4%
   (C)   41%
   (D)   51%
   (E)   64%

10. For the sequence -3,-9,-15, … what is the value of the 50th term?

(A)   -291

(B)   -294

(C)   -297

(D)   -300

(E)   -303

11. For the sequence -3,-9,-15, …what is the sum of the first 50 terms?

(A)   -7,425

(B)   -7,500

(C)   -14,850

(D)   -15,000

(E)   -15,150

12. For the sequence 5,- 7.5, 11.25, -16.875, … what is the 15th term?

(A)   -2189

(B)   -1460

(C)   292

(D)   1460

(E)   2189

13. For the sequence 5,- 7.5, 11.25, -16.875, … what is the sum of the first 15 terms?

(A)   582
(B)   873
(C)   878
(D)   4379
(E)   8780

14. What is the value of the infinite sum 9+3+1+… ?

(A)   13.5
(B)   27.0
(C)   40.5
(D)   54.0
(E)   Does not converge

15. What is the sum of the odd integers between 100 and 300?

(A)   4,900

(B)   9,800

(C)   10,000

(D)   19,800

(E)   20,000

16. John has an ant farm whose population doubles every 5 years. If he started the ant farm 20 years ago and there are now 160,000 ants, how many ants did he have when he started?

(A)   1

(B)   2,500

(C)   5,000

(D)   7,500

(E)   10,000

17. Which of the models below fits the following sequence: 4, 7, 12, 19, 28, …?

(A) $a_n = n^3 - 1$

(B) $a_n = 2^{n+1}$

(C) $a_n = 4 + (n-1)3$

(D) $a_n = n^2 + 3$

(E) $a_n = 3n + 1$

18. Amy wants to invest $1,000 for a period of 10 years, but she cannot decide where to place her investment. Bank A will pay 5.5% interest compounded annually. Bank B will pay 5% interest compounded quarterly. Which is the better deal?

(A)   Bank A is better

(B)   Bank B is better

(C)   Both deals are the same

(D)   Cannot be determined

Solutions to problems on sequences (unit 5.1)

1. (B)
The common difference is -4.
3, -1, -5, -9

2. (A)
$$a_n = a_1 + (n-1)d = 3 + (33-1)(-4)$$
$$= 3 + 32(-4) = -125$$

3. (E)
The common ratio is -2
-3, 6, -12, 24

4. (B)
$$a_n = a_1 (r)^{n-1} = (-3)(-2)^{19-1}$$
$$= -3(-2)^{18} = -786,432$$

5. (B)
First realize that $a_1 = 10$. The "trick" is to realize that the problem is asking for a_5 because four periods of 5 years each will have elapsed after 20 years.
$$a_5 = 10(2)^4 = 160$$

6. (B)
The sum of deposits made into the account forms an arithmetic sequence: 1500, 3000, 4500, etc.
$$a_n = a_1 + (n-1)d$$
19,500=1500+$(n-1)$1,500
$19,500 = 1500n, \ 13 = n$
It will take 13 years until his deposits amount to $19,500.

7. (C)
$$a_n = a_1 \left(\frac{1}{2}\right)^{n-1}$$
$$23,437 = 1,499,968 \left(\frac{1}{2}\right)^{n-1}$$
$$\frac{1}{64} = \left(\frac{1}{2}\right)^{n-1}, \ n-1 = 6, \ n = 7$$
It will take six more years, because the first term is the current value.

8. (D)
$$a_{11} = 20,000(1.07)^{10} = 39,343.03$$

9. (D)
$$(0.8)^3 = 0.512 = 51\%$$
Or substitute values using a starting value of 100:

100, 80, 64, 51.2

10. (C)
This is arithmetic, with d=-6.
$$a_{50} = -3 + (50-1)(-6) = -297$$

11. (B)
$$s_{50} = \frac{50(-3-297)}{2} = -7500$$

12. (D)
This is geometric, with r=-1.5.
$$a_{15} = 5(-1.5)^{15-1} = 1459.646$$

13. (C)
This is geometric, with r=-1.5.
$$s_{15} = \frac{5\left(1-(-1.5)^{15}\right)}{1--1.5} = \frac{5(1+437.89)}{2.5} = 877.79$$ 14. (A)
This is geometric, with r=1/3.
$$s_\infty = \frac{9}{1-\frac{1}{3}} = 13.5$$

15. (E)
This is an arithmetic sequence: 101, 103, …, 299 with d=2 and n=100.
$$s_{100} = \frac{100(101+299)}{2} = 20,000$$

16. (E)
This is a geometric sequence, with r=2. Twenty years later would be the fifth element in the sequence:
$$a_5 = a_1 (2)^{5-1}, \quad 160,000 = 16a_1, \ a_1 = 10,000$$

17. (D)
Sequences can sometimes be neither arithmetic nor geometric. $a_n = n^2 + 3$ is the only model that fits all of the data given.

18. (A)
5.5% compounded annually for 10 years:
$$1000(1.055)^{10} = 1708.14$$
5.0% compounded quarterly for 10 years:
$$1000\left(1+\frac{.05}{4}\right)^{10\cdot4} = 1000(1.0125)^{40} = 1643.62$$
The better deal is the first one, Bank A.

5.2 Absolute value

Absolute value problems can be tricky, especially inequalities. But there is a technique that will help you solve them easily. First, we begin with a definition of absolute value:

$$\text{When } x \geq 0, \ |x| = x. \quad \text{When } x < 0, \ |x| = -x.$$

Note that the absolute value of a number is always positive. If x is positive in the first place, leave the sign alone. If x is negative, change the sign to positive.

Equalities always produce two points

The simplest absolute value problems to solve are equalities, where the absolute value of some expression is set equal to a non-negative constant. The figure below illustrates how two equations are spawned and where the solutions fall on a number line.

For example, the solutions to the equation $|x| = 10$ are $x = 10$ or $x = -10$. In the above scheme, $c \geq 0$. If c were negative then there would be no solution because the absolute value of any number is zero or positive.

When the expression inside the absolute value is more complicated, the process is the same. Simply take the expression and spawn two equations, equating that expression to the positive or negative value of the constant.

Less than (or less than or equal to) always produce barbells

Absolute values can also appear in inequalities. The figure below shows how an inequality is handled when an absolute value is in a less than (or less than or equal to) a quantity. Note that the solution is an interval. The figure illustrates how two inequalities are spawned to find the interval, along with the solution on a number line.

For example, the solution to the equation $|x| < 10$ is the interval $-10 < x < 10$. In the above scheme, $c \geq 0$. If c were negative, no solution for x would work because the absolute value of any number is never negative.

When the expression inside the absolute value is more complicated, the process is the same. Take the expression and spawn two inequalities in order to find the appropriate interval.

Greater than (or greater than or equal to) always produce two intervals

The figure below shows how an inequality is handled when an absolute value is in a greater than (or greater than or equal to) a quantity. Note that the solution is two intervals. The figure illustrates how two inequalities are spawned to find the intervals, along with how the solution looks on a number line.

For example, the solution to the equation $|x| > 10$ are the intervals $-10 > x$ or $x > 10$. In the above scheme, c can be any value, but if c is negative then the inequality holds for any value of x because the absolute value will always be greater than a negative number. It only makes sense to go through the steps above when $c \geq 0$.

When the expression inside the absolute value is more complicated, the process is the same. Take the expression and spawn two inequalities in order to find the appropriate intervals for the solution.

Graphs of absolute value equalities

The graph of an absolute value equality will always have a V shape. Of course the V can be translated (change location) or it can be reflected according the rules given in unit 5.5. The graph of the parent equation, $y = |x|$ looks like this:

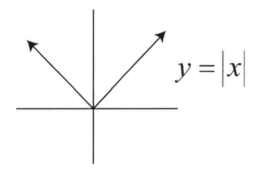

$$y = |x|$$

Problems on absolute value (unit 5.2)

1. The solutions to the equation $5|x-2|=20$ are:

   (A)   x=-2 and x=2

   (B)   x=-2 and x=4

   (C)   x=-2 and x=6

   (D)   x=-4 and x=2

   (E)   x=-4 and x=4

2. The solution to the inequality $2|x+5|<8$ is:

   (A) $-9<x<-1$

   (B) $-9<x<1$

   (C) $-1<x<1$

   (D) $-1<x<9$

   (E) $1<x<9$

3. The solution to the inequality $5|x-3|-5\le0$ is:

   (A) $-4\le x\le-2$

   (B) $-4\le x\le2$

   (C) $-2\le x\le2$

   (D) $-2\le x\le4$

   (E) $2\le x\le4$

4. The solution to the inequality $3|x+8|\ge6$ is:

   (A) $-10\ge x\ or\ x\ge-6$

   (B) $-10\ge x\ or\ x\ge6$

   (C) $-6\ge x\ or\ x\ge6$

   (D) $-6\ge x\ or\ x\ge10$

   (E) $6\ge x\ or\ x\ge10$

5. The solution to the inequality $|2x-5|\ge9$ is:

   (A) $-7\ge x\ or\ x\ge-2$

   (B) $-7\ge x\ or\ x\ge2$

   (C) $-7\ge x\ or\ x\ge7$

   (D) $-2\ge x\ or\ x\ge7$

   (E) $-2\ge x\ or\ x\ge-7$

6. The solution to the inequality $5|3x|>-15$ is:

   (A) $-1\ge x\ or\ x\ge1$

   (B) $1\ge x\ or\ x\ge-1$

   (C) $x\ge0$

   (D)   All values of x

   (E)   No solution

7. The solution to the inequality $|2x|<-2$ is:

   (A) $-2<x<1$

   (B) $-1<x<1$

   (C) $1<x<2$

   (D)   All values of x

   (E)   No solution

8. In order to be admitted to a ride in an amusement park, children must be older than three and younger than seven. Which of the inequalities below represents the admission requirement?

   I. $3<x<7$

   II. $|x-3|<7$

   III. $|x-5|<2$

   (A)   I only
   (B)   II only
   (C)   III only
   (D)   I and II only
   (E)   I and III only

9. A certain auto part must be 2 inches thick, with a tolerance of one-tenth of one inch. Which of the inequalities below represents acceptable thicknesses?

   (A) $|x|\le0.1$

   (B) $|x|\le2$

   (C) $|x-2|\le0.1$

   (D) $|x-0.1|\le2$

   (E)   None of the above

Solutions to problems on absolute value (unit 5.2)

1. (C)

Isolate the absolute value: $|x-2| = \dfrac{20}{5} = 4$

First equation: $x-2=-4, \ x=-2$

Second equation: $x-2=4, \ x=6$

2. (A)

Isolate the absolute value: $|x+5| < \dfrac{8}{2} = 4$

First equation: $-4 < x+5, \ -9 < x$

Second equation: $x+5 < 4, \ x < -1$

Solution: $-9 < x$ and $x < -1$

3. (E)

Isolate the absolute value: $5|x-3| \le 5, \ |x-3| \le 1$

First equation: $-1 \le x-3, \ 2 \le x$

Second equation: $x-3 \le 1, \ x \le 4$

4. (A)

Isolate the absolute value: $3|x+8| \ge 6, \ |x+8| \ge 2$

First equation: $-2 \ge x+8, \ -10 \ge x$

Second equation: $x+8 \ge 2, \ x \ge -6$

5. (D)

First equation: $-9 \ge 2x-5, \ -4 \ge 2x, \ -2 \ge x$

Second equation: $2x-5 \ge 9, \ 2x \ge 14, \ x \ge 7$

6. (D)

Isolate the absolute value: $5|3x| > -15, \ |3x| > -3$

This inequality is true for all values of x. The absolute value of any quantity is always non-negative.

7. (E)

This inequality is never true for any value of x. The absolute value of any quantity is always non-negative.

8. (E)

I. obviously is correct.

II is incorrect:

$|x-3| < 7$

$-7 < x-3 < 7$

$-7+3 < x < 7+3$

$-4 < x < 10$

III is correct

$|x-5| < 2$

$-2 < x-5 < 2$

$-2+5 < x < 2+5$

$3 < x < 7$

9. (C)

$|x-2| \le 0.1$

$-0.1 \le x-2 \le 0.1$

$1.9 \le x \le 2.1$

5.3 Exponents and radicals

The use of exponents is an important part of all of the standardized tests. We begin first with the laws of exponents – these **must** be memorized!

$$x^a \cdot x^b = x^{a+b} \qquad\qquad\qquad x^0 = 1$$

$$\frac{x^a}{x^b} = x^{a-b} \qquad\qquad\qquad (xy)^a = x^a y^a$$

$$\left(x^a\right)^b = x^{ab} \qquad\qquad\qquad \left(\frac{x}{y}\right)^a = \frac{x^a}{y^a}$$

$$x^{-a} = \frac{1}{x^a} \qquad\qquad\qquad \frac{1}{x^{-a}} = x^a$$

In addition to memorizing these laws, of course you must know how to apply them. There are several problems at the end of this unit to test that ability.

Equations involving exponents

Sometimes you will see equations involving exponents. The technique to use here is to convert both sides of the equation to the same base. Once the bases are the same, you can equate the exponents. For example:

$4^x = 128$ original equation

$\left(2^2\right)^x = 2^7$ convert both sides to use base 2

$2^{2x} = 2^7$ simplify the left-hand side using a law of exponents

$2x = 7, \quad x = 3.5$ equate exponents; solve for x.

Radicals and exponents

To some extent, radicals were covered in unit 3.2. However, there we restricted our attention to a particular type of radical, the square root.

Perhaps the best way to deal with square roots and other radicals is to change them into fractional exponents using the law:

$$\sqrt[n]{x} = x^{\frac{1}{n}}.$$

Once the radical is written as a fractional exponent, it can be manipulated using the laws of exponents given above. Also, using fractional exponents permits us to solve problems easily on the calculator

Calculator tip: What if you were asked to find the 7th root of 16,384? That is an easy job for the calculator. Just 16384, ^, (, 1/7,), enter. The calculator returns 4. It turns out that $4^7 = 16,384$, not exactly common knowledge.

Fractional exponents also can be used to simplify combinations of powers and roots, as show in the example below:

$$\sqrt[7]{x^3} = \left(x^3\right)^{\frac{1}{7}} = x^{\frac{3}{7}} \quad \text{and} \quad \left(\sqrt[7]{x}\right)^3 = \left(x^{\frac{1}{7}}\right)^3 = x^{\frac{3}{7}}$$

Problems on exponents and radicals (unit 5.3)

1. The expression $x^3 \cdot x^9$ simplifies to

   (A) x^6

   (B) x^{12}

   (C) x^{27}

   (D) x^3

   (E) x^{-6}

2. The expression $\dfrac{a^8}{a^{11}}$ simplifies to

   (A) a^3

   (B) a^{19}

   (C) a^{88}

   (D) a^{-2}

   (E) a^{-3}

3. The expression $\sqrt{3^{30} x^4}$ simplifies to:

   (A) $(3x)^{68}$

   (B) $(3x)^{34}$

   (C) $(3x)^{17}$

   (D) $3^{15} x^2$

   (E) $3^{60} x^8$

4. The expression $\sqrt[3]{x^3 y^{10}}$ simplifies to:

   (A) $x^{\frac{3}{2}} y^5$

   (B) $x^9 y^{30}$

   (C) $xy\sqrt[3]{y}$

   (D) $xy^2 \sqrt[3]{y}$

   (E) $xy^3 \sqrt[3]{y}$

5. The expression $\dfrac{\left(\sqrt[3]{y}\right)^5}{y^2}$ simplifies to:

   (A) $y^{\frac{11}{3}}$

   (B) y^3

   (C) $y^{\frac{1}{3}}$

   (D) $y^{-\frac{1}{3}}$

   (E) $y^{-\frac{11}{3}}$

6. Simplify $\dfrac{x^2 y}{z} \div \dfrac{x}{zy}$

   (A) xy^2

   (B) $x^2 y^2$

   (C) $x^3 y^2$

   (D) $x^3 y^3$

   (E) $\dfrac{x^3}{z^2}$

7. Simplify $\dfrac{\sqrt[3]{x^{15}} y^{-2}}{x^{-3} y^3}$

   (A) $x^{48} y^{-5}$

   (B) $x^{4.5} y$

   (C) $x^{10.5} y^5$

   (D) $x^5 y^5$

   (E) $\dfrac{x^8}{y^5}$

8. Simplify $\dfrac{x^{12}y^{-2}z^5}{x^3y^4z^{-3}}$

(A) $\quad x^8y^{-6}z^8$

(B) $\quad x^8y^2z^8$

(C) $\quad x^9y^6z^8$

(D) $\quad x^9y^{-6}z^8$

(E) $\quad x^{15}y^2z^2$

9. Solve $x^2 = \sqrt[3]{125}$ for x:

(A) $\quad \sqrt{5}$

(B) $\quad \sqrt[3]{5}$

(C) $\quad 5$

(D) $\quad 25$

(E) $\quad 625$

10. If $\left(x^2y\right)^2 = 45^2$, then y must be:

(A) $\quad 2$

(B) $\quad 3$

(C) $\quad 4$

(D) $\quad 5$

(E) $\quad 9$

11. If $x^{-1} = \dfrac{\sqrt{2}}{2}$, then x^2 must be:

(A) $\quad \dfrac{1}{4}$

(B) $\quad \dfrac{1}{2}$

(C) $\quad 2$

(D) $\quad 4$

(E) $\quad 8$

12. Solve $128 = 4^x$ for x

(A) $\quad 2$

(B) $\quad 2.5$

(C) $\quad 3$

(D) $\quad 3.5$

(E) $\quad 4$

13.. Solve $9^{x+1} = \sqrt{3^{x+2}}$ for x:

(A) $\quad x = -\dfrac{2}{3}$

(B) $\quad x = 0$

(C) $\quad x = \dfrac{2}{3}$

(D) $\quad x = 1$

(E) $\quad$ No solution

14. Solve $81^x = \sqrt[3]{27^2}$ for x:

(A) $\quad x = -\dfrac{4}{3}$

(B) $\quad x = \dfrac{1}{2}$

(C) $\quad x = \dfrac{3}{4}$

(D) $\quad x = \dfrac{4}{3}$

(E) $\quad x = 2$

Solutions to problems on exponents and radicals (unit 5.3)

1. (B)

$$x^3 \cdot x^9 = x^{3+9} = x^{12}$$

2. (E)

$$\frac{a^8}{a^{11}} = a^{8-11} = a^{-3}$$

3. (D)

$$\sqrt{3^{30} x^4} = \left(3^{30}\right)^{\frac{1}{2}} \left(x^4\right)^{\frac{1}{2}} = 3^{15} x^2$$

4. (E)

$$\sqrt[3]{x^3 y^{10}} = \sqrt[3]{x^3 y^9} \sqrt[3]{y} = xy^3 \sqrt[3]{y}$$

5. (D)

$$\frac{\left(\sqrt[3]{y}\right)^5}{y^2} = \frac{y^{\frac{5}{3}}}{y^2} = y^{\frac{5}{3}-\frac{6}{3}} = y^{-\frac{1}{3}}$$

6. (A)

$$\frac{x^2 y}{z} \div \frac{x}{zy} = \left(\frac{x^2 y}{z}\right)\left(\frac{zy}{x}\right) = xy^2$$

7. (E)

$$\frac{\sqrt[3]{x^{15}} y^{-2}}{x^{-3} y^3} = \frac{x^5 y^{-2}}{x^{-3} y^3} = x^{(5--3)} y^{(-2-3)} = x^8 y^{-5} = \frac{x^8}{y^5}$$

8. (D)

$$\frac{x^{12} y^{-2} z^5}{x^3 y^4 z^{-3}} = \left(\frac{x^{12}}{x^3}\right)\left(\frac{y^{-2}}{y^2}\right)\left(\frac{z^5}{z^{-3}}\right) = x^{12-3} y^{-2-4} z^{5--3} = x^9 y^{-6} z^8$$

9. (A)

$$x^2 = \sqrt[3]{125}, \ x^2 = 5, \ x = \pm\sqrt{5}$$

10. (D)

$$45 = 3 \cdot 3 \cdot 5 = x^2 y$$
$$x = 3 \text{ and } y = 5$$

11. (C)

$$x^2 = \left(\frac{1}{x^{-1}}\right)^2 = \left(\frac{2}{\sqrt{2}}\right)^2 = \frac{4}{2} = 2$$

12. (D)

$$128 = 4^x, \ 2^7 = \left(2^2\right)^x, \ 2^7 = 2^{2x}, \ 7 = 2x, \ 3.5 = x$$

13. (A)

$$9^{x+1} = \sqrt{3^{x+2}}, \ \left(3^2\right)^{x+1} = \left(3^{x+2}\right)^{\frac{1}{2}},$$
$$2(x+1) = \frac{1}{2}(x+2), \ \frac{3x}{2} = -1, \ x = \frac{-2}{3}$$

14. (B)

$$81^x = \sqrt[3]{27^2}, \ \left(3^4\right)^x = \left(\left(3^3\right)^2\right)^{\frac{1}{3}}, \ 3^{4x} = 3^2, \ x = 0.5$$

5.4 Quadratic equations and parabolas

A parabola is a graph of a quadratic equation (also called a second degree equation), where y is set equal to an expression involving x^2. You need to be able to recognize quadratic equations, graph them, understand the symmetry of the parabola, find the zeros or roots of the equation, and find the vertex.

Calculator Tip: When solving problems involving quadratic equations, do not forget that you can use your graphing calculator. The calculator can graph the parabola, find the zeros of the equation (use *2nd-calc-zero*), and find its vertex (if the parabola opens up, use *2nd-calc-minimum* if the parabola opens down, use *2nd-calc-maximum*). To find the y-intercept, use the 2nd-calc-value function, plugging in zero for x. The material below demonstrates how to accomplish these tasks by hand.

Equations in Standard Form

A quadratic equation in standard form is $y = ax^2 + bx + c$.

The graph of a quadratic equation is a parabola. The parabola opens up if $a > 0$ and the parabola opens down if $a < 0$. The parabola is symmetric about its axis of symmetry, which is an invisible line running vertically through the vertex. The equation of the axis of symmetry is $x = -b/2a$. This is illustrated in the figures below.

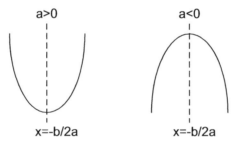

The x-coordinate of the vertex is found by using the formula: $x = -b/2a$. The y-coordinate of the vertex is found by plugging the x-coordinate into the equation.

There are several methods to find the roots. One method is to factor (see unit 3.5) and set each factor to zero. Another method is to use the quadratic formula, which you are expected to memorize:

$$x = \frac{-b \pm \sqrt{b^2 - 4ac}}{2a}.$$

You are also expected to memorize that the sum of the two roots is $\dfrac{-b}{a}$ and that the product of the roots is $\dfrac{c}{a}$.

You can see what kind of roots exist by graphing the equation. If the parabola never crosses the x-axis then the equation has two imaginary roots. If the parabola crosses the x-axis at two points, then the equation has two real roots. If the vertex of the parabola lies on the x-axis then the equation has one real root (also called a double root).

The discriminant

Instead of graphing, the kinds of roots you have can be determined by the sign of the discriminant, $b^2 - 4ac$. When the discriminant is positive, there are two real roots. When the discriminant is negative, there are two imaginary roots. When the discriminant is zero there is one real double root. You are expected to be able to determine the number and type of roots by using the discriminant, rather than solve or graph the equation for its roots.

Equations in vertex form

If the goal is to graph the parabola by hand, it is easier to do so when the equation is written in vertex form rather than standard form. The vertex form of the equation is

$$y = a(x-h)^2 + k$$

The vertex is (h,k) and the axis of symmetry is the equation $x=h$. This is illustrated in the figures below.

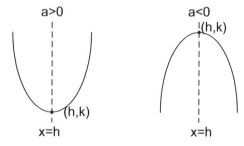

You should be prepared to see quadratic equations in either standard form or vertex form. Remember how to convert an equation from standard form to vertex form using the technique called "completing the square?" This technique is illustrated below.

To find the vertex of the equation $y = x^2 - 12x + 46$:

$$y = x^2 - 12x + 46 \qquad \text{the original equation}$$
$$y - 46 = x^2 - 12x \qquad \text{isolate the x-terms}$$
$$y - 46 + 36 = x^2 - 12x + 36 \qquad \text{add the constant } \left(\frac{b}{2}\right)^2 = \left(\frac{-12}{2}\right)^2 = (-6)^2 = 36$$
$$y + 10 = (x-6)^2 \qquad \text{simplify}$$
$$(6, \ -10) \qquad \text{coordinates of the vertex}$$

Equating quadratic equations

A certain kind of problem shows up on standardized tests with some frequency, so it is worth giving it your attention. If you have an equation that looks like this:

$$ax^2 + bx + c = dx^2 + ex + f$$

then the corresponding coefficients are equal to each other, in this case $a = d$, $b = e$, and $c = f$. For example, if

$$ax^2 + 5x + 4 = x^2 + (k+1)x + k$$

then $a = 1$, and $k = 4$.

Problems on quadratic equations and parabolas (unit 5.4)

TRY TO NOT USE YOUR CALCULATOR TO SOLVE ANY OF THESE PROBLEMS!

1. Which of these parabolas opens up?

    I. $y = 2x^2 - 5x - 3$

    II. $y = -2x^2 - 5x - 5$

    III. $y = 2x^2 + 5x + 3$

  (A)   I only

  (B)   II only

  (C)   III only

  (D)   I and II only

  (E)   I and III only

2. The vertex of the parabola $y = 3x^2 - 6x + 8$ is located at:

  (A)   (-2, 32)

  (B)   (-1, 17)

  (C)   (0, 8)

  (D)   (1, 5)

  (E)   (2, 8)

3. If a parabola crosses the x-axis at (-5,0) and (3,0) then its axis of symmetry must be:

  (A) $x = -5$

  (B) $x = -3$

  (C) $x = -1$

  (D) $x = 1$

  (E) $x = 5$

4. The vertex of the parabola $y + 16 = (x - 1)^2$ is located at:

  (A)   (-1, -16)

  (B)   (-1, 16)

  (C)   (1, -16)

  (D)   (1, 16)

  (E)   (16, 1)

NOTE: Questions 5 and 6 pertain to the parabola: $y = 2x^2 + x - 6$.

5. Find the axis of symmetry:

  (A) $x = -0.5$

  (B) $x = -0.25$

  (C) $x = 0$

  (D) $x = 0.25$

  (E) $x = 0.5$

6. Find the roots (zeros):

  (A) $x = -1, 3$

  (B) $x = 1, 3$

  (C) $x = 1.5, -2$

  (D) $x = -1.5, 2$

  (E)   Cannot be determined

7. In the parabola below, the coordinates (a, b) are:

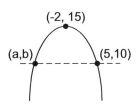

  (A)   (-5, 10)

  (B)   (-5, 15)

  (C)   (-9, 10)

  (D)   (-9, 15)

  (E)   (10, 5)

8. If the roots of a parabola are -3 and 5, then the equation of the parabola could be:

  (A) $y = x^2 - 2x - 15$

  (B) $y = x^2 + 2x - 15$

  (C) $y = x^2 + 8x + 15$

  (D) $y = x^2 - 8x + 15$

  (E)   Cannot be determined

9. If the parabola $2x^2 + bx + 4$ passes through the point (2,18) then the value of b must be:

(A)   5
(B)   6
(C)   9
(D)   18
(E)   36

Problems 10 and 11 are based on the following diagram:

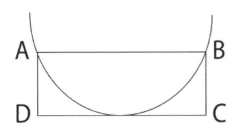

10. If ABCD is a rectangle, DC is 4 units long, and the equation of the parabola is $y = (x-3)^2 + 1$, then how long is BC?

(A)   2

(B)   3

(C)   4

(D)   5

(E)   17

11. If the coordinates of point A are (0,5) and the equation of the parabola is $y = (x-3)^2 + 1$, what is the area of rectangle ABCD?

(A)   6

(B)   12

(C)   18

(D)   24

(E)   30

---

12. If $4x^2 + bx + c = (ax+1)^2$ and $a > 0$, then $a + b + c$ is equal to:

(A)   3
(B)   4
(C)   5
(D)   6
(E)   7

13. If $ax^2 + bx - 9 = (x-k)(2x+k)$ and $b > 0$ then k is equal to:

(A) -3
(B) -1
(C)   0
(D)   1
(E)   3

Extra Credit Problem:

14. If $2x^2 + bx + 36 = ax^2 + (k+a)(k+x) + k$ and $k < 0$ then b is equal to:

(A) -7

(B) -5

(C)   1

(D)   5

(E)   7

15. For the quadratic equation $ax^2 + bx + c$, when the sum of the two roots is added to the product of the two roots, the result is:

(A) $\dfrac{-b}{2a}$

(B) $\dfrac{c}{a}$

(C) $\dfrac{c-b}{a}$

(D) $\dfrac{b-c}{a}$

(E) $\dfrac{-c}{a}$

16. Which of the points below lies on the axis of symmetry for the parabola with the equation of $y = 3x^2 + 12x - 15$?

    (A)   (-4,3)

    (B)   (-2,2)

    (C)   (0,6)

    (D)   (2,5)

    (E)   (4,4)

17. For which of the equations below is the value of the discriminant equal to -23?

    (A) $y = x^2$

    (B) $y = x^2 - x - 3$

    (C) $y = -3x^2 - 2x + 7$

    (D) $y = x^2 - 3x + 2.25$

    (E) $y = 3x^2 - 5x + 4$

18. A parabola never crosses the x-axis if its discriminant is:

    (A)   positive

    (B)   negative

    (C)   zero

    (D)   zero or positive

    (E)   zero or negative

19. One of the solutions to the equation $x^2 - 3x + 2.25 = 0$ is:

    (A)   0.5

    (B)   1.0

    (C)   1.5

    (D)   2.0

    (E)   2.5

20. When the equation $y = x^2 - 6x - 3$ is written in vertex form, it becomes:

    (A) $y = (x+3)^2 - 12$

    (B) $y = (x+3)^2 + 12$

    (C) $y = (x-3)^2 - 12$

    (D) $y = (x-3)^2 + 12$

    (E) $y = (x-3)^2 - 6$

21. If a parabola intersects the x-axis at the points (-3,0) and (3,0), then the equation of the parabola could be:

    I. $y = x^2 - 9$

    II. $y = -x^2 + 9$

    III. $y = (x+3)^2$

    (A)   I only

    (B)   II only

    (C)   III only

    (D)   I and II only

    (E)   I and III only

Solutions to problems on quadratic equations and parabolas (unit 5.4)

1 (E)   A parabola opens up if the coefficient of the x^2 term is positive. That coefficient is positive in the first and third equations.

2. (D) Start by finding the axis of symmetry: $\frac{-b}{2a} = \frac{--6}{2(3)} = 1$. Then substitute x=1 into the equation of the parabola:

$$f(1) = 3 \cdot 1^2 - 6 \cdot 1 + 8 = 3 - 6 + 8 = 5$$

3. (C)   The x-intercepts are equidistant from the axis of symmetry. The value of -1 is 4 units from -5 and 4 units from +3.

4. (C) Rewrite the equation:

$$y + 16 = (x-1)^2$$
$$y = (x-1)^2 - 16$$
$$y = (x-h)^2 + k$$

The vertex is at (h, k) = (1, -16).

5. (B)   The axis of symmetry is

$$x = \frac{-b}{2a} = \frac{-1}{2(2)} = -.25.$$

6. (C)   Factor $y = 2x^2 + x - 6 = (2x-3)(x+2)$. To find the roots, set each factor to zero.

$$2x - 3 = 0, \; x = 1.5$$
$$x + 2 = 0, \; x = -2$$

Note that the roots are equidistant from the axis of symmetry found in the previous problem to be -0.25.

7. (C)   This problem uses symmetry. The axis of symmetry is x=-2. If the point (5, 10) is 7 units from the axis of symmetry then the point (a, 10) must also be 7 units from the axis of symmetry, or (-9, 10).

8. (A)
$$(x+3)(x-5) = 0$$
$$x^2 + 3x - 5x - 15 = 0$$
$$x^2 - 2x - 15 = 0$$

9. (D)
$$18 = 2(2^2) + b(2) + 4, \; 6 = 2b, \; 3 = b$$

10. (C)
The coordinates of the vertex are (3,1). Because DC=4, the coordinates of point C are (5,1).
Therefore the coordinates of point B are (5,y). Solve
$$y = (5-3)^2 + 1 = 5$$

11. (D) The coordinates of the vertex are (3,1).
Therefore the coordinates of point D must be (0,1).
So AD is 4 units. CD is 6 units because the vertex is at the midpoint of CD. The area is 4(6)=24 units.

12. (E)

$$4x^2 + bx + c = (ax+1)^2 = ax^2 + 2ax + 1$$

$a^2 = 4$ or $a = 2$, $b = 2 \cdot 2 = 4$, and $c = 1$. So $a + b + c = 7$

13. (A)

$$ax^2 + bx - 9 = (x-k)(2x+k) = x^2 - kx - k^2$$

$$k^2 = 9, \; k = \pm 3$$

But k must be -3 because b>0 and b = -k.

14. (B)

$$a = 2 \text{ so } ax^2 + (k+a)(k+x) + k = 2x^2 + (k+2)(k+x) + k$$
$$= 2x^2 + (k+2)x + (k^2 + 2k + k) = 2x^2 + (k+2)x + (k+1)^2$$

$$(k+1)^2 = 36, \text{ but } k < 0 \text{ so } k+1 = -6, \text{ and } k = -7.$$

If $k = -7$ and $b = k+2$, then $b = k+5 = -5$.

15. (C)   The sum of the roots is $-b/a$, whereas the product of the roots is c/a. When the sum of the roots is added to the product of the roots we get

$$\frac{-b}{a} + \frac{c}{a} = \frac{c-b}{a}$$

16. (B) In the equation $y = 3x^2 + 12x - 15$, a=3 and b=12. So the axis of symmetry is $-b/2a = -12/6 = -2$. Any point with an x-coordinate of -2 could lie on the axis of symmetry.

17. (E)
Calculate the discriminant for each equation.
  A. D=0-0=0
  B. D=1-4(-3)=13
  C. D=4-4(-21)=88
  D. D=9-4(2.25)=0
  E. D=25-4(12)=-23

18. (B)   If the discriminant is negative, there are no real roots and the parabola never crosses the x-axis.

19. (C) Use the quadratic formula. For

$$x^2 - 3x + 2.25 = 0$$

$$x = \frac{3 \pm \sqrt{9 - 4(2.25)}}{2} = \frac{3 \pm \sqrt{9-9}}{2} = \frac{3}{2}$$

20. (C)   Complete the square.
$$y = x^2 - 6x - 3$$
$$y + 3 = x^2 - 6x$$
$$y + 3 + 9 = x^2 - 6x + 9$$
$$y + 12 = (x-3)^2$$
$$y = (x-3)^2 - 12$$

21. (D)
The first two equations cross the x-axis at the points indicated, whereas the third equation crosses the x-axis at only one point (-3,0).

5.5 Translations and reflections

Translations and reflections are simply movements of the graph of $y = f(x)$. A translation moves the graph horizontally and/or vertically. A reflection causes the graph to flip around an axis. Translations and reflections can take place separately or in combination.

Translations

The table below shows how the graph of $y = f(x)$ is moved vertically and/or horizontally.

Original function $y = f(x)$	Translated function
Move up k units	$y = f(x) + k$
Move down k units	$y = f(x) - k$
Move left h units	$y = f(x + h)$
Move right h units	$y = f(x - h)$

Each movement can take place by itself or in combination with others. For example, to move a graph up k units and right h units you would use $y = f(x - h) + k$.

Reflections

Only the two reflections below are needed:

Original function $y = f(x)$	Reflected function
About the x-axis	$y = -f(x)$
About the y-axis	$y = f(-x)$

Combinations

Translations and reflections are sometimes combined. For example, to move a graph up k units and reflect it about the x-axis would be

$$y = f(x) + k \qquad \text{first translate up k units}$$

$$y = -\big(f(x) + k\big) = -f(x) - k \qquad \text{then reflect about x-axis}$$

Problems on translations and reflections (unit 5.5)

1. If $y = 2x^2 - 3x + 1$ is the result of translating another parabola down 1 unit, what is the equation of that other parabola?

   (A) $y = 2(x+1)^2 - 3(x+1) + 1$

   (B) $y = 3x^2 - 2x$

   (C) $y = 2x^2 - 3x + 2$

   (D) $y = 2x^2 - 3x$

   (E) $y = x^2 - 4x$

2. The equation of the parabola $y = 2x^2 - 3x + 1$ after it has been reflected about the y-axis and then moved up 1 unit is:

   (A) $y = 2(x+1)^2 - 3(x+1) + 1$

   (B) $y = 3x^2 - 2x$

   (C) $y = 2x^2 + 3x + 2$

   (D) $y = 2x^2 - 3x$

   (E) $y = x^2 - 4x$

3. The equation of the parabola $y = 2x^2 - 3x + 1$ after it has been moved right 1 unit and then reflected about the x-axis is:

   (A) $y = 2x^2 - x$

   (B) $y = 2x^2 + x$

   (C) $y = -2x^2 + x$

   (D) $y = -2x^2 + 3x - 1$

   (E) $y = -2x^2 + 7x - 6$

4. The intersection of the line $y = 5x + 3$ and its reflection about the x-axis occurs at the point:

   (A)   (-0.6, 0)

   (B)   (0.6, 0)

   (C)   (0, 0)

   (D)   (0, 3)

   (E)   (3,0)

5. The intersection of the line $y = 5x + 3$ and its reflection about the y-axis occurs at the point:

   (A)   (-0.6, 0)

   (B)   (0.6, 0)

   (C)   (0, 0)

   (D)   (0, 3)

   (E)   (3,0)

6. When the following graph

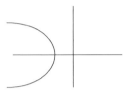

is reflected over the y-axis and then is translated left, it becomes

E. None of the above.

7. If in the diagram below, $g(x) = f(x - h) + k$, then the value of $h + k$ must be:

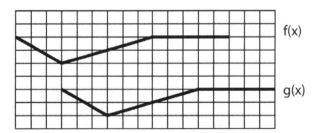

   (A)   --7   (D)   1

   (B)   -1   (E)   7

   (C)   0

Solutions to problems on translations and reflections (unit 5.5)

1. (C)

$$f(x) = 2x^2 - 3x + 2$$
$$f(x) - 1 = 2x^2 - 3x + 1$$

2. (C)

$$f(x) = 2x^2 - 3x + 1$$
$$f(-x) = 2(-x)^2 - 3(-x) + 1$$
$$f(-x) = 2x^2 + 3x + 1$$
$$f(-x) + 1 = 2x^2 + 3x + 2$$

3. (E)

$$f(x) = 2x^2 - 3x + 1$$
$$f(x-1) = 2(x-1)^2 - 3(x-1) + 1$$
$$f(x-1) = 2(x^2 - 2x + 1) - 3(x-1) + 1$$
$$f(x-1) = 2x^2 - 7x + 6$$
$$-f(x-1) = -2x^2 + 7x - 6$$

4. (A)

$$f(x) = 5x + 3$$
$$-f(x) = -5x - 3$$
$$5x + 3 = -5x - 3$$
$$10x = -6, \; x = -0.6$$
$$f(-0.6) = 0$$
$$(-0.6, 0)$$

5. (D)

$$f(x) = 5x + 3$$
$$f(-x) = -5x + 3$$
$$5x + 3 = -5x + 3$$
$$10x = 0, \; x = 0$$
$$f(0) = 3$$
$$(0, 3)$$

6. (C)

Graph A is not reflected and shifted left. Graph B is reflected but not shifted. Graph D is not reflected and shifted right.

7. (B)

The graph f(x) has been translated down 4 units, so $k = -4$. It has also been translated right 3 units, so $h = 3$. Therefore $g(x) = f(x-3) - 4$ and $h + k = 3 + (-4) = -1$

5.6 Functions

A function defines a relation between every possible value that can be accepted by the function (this set is called the domain) to every possible value that can be produced by the function (this set is called the range). For example the function $f(x) = x + 3$ establishes a relationship between every domain value and its corresponding range value. The relationship is simple: take the domain value and add three in order to obtain the range value. A useful graphic representation of a function is shown below.

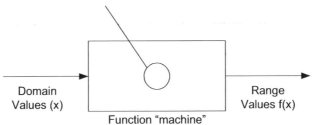

Function "machine"

Imagine that you feed a value from the domain (the x-value) into the function machine. Next, turn the crank on the machine. Then out comes the corresponding value from the range (the y-value or the f(x) value). For a particular domain value that is placed into it, a function can only crank out one range value (otherwise it is not a function). When functions are graphed, they pass the "vertical line test," meaning that if a vertical line is drawn anywhere on the graph, it passes through the graph of the function at one and only one point.

Funny functions

It is pretty easy to ask you to evaluate a traditional function like $f(x) = x^2 + 1$. Instead you could be asked to evaluate functions that use non-mathematical symbols. For example, the # function could be defined as:

$$\# x = \frac{x^2}{2}$$

Then you would be expected to evaluate the # function for various values or expressions in the domain. For example:

$$\#3 = \frac{3^2}{2} = \frac{9}{2} = 4.5$$

$$\#a = \frac{a^2}{2}$$

$$\#(a-2) = \frac{(a-2)^2}{2}$$

Standardized tests may use funny functions with two arguments, such as

$$x \ \psi \ y = 5x - 3y$$

Then you would be expected to evaluate the ψ function for various expressions, such as:

$$2 \ \psi \ 3 = 5(2) - 3(3) = 10 - 9 = 1$$

$$3 \ \psi \ a = 5(3) - 3a = 15 - 3a$$

$$a \ \psi \ (a-1) = 5a - 3(a-1) = 5a - 3a + 3 = 2a + 3$$

Graphs of functions

It is important to be able to navigate graphs of functions. A general graph of a function is

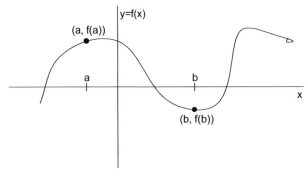

Notice that the domain is the horizontal axis (x-axis) and the range is the vertical axis (y-axis). The function maps each value in the domain to a single value in the range (passes the vertical line test). Any point that lies on the graph must satisfy the function rule. For example if the function were $f(x) = x^2 + 1$ then any arbitrary point on the graph of that function would have the coordinates of $(a, a^2 + 1)$.

Recall that in order for a relation to be a function, it must pass the vertical line test -- each value in the domain can map to one and only one value in the range. Thus $f(x) = x^2$ is a function. However, $f(x) = \pm\sqrt{x}$ is not a function because each value of x maps to two y-values, e.g., 9 maps to 3 and -3.

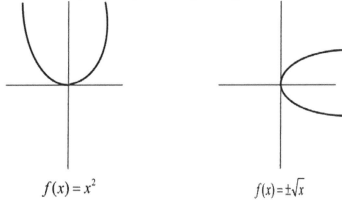

$$f(x) = x^2$$

passes vertical line test (function)
fails horizontal line test (inverse is not a function)

$$f(x) = \pm\sqrt{x}$$

fails vertical line test (not a function)
horizontal line test irrelevant

The inverse $f^{-1}(x)$ of a function $f(x)$

In order for the inverse of a function to be a function, the original relation must be a function (pass the vertical line test) and the original relation must also pass the horizontal line test. For example, the relation $f(x) = x^2$ is a valid function (it passes the vertical line test) but its inverse is not a function because $f(x) = x^2$ fails the horizontal line test (see the diagram above).

To find the inverse, called $f^{-1}(x)$, of a given function, called $f(x)$, first make sure that $f(x)$ is a function (passes the vertical line test). If $f(x)$ is a function then it has an inverse. If $f(x)$ fails the horizontal line test then its inverse is not a function. To find an expression for the inverse function, follow these steps:

- Replace f(x) with y.
- Switch x and y
- Solve for y

For example,

$$f(x) = \frac{x}{5} + 3 \qquad \textit{given the function } f(x)$$

$$y = \frac{x}{5} + 3 \qquad \textit{replace } f(x) \textit{ with } y$$

$$x = \frac{y}{5} + 3 \qquad \textit{switch } x \textit{ and } y$$

$$y = 5x - 15 \qquad \textit{solve for } y$$

$$f^{-1}(x) = 5x - 15$$

If you want to find the inverse function graphically, you can reflect the original function around the line $y = x$. Another graphical technique is to plot points. If the original function goes through point (a,b) then the inverse function will go through point (b,a).

Composite functions

Sometimes functions are combined together to form composite functions. For example, suppose $f(x) = x + 2$ and $g(x) = x^2$. Then we write:

$$f(g(x)) = f(x^2) = x^2 + 2.$$

Note above that the first step is just substituting x^2 for $g(x)$. Then the f-function is applied to the argument x^2, yielding $x^2 + 2$. We could go the other way around, namely

$$g(f(x)) = g(x + 2) = (x + 2)^2$$

The expression $x + 2$ replaces $f(x)$ and then the g-function is applied to the argument $x + 2$, yielding $(x + 2)^2$.

Proving that a given function is an inverse function

To prove that a given function $f^{-1}(x)$ is the inverse of another function $f(x)$, simply examine the composite functions to determine whether

$$f\left(f^{-1}(x)\right) = x \text{ and } f^{-1}\left(f(x)\right) = x.$$

Suppose we wish to determine whether $f(x) = \frac{x}{5} + 3$ and $f^{-1}(x) = 5x - 15$ really are inverses of each other.

$$f\left(f^{-1}(x)\right) = f(5x - 15) = \frac{5x - 15}{5} + 3 = x - 3 + 3 = x$$

$$f^{-1}\left(f(x)\right) = f^{-1}\left(\frac{x}{5} + 3\right) = 5\left(\frac{x}{5} + 3\right) - 15 = x + 15 - 15 = x$$

So now it is possible to conclude that the function $5x - 15$ really is the inverse of the function $\frac{x}{5} + 3$.

Problems on functions (unit 5.6)

NOTE: For problems 1-3, the function $\Uparrow$ is defined as $\Uparrow x = 2x^2 - 3$.

1. The value of $\Uparrow 5$ is:

   (A)   0
   (B)   7
   (C)   10
   (D)   47
   (E)   50

2. The value of $\Uparrow\left(\Uparrow 2\right)$ is:

   (A)   0
   (B)   7
   (C)   10
   (D)   47
   (E)   50

3. Solve for x when $\Uparrow x = \Uparrow(x+1)$

   (A)   -0.5

   (B)   0

   (C)   0.5

   (D)   1

   (E)   No solution

NOTE: For problems 4 and 5, the function $x\Psi y$ is defined as $x\Psi y = x^2 - xy$.

4. Find the expression for $(a+1)\Psi(a-1)$

   (A)   0

   (B)   2

   (C)   2a

   (D)   a+1

   (E)   2a+2

5. If $a\Psi 2 = a\Psi 3b$, then b is equal to:

   (A)   -2/3

   (B)   -3/2

   (C)   2/3

   (D)   3/2

   (E)   2

NOTE: The diagram below is to be used for problems 6-10.

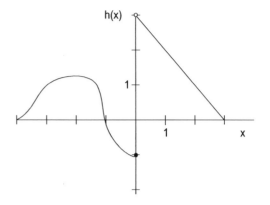

6. The domain of h is:

   (A)   [-4, 1]

   (B)   [-4,0] U (0,3]

   (C)   [-4,3]

   (D)   [-1,1]

   (E)   [-1,3]

7. The range of h is:

   (A)   [-4, 3]
   (B)   [-4,3)
   (C)   (-4,3)
   (D)   [-1, 3)
   (E)   [-1,3]

8. The value of h(0) is:

   (A)   -1
   (B)   0
   (C)   1
   (D)   2
   (E)   3

9. If h(k)=0 then k could be:

   I.   -4
   II. -1
   III. 3
   (A)   I only
   (B)   II only
   (C)   III only
   (D)   I and II only
   (E)   I, II and III

10. For what value of k is h(k) approximately equal to 1?

    I. k= -2
    II. k= 2
    III. k= 3

(A)   I only
(B)   II only
(C)   III only
(D)   I and II only
(E)   I and III only

The table below defines the function f(x). It is to be used for problems 11-13.

x	$f(x)$
1	3
2	2
3	1
4	2
5	3
6	4

11. If $f(x) = 3$, then x could be:

    I.   1
    II. 2
    III. 5

(A)   I only
(B)   II only
(C)   III only
(D)   I and II only
(E)   I and III only

12. The value of $f(3)$ is:

(A)   1
(B)   2
(C)   3
(D)   4
(E)   5

13. An expression for $f(x)$ could be:

(A) $f(x) = x + 2$
(B) $f(x) = x - 2$
(C) $f(x) = x^2 + 2$
(D) $f(x) = x^2 - 2$
(E) $f(x) = |x - 3| + 1$

14. If $f(x) = x^2 + 2x - 1$ then $f(-x)$ is:

(A) $x^2 + 2x - 1$
(B) $x^2 - 2x - 1$
(C) $-x^2 + 2x - 1$
(D) $-x^2 - 2x - 1$
(E) $-x^2 + 2x + 1$

15. If the domain of the function $y = x^2 - 2x - 3$ is restricted to $-1 < x < 3$ then the range is:

(A) $-1 < y < 3$
(B) $1 < y < 3$
(C) $-4 < y < 0$
(D) $y > -4$
(E)   all real numbers

In problems 16-19, find the inverse <u>function</u> of $f(x)$. If $f(x)$ has no inverse <u>function</u>, then choose (E).

16. $f(x) = \dfrac{2x}{3} + 8$

(A) $1.5x - 4$
(B) $1.5x - 8$
(C) $1.5x - 12$
(D) $1.5x - 16$
(E)   The inverse is not a function

17. $f(x) = x^2 + 6x + 9$

(A) $y = x^2$
(B) $y = x^2 - x - 3$
(C) $y = -3x^2 - 2x + 7$
(D) $y = x^2 - 3x + 2.25$
(E)   The inverse is not a function

18. $f(x) = \dfrac{x^3 + 2}{5}$

(A) $\sqrt[3]{2x + 5}$
(B) $\sqrt[3]{5x + 2}$
(C) $\sqrt[3]{\dfrac{x - 5}{2}}$
(D) $\sqrt[3]{5x - 2}$
(E)   The inverse is not a function

19. $f(x) = |x - 5| + 3$

    (A) $x + 2$

    (B) $x - 2$

    (C) $x - 8$

    (D) $8 - x$

    (E)   The inverse is not a function

20. If the inverse of a function is $\dfrac{x + 2}{2}$ then the

original function is:

    (A) $\dfrac{x + 2}{2}$

    (B) $\dfrac{x - 2}{2}$

    (C) $x - 1$

    (D) $2x - 2$

    (E)   Cannot be determined

In problems 21-24, let $f(x) = x^2 - 1$ and $g(x) = x - 1$.

21. What is $f(g(x))$?

    (A) $x - 1$

    (B) $x + 1$

    (C) $x^2 - 2x$

    (D) $x^2 - 2x + 1$

    (E) $x^2 - 2$

22. What is $g(f(x))$?

    (A) x^2

    (B) $x^2 + 1$

    (C) $x^2 + 2$

    (D) $x^2 - 1$

    (E) $x^2 - 2$

23. What is $f(f(-1))$?

    (A) -2

    (B) -1

    (C) 0

    (D) 1

    (E) 2

24. What is $g(g(x))$?

    (A) $x - 2$

    (B) $x - 1$

    (C) x

    (D) $x + 1$

    (E) $x + 2$

Solutions to problems on functions (unit 5.6)

1. (D)

$\Uparrow 5 = 2(5)^2 - 3 = 50 - 3 = 47$

2. (D)

$\Uparrow(\Uparrow 2) = \Uparrow(2 \cdot 2^2 - 3) = \Uparrow(5)$

$\Uparrow 5 = 2(5)^2 - 3 = 50 - 3 = 47$

3. (A)

$\Uparrow x = 2x^2 - 3$

$\Uparrow(x+1) = 2(x+1)^2 - 3 = 2(x^2 + 2x + 1) - 3$

$\Uparrow(x+1) = 2x^2 + 4x - 1$

$2x^2 - 3 = 2x^2 + 4x - 1$

$-2 = 4x, \quad -0.5 = x$

4. (E)

$(a+1)\Psi(a-1) = (a+1)^2 - (a+1)(a-1)$

$\quad\quad\quad = (a^2 + 2a + 1) - (a^2 - 1) = 2a + 2$

5. (C)

$a\Psi 2 = a\Psi 3b$

$a^2 - 2a = a^2 - 3ab$

$b = \dfrac{-2a}{-3a} = 2/3$

6. (C)

The function is defined for all x within [-4,3].

7. (D)

The height of the function ranges from -1 up to almost 3.

8. (A)

 h(0)=-1

9. (E)

Find the points where the curve crosses the x-axis. These are approximately -4, -1 and 3.

10. (D)

Draw the horizontal line y=1. It intersects the graph at -2 and 2.

11. (E)

I. f(1)=3 true. II. f(2)=2 false. III. f(5)=3 true.

12. (A)

13. (E)

(A) $f(x) = x + 2$ works for x=1 only.

(B) $f(x) = x - 2$ works for x=3,4,5,and 6 only.

(C) $f(x) = x^2 + 2$ works for x=1 only.

(D) $f(x) = x^2 - 2$ works for x=2 only.

(E) $f(x) = |x - 3| + 1$ works for all values in the table

14. (B)

$f(-x) = (-x)^2 + 2(-x) - 1 = x^2 - 2x - 1$

15. (C) The graph looks like:

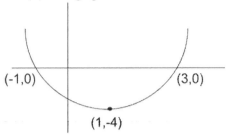

(-1,0)   (3,0)

(1,-4)

Keep in mind that we are only looking at -1<x<3.

16. (C)

$f(x) = \dfrac{2x}{3} + 8$

$x = \dfrac{2y}{3} + 8$

$y = f^{-1}(x) = \dfrac{3(x-8)}{2} = 1.5x - 12$

17. (E) $y = x^2 + 6x + 9$ fails the horizontal line test and therefore its inverse is not a function.

18. (D)

$f(x) = \dfrac{x^3 + 2}{5}$

$x = \dfrac{y^3 + 2}{5}$

$y = \sqrt[3]{5x - 2}$

19. (E)

$y = |x - 5| + 3$ fails the horizontal line test and therefore its inverse is not a function.

20. (D) To find the original function, take the inverse of the inverse. Or you can solve this by taking the inverse of each of the answers to see which one matches the inverse that was given.

$f^{-1}(x) = \dfrac{x+2}{2}$

$x = \dfrac{y+2}{2}$

$f(x) = y = 2x - 2$

21. (C)

$f(g(x)) = f(x-1) = (x-1)^2 - 1$

$\quad\quad\quad = (x^2 - 2x + 1) - 1 = x^2 - 2x$

22. (E)

$g(f(x)) = g(x^2 - 1) = (x^2 - 1) - 1 = x^2 - 2$

23. (B)

$f(f(-1)) = f((-1)^2 - 1) = f(1 - 1) = f(0) = 0 - 1 = -1$

24. (A)

$g(g(x)) = g(x-1) = (x-1) - 1 = x - 2$

5.7 Logarithms

It is rare when a formal definition in math is particularly useful when solving problems, but that is the case with logarithms. Take a close look at the definition:

$$\text{If } y = \log_b x \text{ then } b^y = x.$$
$$\text{If } x = b^y \text{ then } y = \log_b x$$

There are many problems that make use of this definition and you can get them easily with a little practice. But first, take a look at two special cases of the base, b.

$$\text{If } b = 10 \text{ then we write } \log x \text{ instead of } \log_{10} x$$
$$\text{If } b = e \text{ then we write } \ln x \text{ instead of } \log_e x$$

$\ln x$ is called the "natural logarithm" of x.

Calculator tip: The values of $\log x$ and $\ln x$ can be found on the graphing calculator, using the keys marked "LOG" and "LN". Use your calculator to find that $\log 250 = 2.4$ and $\ln 250 = 5.5$.

Practice translating the following log expressions to exponentials

$$\log x = 5 \text{ translates to } 10^5 = x, \text{ or } x = 100,000$$

$$\ln x = 3 \text{ translates to } e^3 = x, \text{ or } x = 20.08$$

$$\log_3 x = 5 \text{ translates to } 3^5 = x, \text{ or } x = 243.$$

Practice translating the following exponential expressions to logs:

$$x = 10^2 \text{ translates to } \log x = 2$$

$$x = e^3 \text{ translates to } \ln x = 3$$

$$x = 5^{12} \text{ translates to } \log_5 x = 12.$$

Laws of Logarithms

Now that you have refreshed the way logarithms work and their relationship to exponentials, it is necessary to memorize and know how to use the four laws of logarithms. They are

$$\log_b xy = \log_b x + \log_b y$$

$$\log_b \frac{x}{y} = \log_b x - \log_b y$$

$$\log_b x^y = y \log_b x$$

$$\log_b x = \frac{\log x}{\log b} = \frac{\ln x}{\ln b}$$

The last law, called the "change of base formula," is very useful when calculating the numeric value of a log that is using a base other than 10 or e.

A simple illustration of the first three laws:

$$\log_b \left(\frac{xy}{z} \right)^5 = 5 \log_b \left(\frac{xy}{z} \right) = 5 \left(\log_b xy - \log_b z \right) = 5 \left(\log_b x + \log_b y - \log_b z \right)$$

Some illustrations of the change of base formula are:

$$\log_5 170 = \frac{\log 170}{\log 5} = \frac{2.23}{0.70} = 3.2$$

or

$$\log_5 170 = \frac{\ln 170}{\ln 5} = \frac{5.14}{1.61} = 3.2$$

Problems on logarithms (unit 5.7)

1. The equation $x^3 = e^{57}$ is equivalent to:

   (A) $\log x = 19$

   (B) $\log x = 57$

   (C) $\ln x = 19$

   (D) $\ln x = 57$

   (E) None of the above

2. The equation $5^x = y$ is equivalent to:

   I. $\log_5 x = y$

   II. $\log_5 y = x$

   III. $\dfrac{\log y}{\log 5} = x$

   (A) I only

   (B) II only

   (C) III only

   (D) I and III only

   (E) II and III only

3. If $x = \left(\dfrac{a^2 b^3}{a + c^2}\right)^5$, then $\log x$ is:

   (A) $5\log a + 15\log b - 10\log c$

   (B) $10\log a + 15\log b - 5\log(a + c^2)$

   (C) $5\log a + 15\log b - 5\log c$

   (D) $15\log a + 15\log b + 10\log c$

   (E) None of the above

4. If $x = \log_3 45 - \log_3 5$, then x is equal to

   (A) -1

   (B) 0

   (C) 1

   (D) 2

   (E) 3

5. If $x = 15\log_{15} 3 + 15\log_{15} 5$ then x is equal to:

   (A) 0

   (B) 1

   (C) 3

   (D) 5

   (E) 15

6. If $5^x = 125^{x+4}$ then x is equal to:

   (A) -6

   (B) -2

   (C) 2

   (D) 6

   (E) 10

7. If $\log_3(2x - 1) = 2$ then x is equal to:

   (A) 3

   (B) 3.5

   (C) 4

   (D) 5

   (E) 6

8. If $\log x + \log 2 = 2$ then x is equal to:

   (A) 5

   (B) 10

   (C) 25

   (D) 50

   (E) 100

9. Without a calculator, find the value of $\dfrac{\ln 8}{\ln 2}$

   (A) 2

   (B) 3

   (C) 4

   (D) 6

   (E) 8

Solutions to problems on logarithms (unit 5.7)

1. (C)

$x^3 = e^{57}$

$\ln x^3 = 57, \ 3\ln x = 57, \ \ln x = \dfrac{57}{3} = 19$

2. (E)

By definition, I is false and II is true. Use the change of base formula to see that if II is true then III is true.

$x = \log_5 y = \dfrac{\log y}{\log 5}$

3. (B)

$x = \left(\dfrac{a^2 b^3}{a + c^2} \right)^5, \ \log x = 5\log\left(\dfrac{a^2 b^3}{a + c^2} \right)$

$\log x = 5\left(\log a^2 b^3 - \log\left(a + c^2 \right) \right)$

$\log x = 5\left(2\log a + 3\log b - \log\left(a + c^2 \right) \right)$

$\log x = 10\log a + 15\log b - 5\log(a + c^2)$

4. (D)

$x = \log_3 45 - \log_3 5 = \log_3\left(\dfrac{45}{5} \right) = \log_3 9$

$x = \log_3 9$ translates to $3^x = 9, \ x = 2$

5. (E)

$x = 15\log_{15} 3 + 15\log_{15} 5$

$x = 15(\log_{15} 3 + \log_{15} 5)$

$x = 15\log_{15}\left(3 \cdot 5 \right) = 15\log_{15} 15 = 15 \cdot 1 = 15$

6. (A)

$5^x = 125^{x+4}$

$5^x = \left(5^3 \right)^{x+4} = 5^{3x+12}$

$x = 3x + 12, \ x = -6$

7. (D)

$\log_3\left(2x - 1 \right) = 2$

$3^2 = 2x - 1$

$9 = 2x - 1, \ x = 5$

8. (D)

$\log x + \log 2 = 2$

$\log 2x = 2$

$10^2 = 2x, \ 100 = 2x, \ x = 50$

9. (B)

Use the change of base formula

$\dfrac{\ln 8}{\ln 2} = \log_2 8$

$x = \log_2 8, \ 2^x = 8, \ x = 3$

5.8 Matrix algebra

A matrix is a collection of numbers arranged into rows and columns. A matrix is denoted by a capital letter, and its members are denoted by lower case letters. There are only a few basic operations that you need to know.

In the material below, we will use these two general expressions for the matrices A and B

$$A = \begin{pmatrix} a_{1,1} & a_{1,2} \\ a_{2,1} & a_{2,2} \end{pmatrix} \quad B = \begin{pmatrix} b_{1,1} & b_{1,2} \\ b_{2,1} & b_{2,2} \end{pmatrix}$$

It will also help to use a specific example, so we will let

$$A = \begin{pmatrix} 1 & 2 \\ 3 & 4 \end{pmatrix} \quad B = \begin{pmatrix} 5 & 6 \\ 7 & 8 \end{pmatrix}$$

Multiplication by a scalar

If k is a scalar, then $kA = \begin{pmatrix} ka_{1,1} & ka_{1,2} \\ ka_{2,1} & ka_{2,2} \end{pmatrix} \quad kB = \begin{pmatrix} kb_{1,1} & kb_{1,2} \\ kb_{2,1} & kb_{2,2} \end{pmatrix}$

Suppose k=5. Then $kA = \begin{pmatrix} 5 \cdot 1 & 5 \cdot 2 \\ 5 \cdot 3 & 5 \cdot 4 \end{pmatrix} = \begin{pmatrix} 5 & 10 \\ 15 & 20 \end{pmatrix} \quad kB = \begin{pmatrix} 5 \cdot 5 & 5 \cdot 6 \\ 5 \cdot 7 & 5 \cdot 8 \end{pmatrix} = \begin{pmatrix} 25 & 30 \\ 35 & 40 \end{pmatrix}$

Addition and subtraction

Addition and subtraction can only take place when both matrices have the same dimensions. When this occurs, simply add or subtract corresponding elements:

$$A \pm B = \begin{pmatrix} a_{1,1} & a_{1,2} \\ a_{2,1} & a_{2,2} \end{pmatrix} \pm \begin{pmatrix} b_{1,1} & b_{1,2} \\ b_{2,1} & b_{2,2} \end{pmatrix} = \begin{pmatrix} a_{1,1} \pm b_{1,1} & a_{1,2} \pm b_{1,2} \\ a_{2,1} \pm b_{2,1} & a_{2,2} \pm b_{2,2} \end{pmatrix}$$

Suppose we want to calculate **5A - 2B**. This would be

$$5A - 2B = \begin{pmatrix} 5 \cdot 1 & 5 \cdot 2 \\ 5 \cdot 3 & 5 \cdot 4 \end{pmatrix} - \begin{pmatrix} 2 \cdot 5 & 2 \cdot 6 \\ 2 \cdot 7 & 2 \cdot 8 \end{pmatrix} = \begin{pmatrix} 5 & 10 \\ 15 & 20 \end{pmatrix} - \begin{pmatrix} 10 & 12 \\ 14 & 16 \end{pmatrix} = \begin{pmatrix} 5-10 & 10-12 \\ 15-14 & 20-16 \end{pmatrix} = \begin{pmatrix} -5 & -2 \\ 1 & 4 \end{pmatrix}$$

Multiplication

Multiplication is the most difficult of the matrix operations. Remember that multiplication may only take place when the inner dimensions of the two matrices are identical. The dimensions of the resulting product will have the outer dimensions of the matrices that have been multiplied. This sounds complicated, but it's not.

Suppose **C** is a matrix with dimensions (2x3) and **D** is a matrix with dimensions (3x2). The product **CD** will have dimensions (2x2) because:

$$\mathbf{CD} = \underset{(2x3)}{\mathbf{C}} \cdot \underset{(3x2)}{\mathbf{D}} = \underset{(2x2)}{\mathbf{E}}$$

he inner dimensions sort of "cancel out" leaving the outer dimensions for the result.

The product DC will have dimensions (3x3) because:

$$\mathbf{DC} = \underset{(3x2)}{\mathbf{D}} \cdot \underset{(2x3)}{\mathbf{C}} = \underset{(3x3)}{\mathbf{F}}$$

It's important to understand dimensions before actually doing some problems because dimensions are used to guide the way things are set up. Notice that **E** and **F** are different matrices with different dimensions, proving that in the world of matrices $\mathbf{C} \cdot \mathbf{D} \neq \mathbf{D} \cdot \mathbf{C}$. So now we are ready to take a look at how multiplication actually works. Suppose:

$$\mathbf{C} = \begin{pmatrix} 1 & 3 & -1 \\ 0 & -2 & 1 \end{pmatrix} \quad \mathbf{D} = \begin{pmatrix} 1 & 2 \\ 0 & -1 \\ -2 & 1 \end{pmatrix}$$

Then

$$\mathbf{CD} = \begin{pmatrix} 1\cdot1+3\cdot0+-1\cdot\cdot-2 & 1\cdot2+3\cdot\cdot-1+-1\cdot1 \\ 0\cdot1+-2\cdot0+1\cdot\cdot-2 & 0\cdot2+-2\cdot\cdot-1+1\cdot1 \end{pmatrix} = \begin{pmatrix} 1+0+2 & 2-3-1 \\ 0+0-2 & 0+2+1 \end{pmatrix} = \begin{pmatrix} 3 & -2 \\ -2 & 3 \end{pmatrix}$$

Notice that the first row and first column of the resulting product matrix consists of the first row of **C** multiplied by the first column of **D**. The first row and second column consists of the first row of **C** multiplied by the second column of **D**, etc.

Now take a look at **DC**. Notice that $\mathbf{DC} \neq \mathbf{CD}$.

$$\mathbf{DC} = \begin{pmatrix} 1\cdot1+2\cdot0 & 1\cdot3+2\cdot\cdot-2 & 1\cdot\cdot-1+2\cdot1 \\ 0\cdot1-1\cdot0 & 0\cdot3-1\cdot\cdot-2 & 0\cdot\cdot-1-1\cdot1 \\ -2\cdot1+1\cdot0 & -2\cdot3+1\cdot\cdot-2 & -2\cdot\cdot-1+1\cdot1 \end{pmatrix} = \begin{pmatrix} 1+0 & 3-4 & -1+2 \\ 0-0 & 0+2 & 0-1 \\ -2+0 & -6-2 & 2+1 \end{pmatrix} = \begin{pmatrix} 1 & -1 & 1 \\ 0 & 2 & -1 \\ -2 & -8 & 3 \end{pmatrix}$$

Problems on matrix algebra (unit 5.8)

Use these matrices to solve problems 1-5 below:

$$A = \begin{pmatrix} 1 & 0 \\ 2 & -1 \end{pmatrix} \quad B = \begin{pmatrix} 0 & 2 \\ 1 & 1 \end{pmatrix} \quad C = \begin{pmatrix} 1 & 2 & -1 \\ 2 & 0 & 1 \end{pmatrix}$$

1. The sum of **A** and **B** is:

   (A) $\begin{pmatrix} 1 & -2 \\ 1 & -2 \end{pmatrix}$

   (B) $\begin{pmatrix} -1 & 2 \\ -1 & -2 \end{pmatrix}$

   (C) $\begin{pmatrix} 1 & 2 \\ 3 & 0 \end{pmatrix}$

   (D) $\begin{pmatrix} 3 & 0 \\ 3 & 0 \end{pmatrix}$

   (E) Cannot be determined

2. The value of **B − 2A** is:

   (A) $\begin{pmatrix} 0 & 2 \\ -3 & 0 \end{pmatrix}$

   (B) $\begin{pmatrix} -2 & 2 \\ -3 & 3 \end{pmatrix}$

   (C) $\begin{pmatrix} -1 & 2 \\ -1 & -2 \end{pmatrix}$

   (D) $\begin{pmatrix} 1 & 2 \\ 3 & 0 \end{pmatrix}$

   (E) Cannot be determined

3. The value of **BA** is:

   (A) $\begin{pmatrix} 4 & -2 \\ 3 & -1 \end{pmatrix}$

   (B) $\begin{pmatrix} 0 & 2 \\ 1 & 3 \end{pmatrix}$

   (C) $\begin{pmatrix} 4 & 2 \\ 3 & -1 \end{pmatrix}$

   (D) $\begin{pmatrix} 0 & 2 \\ 3 & 3 \end{pmatrix}$

   (E) Cannot be determined

4. The value of **A + C** is:

   (A) $\begin{pmatrix} 2 & 2 & -1 \\ 4 & -1 & 1 \end{pmatrix}$

   (B) $\begin{pmatrix} 1 & 4 & -1 \\ 3 & 1 & 1 \end{pmatrix}$

   (C) $\begin{pmatrix} 1 & 3 & -1 \\ 2 & 2 & 0 \end{pmatrix}$

   (D) $\begin{pmatrix} 1 & 2 & 1 \\ 2 & 1 & 2 \end{pmatrix}$

   (E) Cannot be determined

5. The value of **AC** is:

   (A) $\begin{pmatrix} 4 & 0 & 2 \\ 3 & 2 & 0 \end{pmatrix}$

   (B) $\begin{pmatrix} 4 & 0 & 1 \\ 3 & 2 & 0 \end{pmatrix}$

   (C) $\begin{pmatrix} 1 & 2 & 1 \\ 0 & 3 & -3 \end{pmatrix}$

   (D) $\begin{pmatrix} 1 & 2 & -1 \\ 0 & 4 & -3 \end{pmatrix}$

   (E) Cannot be determined

6. If $\begin{pmatrix} 1 & 0 \\ 2 & -1 \end{pmatrix}\begin{pmatrix} x \\ y \end{pmatrix} = \begin{pmatrix} 3 \\ -6 \end{pmatrix}$, find the value of y.

   (A)   -12

   (B)   -6

   (C)   0

   (D)   6

   (E)   12

Solutions to problems on matrix algebra (unit 5.8)

1. (C)

$$\mathbf{A} + \mathbf{B} = \begin{pmatrix} 1+0 & 0+2 \\ 2+1 & -1+1 \end{pmatrix} = \begin{pmatrix} 1 & 2 \\ 3 & 0 \end{pmatrix}$$

2. (B)

$$\mathbf{B} - 2\mathbf{A} = \begin{pmatrix} 0 & 2 \\ 1 & 1 \end{pmatrix} - \begin{pmatrix} 2 & 0 \\ 4 & -2 \end{pmatrix} = \begin{pmatrix} -2 & 2 \\ -3 & 3 \end{pmatrix}$$

3. (A)

$$\mathbf{BA} = \begin{pmatrix} 0\cdot1+2\cdot2 & 0\cdot0+2\cdot-1 \\ 1\cdot1+1\cdot2 & 1\cdot0+1\cdot-1 \end{pmatrix} = \begin{pmatrix} 4 & -2 \\ 3 & -1 \end{pmatrix}$$

4. (E)

These matrices cannot be added because they have different dimensions.

5. (D)

$$\mathbf{AC} = \begin{pmatrix} 1\cdot1+0\cdot2 & 1\cdot2+0\cdot0 & 1\cdot-1+0\cdot1 \\ 2\cdot1-1\cdot2 & 2\cdot2-1\cdot0 & 2\cdot-1-1\cdot1 \end{pmatrix} = \begin{pmatrix} 1 & 2 & -1 \\ 0 & 4 & -3 \end{pmatrix}$$

6. (E)

$$\begin{pmatrix} 1 & 0 \\ 2 & -1 \end{pmatrix} \begin{pmatrix} x \\ y \end{pmatrix} = \begin{pmatrix} 3 \\ -6 \end{pmatrix}$$

$x = 3$

$2x - y = -6$

$2(3) - y = -6, \; y = 12$

Unit 5.9 Complex numbers and rational numbers

Relationships between different types of numbers are shown in the diagram below. All numbers are complex numbers because they can be expressed as $a + bi$, where a and b are real numbers (note that a and b do not have to be integers) and $i^2 = -1$. If $b = 0$ the complex number is real, but if $b \neq 0$ the complex number is imaginary.

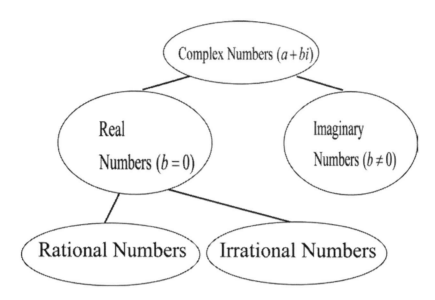

Rational Numbers

A real number is rational if it can be expressed as the ratio of two integers. An easy way to recognize a rational number is to use the calculator to express it as a decimal. The number is rational if the decimal portion of the number terminates or repeats. For example:

The number	Is	Because
$2\dfrac{1}{2}$	Rational	(a) It can be expressed as 5/2, which is a ratio of integers; or (b) It can be expressed as 2.5, which is a terminating decimal.
0.833333333......	Rational	(a). It can be expressed as 5/6, or (b) It is a repeating decimal (the repeating group is 3).
$\sqrt{2}$	Irrational	(a) It cannot be expressed as a ratio of integers; or (b) When converted to decimal it does not repeat.
1.123123123123123......	Rational	(a) It can be expressed as 1122/999; or (b).It is a repeating decimal (the repeating group is 123)

Calculator Tip: It is easy to convert from a decimal to a fraction. Type 1.33333333333333 into your calculator and press Math-Frac-Enter. The calculator will return 4/3.

Imaginary Numbers

Suppose we want to solve the equation

$$x^2 + 9 = 0 \ .$$

We would perform two steps and then be stuck:

$$x^2 = \text{-}9$$
$$x = \pm\sqrt{\text{-}9}$$

We are stuck because a negative number cannot have a real square root. So to get around this, mathematicians invented i which is called the imaginary number. By definition, $i = \sqrt{\text{-}1}$ and $i^2 = \text{-}1$. So now we can finish the problem by writing:

$$x = \pm\sqrt{\text{-}9} = \pm\sqrt{9} \cdot \sqrt{\text{-}1} = \pm 3i$$

The expression $3i$ is a special form of complex number called an imaginary number.

Addition, subtraction and multiplication of imaginary numbers

Now that you understand what imaginary numbers are and one of the reasons why they were invented, you need to be able to perform three operations: addition, subtraction, and multiplication.

Suppose we have two imaginary numbers, $a + bi$ and $c + di$. Then:

$$(a+bi)+(c+di)=(a+c)+(b+d)i$$
$$(a+bi)-(c+di)=(a-c)+(b-d)i$$

For example

$$(2+i)+(3-2i)=2+3+i-2i=5-i$$
$$(2+i)-(3-2i)=2-3+i+2i=\text{-}1+3i$$

As you can see above, addition and subtraction are what you would expect. Treat i as though it were a variable. The same applies to multiplication—the imaginary numbers are FOILed:

$$(a+bi)(c+di)=ac+adi+bci+bdi^2=(ac-bd)+(ad+bc)i$$

For example:

$$(2+i)(3-2i)=2\cdot3-4i+3i-2i^2=6-i-2(-1)=8-i$$

Division of imaginary numbers (the use of conjugates)

You must know how to simplify expressions with imaginary numbers in the denominator. This is done using conjugates. The conjugate of $a+bi$ is $a-bi$. In other words, to find the conjugate of an imaginary number just change the sign of the imaginary portion of the number.

For example, the conjugate of $3-5i$ is $3+5i$. We use this fact to simplify fractions, as in the following

$$\frac{2}{3-5i}=\left(\frac{2}{3-5i}\right)\left(\frac{3+5i}{3+5i}\right)=\frac{2(3+5i)}{9-15i+15i-25i^2}=\frac{2(3+5i)}{9+25}=\frac{2(3+5i)}{34}=\frac{3+5i}{17}$$

Powers of i

A favorite type of problem involves powers of i. These follow a pattern that is easy to find, once you get the hang of it.

$$i=i$$
$$i^2=-1$$
$$i^3=i\cdot i^2=-i$$
$$i^4=\left(i^2\right)^2=\left(-1\right)^2=1$$

Powers of i will always equal 1 or -1 when the power is even; and i or $-i$ when the power is odd. Some examples:

$$i^{18}=\left(i^2\right)^9=\left(-1\right)^9=-1$$
$$i^{52}=\left(i^2\right)^{26}=\left(-1\right)^{26}=1$$
$$i^{17}=i^{16}\cdot i=\left(i^2\right)^8\cdot i=\left(-1\right)^8\cdot i=i$$
$$i^{51}=i^{50}\cdot i=\left(i^2\right)^{25}\cdot i=\left(-1\right)^{25}\cdot i=-i$$

Problems on complex numbers and rational numbers (unit 5.9)

1. Which of the following numbers are rational?
   I. $0.101010\ldots$

   II. $6/7$

   III. $\sqrt{25}$

   (A)   I only
   (B)   II only
   (C)   III only
   (D)   I and II only
   (E)   I, II, and III

2. Which of the following numbers are irrational?
   I. π

   II. $\sqrt{10}$

   III. $1.875875875\ldots$

   (A)   I only
   (B)   II only
   (C)   III only
   (D)   I and II only
   (E)   I, II, and III

3. The sum of $2-3i$ and its conjugate is:
   (A)   4
   (B) $4-6i$
   (C) $4+6i$
   (D) $-6i$
   (E) $6i$

4. The product of $2-3i$ and its conjugate is:
   (A)   -5
   (B)   13
   (C)   14
   (D) $-5-6i$
   (E) $13-6i$

5. The expression $\left(2-5i\right)^2$ simplifies to:
   (A)   -21
   (B)   29
   (C) $-1-20i$
   (D) $-21-20i$
   (E) $-21-10i$

6. The expression $\dfrac{3}{3+2i}$ simplifies to:
   (A) $(9-2i)/13$
   (B) $(9-6i)/13$
   (C) $(9-2i)/6$
   (D) $(3-2i)/2$
   (E) $(9-6i)/5$

7. The expression $\dfrac{8-3i}{2-5i}$ simplifies to:
   (A) $-31/21$
   (B) $-(31+34i)/21$
   (C) $(1-34i)/29$
   (D) $(1+34i)/29$
   (E) $(31+34i)/29$

8. The value of i^8 is:
   (A) -1
   (B) 1
   (C) $-i$
   (D) i

9. .The value of i^{886} is:
   (A) -1
   (B) 1
   (C) $-i$
   (D) i

10. The value of i^{21} is:
    (A) -1
    (B) 1
    (C) $-i$
    (D) i

11. The value of i^{355} is:
    (A) -1
    (B) 1
    (C) $-i$
    (D) i

Solutions to problems on complex numbers and rational numbers (unit 5.9)

1. (E)

0.101010... is rational because it is repeating. The repeating group is 10.

6/7 is rational because it is the ratio of two integers.

$\sqrt{25} = 5$ is rational because 5=5/1.

2. (D)

π is irrational. When expressed in decimal it does not repeat and it does not terminate

$\sqrt{10}$ is irrational. When expressed in decimal it does not repeat and it does not terminate.

1.875875875... is rational because it is repeating. The repeating group is 875.

3. (A)

$(2-3i)+(2+3i) = 2+2-3i+3i = 4$

4. (B)

$(2-3i)(2+3i) = 4+6i-6i-9i^2$
$= 4-9(-1) = 13$

5. (D)

$(2-5i)^2 = (2-5i)(2-5i)$
$= 4-10i-10i+25i^2 = -21-20i$

6. (B)

$\dfrac{3}{3+2i} = \left(\dfrac{3}{3+2i}\right)\left(\dfrac{3-2i}{3-2i}\right) = \dfrac{9-6i}{9-4i^2} = \dfrac{9-6i}{13}$

7. (E)

$\dfrac{8-3i}{2-5i} = \left(\dfrac{8-3i}{2-5i}\right)\left(\dfrac{2+5i}{2+5i}\right) = \dfrac{16-6i+40i-15i^2}{4-25i^2}$
$= \dfrac{31+34i}{29}$

8. (B)

$i^8 = \left(i^2\right)^4 = (-1)^4 = 1$

9. (A)

$i^{886} = \left(i^2\right)^{443} = (-1)^{443} = -1$

10. (D)

$i^{21} = i^{20} \cdot i = \left(i^2\right)^{10} i = (-1)^{10} i = i$

11. (C)

$i^{355} = i^{354} \cdot i = \left(i^2\right)^{177} i = -i$

Unit 5.10 Polynomial division

In unit 5.4 we covered second degree polynomials (called quadratic equations) and their graphs (called parabolas). In this unit we cover general $n^{\underline{th}}$ degree polynomials that take the form

$$p(x) = c_n x^n + c_{n-1} x^{n-1} + \ldots + c_1 x + c_0$$

One of the skills that you are expected to have is the ability to divide two polynomials using long division. Suppose

$$\frac{p(x)}{q(x)} = \frac{x^4 + x^3 - 6x^2 - 5x - 1}{x^2 - 2x - 1}.$$

Sometimes you get lucky and $p(x)$ and/or $q(x)$ factors. When that happens, just factor each polynomial and simplify. In this example, the polynomials do not factor so the only thing left to do is polynomial long division.

Step 1. Set up the long division

$$x^2 - 2x - 1 \overline{\smash{\big)} x^4 + x^3 - 6x^2 - 5x - 1}$$

Step 2. Multiply by x^2

$$
\begin{array}{r}
x^2 \\
x^2 - 2x - 1 \overline{\smash{\big)} x^4 + x^3 - 6x^2 - 5x - 1} \\
x^4 - 2x^3 - x^2
\end{array}
$$

Step 3. Subtract

$$
\begin{array}{r}
x^2 \\
x^2 - 2x - 1 \overline{\smash{\big)} x^4 + x^3 - 6x^2 - 5x - 1} \\
\underline{x^4 - 2x^3 - x^2} \\
3x^3 - 5x^2 - 5x - 1
\end{array}
$$

Step 4. Multiply by $3x$

$$
\begin{array}{r}
x^2 + 3x \\
x^2 - 2x - 1 \overline{\smash{\big)} x^4 + x^3 - 6x^2 - 5x - 1} \\
\underline{x^4 - 2x^3 - x^2} \\
3x^3 - 5x^2 - 5x - 1 \\
3x^3 - 6x^2 - 3x
\end{array}
$$

Step 5. Subtract

$$
\begin{array}{r}
x^2 + 3x \\
x^2 - 2x - 1 \overline{\smash{\big)} x^4 + x^3 - 6x^2 - 5x - 1} \\
\underline{x^4 - 2x^3 - x^2} \\
3x^3 - 5x^2 - 5x - 1 \\
\underline{3x^3 - 6x^2 - 3x} \\
x^2 - 2x - 1
\end{array}
$$

Step 6. Multiply by 1

$$\begin{array}{r} x^2 +3x+1 \\ x^2-2x-1\overline{\smash{\big)}\,x^4 +x^3 -6x^2 -5x-1} \\ \underline{x^4 -2x^3 -x^2} \\ 3x^3 -5x^2 -5x-1 \\ \underline{3x^3 -6x^2 -3x} \\ x^2 -2x-1 \\ x^2 -2x-1 \end{array}$$

Step 7. Subtract to find the remainder is zero

$$\begin{array}{r} x^2 +3x+1 \\ x^2-2x-1\overline{\smash{\big)}\,x^4 +x^3 -6x^2 -5x-1} \\ \underline{x^4 -2x^3 -x^2} \\ 3x^3 -5x^2 -5x-1 \\ \underline{3x^3 -6x^2 -3x} \\ x^2 -2x-1 \\ \underline{x^2 -2x-1} \\ 0 \end{array}$$

In this problem the remainder is zero, and we can write that

$$p(x) = x^4 +x^3 -6x^2 -5x-1 = (x^2 +3x+1)(x^2 -2x-1) + \frac{0}{x^2 -2x-1}$$

Because the remainder is zero we can say that $x^2 +3x+1$ and $x^2 -2x-1$ are factors of $x^4 +x^3 -6x^2 -5x-1$. If we wanted to find the zeros or roots of $x^4 +x^3 -6x^2 -5x-1$ we would find the values of x for which either of its factors are equal to zero. This is the same process that we followed in unit 5.4 with quadratic equations, though polynomial long division was not needed because if the quadratic did not factor we could use the quadratic formula.

Special case where $q(x) = x - c$ (synthetic division)

Sometimes the denominator q(x) is equal to x plus or minus a constant. When that occurs you could still use polynomial long division. For example

$$\frac{p(x)}{q(x)} = \frac{x^3 +7x^2 +13x+15}{x+5}.$$

The solution using long division looks like this:

$$\begin{array}{r} x^2 +2x+3 \\ x+5\overline{\smash{\big)}\,x^3 +7x^2 +13x+15} \\ \underline{x^3 +5x^2} \\ 2x^2 +13x+15 \\ \underline{2x^2 +10x} \\ 3x+15 \\ \underline{3x+15} \\ 0 \end{array}$$

But there is a much faster way to get the same result, and that is called synthetic division. The steps are as follows:

Step 1. Set up the synthetic division

$$-5 \,\big|\, \begin{array}{ccc} 1 & 7 & 13 & 15 \end{array}$$

Step 2. Bring down the first coefficient

$$-5 \,\big|\, \begin{array}{ccc} 1 & 7 & 13 & 15 \\ \hline 1 & & & \end{array}$$

Step 3. Multiply $(-5)(1)$

$$-5 \,\big|\, \begin{array}{ccc} 1 & 7 & 13 & 15 \\ & \text{-5} & & \\ \hline 1 & & & \end{array}$$

Step 4. Add $7+(-5)$

$$-5 \,\big|\, \begin{array}{ccc} 1 & 7 & 13 & 15 \\ & \text{-5} & & \\ \hline 1 & 2 & & \end{array}$$

Steps 5+. Continue multiplying and adding

$$-5 \,\big|\, \begin{array}{ccc} 1 & 7 & 13 & 15 \\ & \text{-5} & \text{-10} & \text{-15} \\ \hline 1 & 2 & 3 & 0 \end{array}$$

From the coefficients in the bottom row, we can see that the answer is $1x^2 + 2x + 3$ with no remainder. Thus we conclude that $x+5$ and $1x^2 + 2x + 3$ are factors of $x^3 + 7x^2 + 13x + 15$ and that -5 is a zero or root of $x^3 + 7x^2 + 13x + 15$.

Finding the zeros (roots) of a polynomial

In unit 5.4, we found the roots (zeros) of a second-degree polynomial by factoring and setting each factor to zero. If the quadratic polynomial could not be factored, we used the quadratic formula to find them.

The process for finding the roots for a higher order polynomial is a little bit different. The first step is to put the original polynomial into the equation editor (Y=) of your graphing calculator and press the graph button. Look at the graph and see where the graph crosses the x-axis. That is a root. Its exact value can be found by using 2nd-calc-zero. Once you have identified a zero, use synthetic division to find the "reduced polynomial." This is the polynomial with the coefficients in the bottom row of the synthetic division, assuming the remainder is zero and you do indeed have a root. If the order of reduced polynomial is greater than two, then enter the reduced polynomial into your calculator, find another zero, and use synthetic division to find the next reduce polynomial. Continue the process until you get a quadratic reduced polynomial. Then factor or use the quadratic formula to find the two other zeros.

An example will illustrate this process. Suppose you want to find the zeros of the polynomial $x^4 + 3x^3 - x^2 - 13x - 10$. Graphing this in the calculator suggests that 2 and -1 may be roots. We decide to try 2 first, using synthetic division. The result is

$$
\begin{array}{r|rrrrr}
 & 1 & 3 & -1 & -13 & -10 \\
2 & & 2 & 10 & 18 & 10 \\
\hline
 & 1 & 5 & 9 & 5 & 0
\end{array}
$$

Next we graph the reduce polynomial $x^3 + 5x^2 + 9x + 5$ on our calculator, and we see that -1 is a root (it can be confirmed by using 2nd-calc-zero). This sets up the next synthetic division

$$
\begin{array}{r|rrrr}
 & 1 & 5 & 9 & 5 \\
-1 & & -1 & -4 & -5 \\
\hline
 & 1 & 4 & 5 & 0
\end{array}
$$

Finally we have a reduced polynomial that is a quadratic! It is $x^2 + 4x + 5$. At first it looks like it might factor but it does not. So we use the quadratic formula to find the other two zeros:

$$
x = \frac{-4 \pm \sqrt{16 - 20}}{2} = \frac{-4 \pm 2i}{2} = -2 \pm i
$$

We can now say that the zeros (roots) of $x^4 + 3x^3 - x^2 - 13x - 10$ are $2, -1, -2 + i,$ and $-2 - i$. An equivalent statement is that

$$
x^4 + 3x^3 - x^2 - 13x - 10 = (x-2)(x+1)(x-(-2+i))(x-(-2-i))
$$

Problems on polynomial division (unit 5.10)

1. Which of the following are zeros (roots) of $x^3 + 2x^2 - 3x$?

   I. -3

   II. 0

   III 1

(A) I only
(B) II only
(C) III only
(D) I and II only
(E) I, II, and III

2. If 5 is a zero (root) of $x^3 - 5x^2 - x + 5$ then another zero (root) is:

(A) $-i$
(B) i
(C)   -5
(D)   -1
(E)   0

3. What is the remainder when $x^3 + x^2 - x + 2$ is divided by $x + 1$?

(A)   0
(B)   1
(C)   3
(D) $x + 1$
(E) $x^2 - 1$

4. What is the remainder when $x^3 + x^2 - x + 2$ is divided by $x^2 - x - 1$?

(A) $2x + 4$
(B) $x + 2$
(C) $2x$
(D) x
(E)   0

5. For what value of x is $x^3 + x^2 - x + 2$ equal to zero?

(A)   -1
(B)   0
(C)   1
(D)   2
(E) $0.5 + 1.5i$

6. Which of the following is <u>NOT</u> a zero (root) of $x^4 + 5x^2 - 36$?

(A) $-3i$
(B)   -2
(C)   2
(D)   3
(E) $3i$

Solutions to problems on polynomial division (unit 5.10)

1. (E)

$$x^3 + 2x^2 - 3x = x(x^2 + 2x - 3) = x(x+3)(x-1)$$

2. (D)

$$\begin{array}{r|rrrr} & 1 & -5 & -1 & 5 \\ 5 & & 5 & 0 & -5 \\ \hline & 1 & 0 & -1 & 0 \end{array}$$

The reduced polynomial is $x^2 - 1 = (x+1)(x-1)$

3. (C)

$$\begin{array}{r|rrrr} & 1 & 1 & -1 & 2 \\ -1 & & -1 & 0 & 1 \\ \hline & 1 & 0 & -1 & 3 \end{array}$$

$$\frac{x^3 + x^2 - x + 2}{x+1} = x^2 - 1 + \frac{3}{x+1}$$

4. (A)

$$\begin{array}{r} x+2 \\ x^2 - x - 1 \overline{\smash{\big)}\ x^3 + x^2 - x + 2} \\ \underline{\lfloor x^3 - x^2 - x} \\ 2x^2 + 2 \\ \underline{\lfloor 2x^2 - 2x - 2} \\ 2x + 4 \end{array}$$

5. (E)

$$\begin{array}{r|rrrr} & 1 & 1 & -1 & 2 \\ -2 & & -2 & 2 & -2 \\ \hline & 1 & -1 & 1 & 0 \end{array}$$

Use quadratic formula to solve the reduced polynomial $x^2 - x + 1 = 0$.

$$x = \frac{1 \pm \sqrt{1-4}}{2} = \frac{1 \pm 3i}{2}$$

6. (D)

On the calculator, 2 looks like a root. Make sure to use zeroes for the x^3 and x terms.

$$\begin{array}{r|rrrrr} & 1 & 0 & 5 & 0 & -36 \\ 2 & & 2 & 4 & 18 & 36 \\ \hline & 1 & 2 & 9 & 18 & 0 \end{array}$$

Looking at the reduced polynomial $x^3 + 2x^2 + 9x + 18$ on the calculator, -2 looks like a root. So do another synthetic division.

$$\begin{array}{r|rrrr} & 1 & 2 & 9 & 18 \\ -2 & & -2 & 0 & -18 \\ \hline & 1 & 0 & 9 & 0 \end{array}$$

You are left with $x^2 + 9$ which gives $\pm 3i$ as the

6. MISCELLANEOUS TOPICS

This chapter contains some topics from probability and statistics, word problems and topics from trigonometry. Many students are not exposed to probability or statistics in high school and others do not get much exposure to trigonometry, so this chapter is worth some of your time.

6.1 Counting and probability

You may be thinking "I already know how to count!" but I think you will find that counting on standardized tests has its challenges.

Suppose you are having a contest and there are three contestants, Alan, Bob and Charlie. One will be awarded first prize, one will be awarded second prize and one will be awarded third prize. How many different outcomes could there be? You could make a list of outcomes: ABC, ACB, BAC, BCA, CAB, and CBA. That makes six outcomes. A faster way is to use this rule:

The number of ways that n objects can be arranged sequentially is $n!$

You may not recognize the **factorial** symbol, (!). It is used widely in counting problems. The formal definition is

$$n! = n(n-1)(n-2)(n-3).....1$$

Also it is useful to note that $0! = 1$.

Calculator Tip: The factorial key may be found on your graphing calculator by pressing math-prb-!. Try using the calculator to solve the problem above by finding that $3! = 3 \cdot 2 \cdot 1 = 6$. Just press 3-math-prb-!-enter.

Now that you have mastered ordering n objects sequentially it is time to consider changing the problem (you didn't think things were going to stay so simple did you?). Let's say that there are four contestants (Alan, Bob, Charlie, and David) and we are going to award two prizes: a first prize and a second prize. Now how many outcomes will there be? You could make a list: AB, AC, AD, BA, BC, BD, CA, CB, CD, DA, DB, and DC. That makes 12 outcomes. A faster way is to use this rule, called **permutations**:

The number of ways that n objects can be arranged sequentially, r at a time is $_nP_r = \dfrac{n!}{(n-r)!}$

Calculator Tip: The permutation key may be found on your graphing calculator by pressing math-prb-nPr. Try using your calculator to solve the problem above by finding that $_4P_2 = \dfrac{4!}{(4-2)!} = \dfrac{4 \cdot 3 \cdot 2 \cdot 1}{2 \cdot 1} = 12$. Just press 4-math-prb-nPr-2-enter.

Now that you have mastered selecting where order matters (permutations), we will discuss selecting where order does not matter (combinations). Let's say that there are four contestants (Alan, Bob, Charlie, and David) and two of them will be selected to continue into the next round of the competition. In this situation, order does not matter. The outcome AB is the same as the outcome BA because both Alan and Bob will make it into the next round. The list of outcomes would be: AB, AC,. AD, BC, BD, and CD. That makes six outcomes. A faster way is to use this rule, called **combinations**:

The number of ways that n objects can be selected (without order), r at a time is: $_nC_r = \dfrac{n!}{r!(n-r)!}$

Calculator Tip: The combination key may be found on your graphing calculator by pressing math-prb-nCr. Try using your calculator to solve the problem above by finding that $_4C_2 = \dfrac{4!}{2!(4-2)!} = \dfrac{4 \cdot 3 \cdot 2 \cdot 1}{2 \cdot 1 \cdot 2 \cdot 1} = 6$. Just press 4-math-prb-nCr-2-enter.

Probability

You may be wondering what counting has to do with probability. One way to define the probability of an event is:

$$\text{probability of an event} = \frac{\text{number of outcomes that include the event}}{\text{number of all possible outcomes}}$$

To illustrate this let's go back to the first example, where there are three contestants, Alan, Bob and Charlie. One will be awarded first prize, one will be awarded second prize and one will be awarded third prize.

$$\text{probability of Bob winning second prize} = \frac{ABC, CBA}{ABC, ACB, BAC, BCA, CAB, CBA} = \frac{2}{6} = \frac{1}{3}$$

In this case the event is that Bob wins second prize. That happens in two outcomes, and there is a total of six possible outcomes.

Now we will use this definition of probability with the second example, where there are four contestants (Alan, Bob, Charlie, and David) and we are going to award two prizes: a first prize and a second prize.

$$\text{probability of Bob winning second prize} = \frac{AB, CB, DB}{AB, AC, AD, BA, BC, BD, CA, CB, CD, DA, DB, DC} = \frac{3}{12} = \frac{1}{4}$$

In this case the event is that Bob wins second prize. This happens in two outcomes, and there is a total of twelve possible outcomes.

To wrap up the discussion of probability (there is more on probability in the next unit), consider applying the definition of probability to the third example above, where there are four contestants (Alan, Bob, Charlie, and David) and two of them will be selected to continue into the next round of the competition.

$$\text{probability of Bob entering the next round} = \frac{AB, BC, BD}{AB, AC, AD, BC, BD, CD} = \frac{3}{6} = \frac{1}{2}$$

In this case the event is that Bob enters the next round. This happens in three outcomes and there is a total of six possible outcomes.

Problems on counting and probability (unit 6.1)

NOTE: In problems 1-3, the pizza place in town offers two kinds of crust (regular and whole wheat) and four different toppings (mushroom, onion, pepperoni, and sausage).

1. How many different pizzas (each with one topping) could a person order?

    (A)   6

    (B)   8

    (C)   12

    (D)   16

    (E)   18

2. How many different pizzas with regular crust and two toppings could a person order?

    (A)   4

    (B)   6

    (C)   8

    (D)   12

    (E)   16

3. A big birthday party ordered five different pizzas. If they are to be arranged along a buffet table, how many arrangements could there be?

    (A)   5

    (B)   10

    (C)   20

    (D)   40

    (E)   120

4. The expression $\dfrac{(n+2)!}{n!}$ reduces to:

    (A)   2

    (B)   3

    (C) n

    (D) n^2

    (E) $n^2 + 3n + 2$

5. Caroline has unusual taste in clothes. She never will wear two pieces of clothing that are the same color. If the colors of her shirts are red, white, and blue, and the colors of her pants are red white, and blue, how many different outfits could Caroline wear?

    (A)   2

    (B)   3

    (C)   5

    (D)   6

    (E)   9

6. John has the difficult job of casting for the school musical. He has 10 singers on stage and will choose the best singer to play the hero, and the next best singer to play the villain. How many possible choices does John have for casting these roles in the musical?

    (A)   45

    (B)   60

    (C)   75

    (D)   90

    (E)   105

In problems 7-8, Amy, Bill, Caroline, and David must line up in single file

7. How many arrangements of students can there be in that single file line?

    (A)   10

    (B)   12

    (C)   24

    (D)   36

    (E)   72

8. What is the probability that Amy and Bill will stand next to each other?

    (A)   1/9

    (B)   1/4

    (C)   1/3

    (D)   1/2

    (E)   4/9

Solutions to problems on counting and probability (unit 6.1)

1. (B)

Multiply 2x4=8 or count: RM, RO, RP, RS, WM, WO, WP, WS.

2. (B)

Use $_4C_2 = 6$ or count: MO, MP, MS, OP, OS, PS.

3. (E)

$$5! = 5 \cdot 4 \cdot 3 \cdot 2 \cdot 1 = 120$$

4. (E)

$$\frac{(n+2)!}{n!} = \frac{(n+2)(n+1)n!}{n!} = (n+2)(n+1) = n^2 + 3n + 2$$

5. (D)

Count: RW,RB,WR,WB,BW,BR. Six. Or, given three possibilities of shirts there are only two possibilities of pants. Multiply 3x2.

6. (D)

$$_{10}P_2 = \frac{10!}{(10-2)!} = 10 \cdot 9 = 90$$

7. (C)

$$4! = 4 \cdot 3 \cdot 2 \cdot 1 = 24$$

8. (D)

Of the 24 possible arrangements, they stand next two each other in 12 of them. 12/24 = 1/2.

A BCD, ABDC, DABC, CABD, CDAB, DCAB,

BACD, BADC, DBAC, CBAD, CDBA, DCBA

6.2 Sets and more probability

Sets

A set is a collection of numbers (or other objects). Each number in the set is called a member or element of the set. A set may be finite or infinite. For example:

$$A = \{1,2,3\} \quad \text{and} \quad B = \{1,3,5,...\}.$$

Set A is finite with three members. Set B contains the positive odd integers. It is infinite.

There are two operations to be done with sets: union and intersection. The union of two sets, denoted by $\cup$, is a collection of elements that belong to either of the parent sets. The intersection of two sets, denoted by $\cap$, is a collection of elements that belong to both of the parent sets. In the example above:

$$A \cup B = \{1,2,3,5,7,9,11,...\} \quad \text{and} \quad A \cap B = \{1,3\}.$$

Union and intersection may also be depicted graphically in what is called a Venn diagram. A general Venn diagram for two sets is shown below.

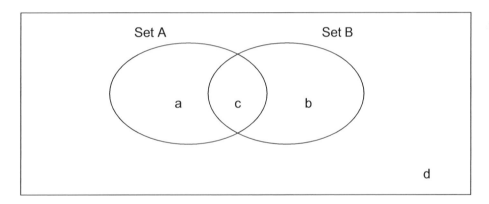

In this diagram, the quantity a represents elements that are in Set A but not Set B. Quantity b represents elements that are in Set B but not in Set A. Quantity c represents elements that are in Set A and Set B. Quantity d contains elements that are not in Set A and are not in Set B. When expressed in terms of union and intersection,

$$A \cup B = \{a,b,c\} \quad \text{and} \quad A \cap B = \{c\}.$$

More Probability

In Unit 6.1, we defined probability in terms of counting outcomes. In this unit, we take that general idea and expand it. Take a look at the Venn diagram above. It should be intuitive that the

$$\text{probability of an element being in Set A} = \frac{a+c}{a+b+c+d}$$

$$\text{probability of an element being in Set B} = \frac{b+c}{a+b+c+d}$$

$$\text{probability of an element not being in Set A and not in Set B} = \frac{d}{a+b+c+d}$$

In some problems you will see probability expressed in terms of area. Suppose that without looking, you drop a ball into this special carton shown below, divided into three sections:

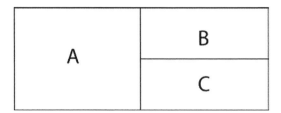

If the special carton were drawn to scale (trust what your eye is telling you), it should be intuitive that the

$$\text{probability of the ball landing in Section A} = \frac{1}{2}$$

$$\text{probability of the ball landing in Section B} = \frac{1}{4} = \text{probability of the ball landing in Section C}$$

Independent Events

If you don't much care for the topic of probability, you are not alone. There is just one more concept to be covered: independent events.

> If event A and event B are independent, then the probability of event A happening and event B happening is the product of their individual probabilities.

This sounds like a lot to learn, but it is simple and intuitive.

Suppose your are throwing a die (a die is a cube with six sides, each with a different number of dots showing). We know that the probability of throwing any particular number is 1/6. We also know that each throw of the die is independent of the other throws. So using the rule above, the

$$\text{probability of throwing a 1 followed by a 2} = (\text{prob of throwing 1})(\text{prob of throwing 2}) = \frac{1}{6} \cdot \frac{1}{6} = \frac{1}{36}$$

Consider another simple example. If Andy has three different hats -- one red one white and one blue; and Bob has three different hats -- one red one white and one blue, and if Andy and Bob choose their hats independently then the probability that they both choose red hats is:

$$\text{probability of the two reds} = (\text{probability of Andy red})(\text{probability of Bob red}) = \frac{1}{3} \cdot \frac{1}{3} = \frac{1}{9}$$

Problems on sets and more probability (unit 6.2)

NOTE: Use the sets: $A = \{1, 2, 3\}$ and $B = \{3, 4\}$ to answer questions 1-3.

1. The elements of $A \cup B$ are:
   - (A) $\{2\}$
   - (B) $\{3\}$
   - (C) $\{2, 3\}$
   - (D) $\{1, 2, 3\}$
   - (E) $\{1, 2, 3, 4\}$

2. If two numbers are chosen at random from set A, what is the probability that their sum is three?
   - (A)   0
   - (B)   1/2
   - (C)   1/3
   - (D)   2/3
   - (E)   3/4

3. How many distinct ratios are formed when the numerator is taken from set A and the denominator is taken from set B?
   - (A)   0
   - (B)   2
   - (C)   4
   - (D)   6
   - (E)   8

---

4. Sarah wants to form a rock band consisting of three guitars and one drums. She will choose them from 20 guitarists and 5 drummers. How many different rock bands could she form?
   - (A)   100
   - (B)   120
   - (C)   1,140
   - (D)   5,700
   - (E)   6,840

NOTE: Use the diagram below for questions 5-6. It illustrates band and orchestra participation for the 1000 students at Central High School.

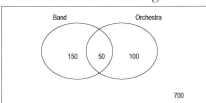

5. What is the probability that a student will play in the band?
   - (A)   0.15
   - (B)   0.20
   - (C)   0.30
   - (D)   0.50
   - (E)   0.67

6. Suppose the band and orchestra each play once at different times on the same day. How many student performances will there be on that day?
   - (A)   50
   - (B)   200
   - (C)   250
   - (D)   300
   - (E)   350

NOTE: The diagram below is to be used for problems 7 and 8.

In the diagram below a dart board consists of three concentric circles. The smallest circle (the bull's eye) has a radius of 1 unit; the middle circle has a radius of 2 units; and the outer circle has a radius of 3 units.

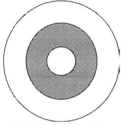

7. What is the probability that a dart will land in the bull's eye?
   - (A)   1/9
   - (B)   1/3
   - (C)   2/9
   - (D)   2/3
   - (E)   4/9

8. What is the probability that a dart will land in the shaded area?
   - (A)   1/9
   - (B)   1/4
   - (C)   1/3
   - (D)   1/2
   - (E)   4/9

Solutions to problems on sets and more probability (unit 6.2)

1. (E)

The union consists of elements in either A or B.

$A \cup B = \{1, 2, 3, 4\}$

2. (C)

There are $_3C_2 = 3$ ways to choose two numbers from a set of three numbers. The ways are:

{1,2} sum=3

{1,3} sum=4

{2,3} sum=5

The sum is three for only one way. Therefore the probability is 1/3.

3. (D)

Possible ratios are $\dfrac{1}{3}, \dfrac{1}{4}, \dfrac{2}{3}, \dfrac{2}{4}, \dfrac{3}{3}, \dfrac{3}{4}$ and they all have distinct values. So there are six of them.

4. (D)

Start with the easy one, the drummer. There are 5 choices of drummer. For guitarists, the order of selection does not matter. So

$_{20}C_3 = \dfrac{20!}{3!(20-3)!} = \dfrac{20 \cdot 19 \cdot 18}{3 \cdot 2 \cdot 1} = 1,140$ choices of

guitarists. The number of possible bands is

$5(1,140) = 5,700$ bands.

5. (B)

$\dfrac{150 + 50}{1000} = \dfrac{200}{1000} = \dfrac{1}{5} = 0.20$

6. (E)

There will be 200 band student performances plus 150 orchestra student performances, or a total of 350 student performances.

7. (A)

$\dfrac{\text{area of bulls eye}}{\text{area of board}} = \dfrac{\pi 1^2}{\pi 3^2} = \dfrac{1}{9}$

8. (C)

$\dfrac{\text{shaded area}}{\text{area of board}} = \dfrac{\pi 2^2 - \pi 1^2}{\pi 3^2} = \dfrac{3}{9} = \dfrac{1}{3}$

6.3 Statistics

This section covers descriptive statistics, which are numbers that tell you something about a data set (set of numbers). The idea is to convey some general idea of what the data are like without having to look at every data point in the set. Mean, median and mode tell you something about the center of the data set; whereas the variance and standard deviation tell you something about how widely the numbers are spread about that center.

Mean

Standardized tests contain the phrase "average (arithmetic mean)." Don't let this confuse you. That phrase refers to the good ole average, something you learned in grade school. It is the sum over the count. Although details are in unit 2.7, a simple example is:

> "Find the average (arithmetic mean) of 2, 3, -1 and 0." The sum is 4 and the count is 4. So the average is 4/4 or 1.

Median

The value of the median depends on whether the count is odd or even. To find the median, list the numbers from smallest to largest. If the count is odd, the median is the middle number. If the count is even, the median is the mean of the middle two numbers.

> "Find the median of 5, -1, 6, 2, and 0." First, list the numbers from smallest to largest. The ordered list is: -1, 0, 2, 5 and 6. Next we notice that the count is odd (the count is 5). The median is the middle number, 2.

> "Find the median of 5, -1, 6, -3, 2, and 0." First, list the numbers from smallest to largest. The ordered list is: -3, -1, 0, 2, 5 and 6. Next we notice that the count is even (the count is 6). The median is mean of the middle two numbers, which is $\dfrac{0+2}{2} = 1$.

Mode

The mode is the number that appears most frequently. Remember that there can be more than one mode (this is called multi-modal). To find the mode(s), list the numbers from smallest to largest. The mode(s) are the numbers that appear most frequently.

> "Find the mode of 5, -1, 6, -3, 2, 0, and 6." First, list the numbers from smallest to largest. The ordered list is -3, -1, 0, 2, 5, 6, 6. The mode is 6 because it is the only number that appears twice.

> "Find the mode of 2, -1, 6, -3, 2, 0, and 6." First, list the numbers from smallest to largest. The ordered list is -3, -1, 0, 2, 2, 6, 6. The modes are 2 and 6 because they are the only numbers that appear twice.

Variance and Standard Deviation

The variance is the average of the sum of all the squared differences from each number in the data set to the mean of the data set. If m is the mean of n numbers,

$$\text{variance} = \frac{1}{n}\left[\left(x_1 - m\right)^2 + \left(x_2 - m\right)^2 + \left(x_3 - m\right)^2 + \ldots + \left(x_n - m\right)^2\right]$$

The standard deviation is the square root of the variance.

Problems on statistics (unit 6.3)

1. For the following data set: 5, -3, 0, -1, 6, -3, 1 the sum of the median and the mode is:

(A)   -3
(B)   -2
(C)   -1
(D)   0
(E)   1

NOTE: The following data set is to be used to answer questions 2-5.

$$-1, -1, 5, 6, -4, 5$$

2. The difference between the median and mean is:

(A)   -2
(B)   -1
(C)   1/3
(D)   1
(E)   2

3. The number of modes is:

(A)   0

(B)   1

(C)   2

(D)   3

(E)   4

4. The variance of the data set is:

(A)   4

(B)   14

(C)   87

(D)   350

(E)   786

5. The standard deviation of the data set is:

(A)   2

(B)   4

(C)   9

(D)   19

(E)   28

6. The expression for the average (arithmetic mean) of x, x+2, and 4x+10 is:

(A) $x+2$

(B) $2x+4$

(C) $3x+6$

(D) $4x+8$

(E) $6x+12$

7. If the average (arithmetic mean) of x and 3x is equal to 100, what is the value of x?

(A)   25

(B)   50

(C)   75

(D)   100

(E)   200

NOTE: The table below is to be used to answer questions 8-11.

Mr. Corn asked the 15 students in his math class to report how many television sets are in their homes. The results are tabulated below.

Number of television sets per home	Number of homes
0	1
1	2
2	3
3	4
4	5

8. The average (arithmetic mean) number of televisions per home is:

(A)   2/3
(B)   4/3
(C)   6/3
(D)   8/3
(E)   10/3

9. The median number of televisions per home is:

(A)   2

(B)   2.5

(C)   3

(D)   3.5

(E)   4

10. The mode number of television per home is:

(A)   1

(B)   2

(C)   3

(D)   4

(E)   5

11. Suppose there are 16 students in the class, but one was absent that day. When he returns to class he reports the number of television sets in his home. The new median would be:

(A)   2

(B)   2.5

(C)   3

(D)   3.5

(E)   Cannot be determined

_____

12. If the constant k is added to every member of a data set whose mean is m, then the mean of the new data set would be:

(A) m

(B) k

(C) $m + k$

(D) $m - k$

(E) $\dfrac{m}{k}$

13. If every member in a data set whose mean is m were to be multiplied by the constant k, then the mean of the new data set would be:

(A) m

(B) k

(C) $m + k$

(D) mk

(E) $\dfrac{m}{k}$

14. A data set contains five different positive integers. If the largest number is ten, what is the difference between the largest possible mean and the smallest possible mean?

(A)   1

(B)   2

(C)   3

(D)   4

(E)   5

15. A data set contains five different positive integers. If the largest number is ten, what is the difference between the largest possible median and the smallest possible median?

(A)   1

(B)   2

(C)   3

(D)   4

(E)   5

Solutions to problems on statistics (unit 6.3)

1. (A)

The ordered numbers are: -3, -3, -1, 0, 1, 5, 6. The median is 0 because it is the middle number. The mode is -3 because it appears twice. The sum of the median and mode is 0+-3=-3.

2. (C)

The ordered numbers are -4, -1, -1, 5, 5, 6. The median is the mean of -1 and 5. So the median is $\frac{-1+5}{2} = \frac{4}{2} = 2$. The sum is 10 and the count is 6. The mean is 10/6=5/3. The difference between the median and the mean is $2 - \frac{5}{3} = \frac{6}{3} - \frac{5}{3} = \frac{1}{3}$.

3. (C)

The values -1 and 5 each appear twice and no value appears three times, so they are both modes.

4. (B)

$$\left(1/6\right)\left[(-4-5/3)^2 + 2(-1-5/3)^2 + 2(5-5/3)^2 + (6-5/3)^2\right]$$

$$(1/6)\left[(-17/3)^2 + 2(-8/3)^2 + 2(10/3)^2 + (13/3)^2\right] = 786/54 = 14.5$$

5. (B)

From question 4 above, $\sqrt{14.5} = 3.81$

6. (B)

$$\frac{sum}{count} = \frac{x+(x+2)+(4x+10)}{3} = \frac{6x+12}{3} = 2x+4$$

7. (B)

$$\frac{x+3x}{2} = 100, \quad x+3x = 200, \quad 4x = 200, \quad x = 50$$

8. (D)

$$sum = 0(1) + 1(2) + 2(3) + 3(4) + 4(5)$$
$$sum = 0 + 2 + 6 + 12 + 20 = 40$$
$$avg = sum/count = 40/15 = 8/3$$

9. (C)

The ordered numbers are 0,1,1,2,2,2,3,3,3,3,4,4,4,4,4. The middle number is 3.

10. (D)

More homes have 4 television sets than any other number of television sets.

11. (C)

The median remains unchanged regardless of how many televisions the sixteenth student has in his home.
If he had 4 or more television sets, the new data would be:
0,1,1,2,2,2,3,3,3,3,4,4,4,4,4,?
If he had less than 3 television sets, the new data would be
0,1,1,2,2,2,?,3,3,3,3,4,4,4,4,4
In either case, the median remains three because the middle two numbers are three.

12. (C)

old mean $= m = (1/n)(x_1 + x_2 + ... + x_n)$

new mean $= \left(1/n\right)\left[(x_1+k)+(x_2+k)+...+(x_n+k)\right]$
$= (1/n)\left[(x_1+x_2+...+x_n)+nk\right] = m+k$

13. (D)

old mean $= m = (1/n)(x_1 + x_2 + ... + x_n)$

new mean $= \left(1/n\right)\left[kx_1 + kx_2 + kx_3 + ... + kx_n\right]$
$= (1/n)\left[(x_1+x_2+...+x_n)k\right] = mk$

14. (D)

The data set for the largest possible mean is 6,7,8,9,10 and this has a mean of 8. The data set for the smallest possible mean is 1,2,3,4,10 and this has a mean of 4. The difference is 8-4=4.

15. (E)

The data set for the largest possible median is 6,7,8,9,10 and this has a median of 8. The data set for the smallest possible median is 1,2,3,4,10 and this has a mean of 3. The difference is 8-3=5.

6.4 Word problems

Almost all students have trouble with word problems, so do not feel like you are alone. The good news is that if you have been working through this book in sequence, then you have already done quite a few word problems. Earlier word problems can be found:

Type of word problem	Unit covered
Averages	2.6
Direct and inverse variation	3.6
Mixture	3.6
Percentages	2.5
Probability and Statistics	6.1, 6.2, 6.3
Ratios	3.6
Remainders	2.3
Sequences	5.1

If you have not been moving through this book in sequence, you should backtrack through these earlier sections to make sure you can do the types of problems listed above. Most of what follows in this section are types of word problems that are not covered earlier.

Algebraic Problems

Most of the word problems on the ACT® are algebraic in nature. They may use the keywords below or special keywords that were covered earlier in the book such as average, percentage increase/decrease, or remainder. Typically the skill that is required is to take words and translate them into an equation.

Keyword	Operation	Example	Expression
Sum	Addition	The sum of a number and 25 is 30.	$x + 25 = 30$
Difference	Subtraction	When the difference of a number and 30 is multiplied by 5, the result is 25.	$5(x - 30) = 25$
Product	Multiplication	The product of a number with 5 is equal to the square root of the number.	$5x = \sqrt{x}$
Quotient	Division	The quotient of a number with 5 is equal to the square of the number.	$\dfrac{x}{5} = x^2$

Distance, Rate, and Time

Distance rate and time problems are probably the best known of the word problems. They are based on the equation:

$$\text{Distance} = \text{Rate x Time.}$$

Consider the following problem and its solution:

Ellen and William started driving from the same spot at the same time, Ellen driving due East and William driving due West. If Ellen drove at 55 mph and William drove at 70 mph, how far apart were they after 5 hours have elapsed?

	Rate	x Time	=Distance
Ellen	55	5	275
William	70	5	350
TOTAL			625

They were 625 miles apart. The solution is found by building a table based on the equation, then filling in what is given, and calculating the rest. In this problem, it was simple to fill in the table and solve.

Tabular (equation)

Though they are popular, distance rate and time problems are not the only word problems based on a simple equation that may be used to construct a table. Consider the following:

The senior class at Central High School is selling tickets to the school play. Adult tickets cost $15 and student tickets cost $5. If the seniors raised $2,750 from ticket sales and they sold 100 adult tickets, how many student tickets did they sell?

	Price	x Quantity	= Revenue
Adult	15	100	1500
Student	5	x	
TOTAL			2750

The information given in the problem permits a table to be constructed and filled as shown above. We can deduce that $1,250 was raised from student tickets by subtracting 1500 from 2750. Now we solve a simple equation

$$5x = 1250, \quad x = 250.$$

Word problems (unit 6.4)

1. Mary has to drive to her Grandmother's house and be back by 4:00. It is now 3:00 and she needs to spend 15 minutes with her Grandma. How far away is her Grandma's house if she can run this errand driving an average speed of 32 miles per hour?

(A)   12 miles
(B)   16 miles
(C)   24 miles
(D)   32 miles
(E)   36 miles

2. Alan and Bob are running a relay race where each person runs 1000 meters. If Alan's best time is 5 minutes, how fast would Bob have to run in order for their combined time to be less than 9 minutes?

(A)   100 m/min
(B)   150 m/min
(C)   200 m/min
(D)   250 m/min
(E)   300 m/min

3. One train leaves Boston and travels toward NYC at 40 mph. At the same time, a second train leaves NYC and travels toward Boston on a parallel track. After 3 hours, the trains pass each other. What is the speed of the second train if the total distance between Boston and NYC is 270 miles?

(A)   25 mph
(B)   50 mph
(C)   100 mph
(D)   125 mph
(E)   150 mph

4. You have bought 30 oz of lemonade which is 10% lemon juice. How much water must be added in order to dilute it to 3% lemon juice?

(A)   61 oz
(B)   64 oz
(C)   67 oz
(D)   70 oz
(E)   73 oz

5. Mr. Corn needs to spray his yard with 20 liters of a solution that is 30% pesticide. But the only ready-made solutions sold in his local store are 25% pesticide and 50% pesticide. How many liters of the 25% ready-made solution should he buy so that when mixed with the 50% solution, together they form 20 liters of the desired 30% solution?

(A)   8 liters
(B)   10 liters
(C)   12 liters
(D)   14 liters
(E)   16 liters

6. When the difference between a number and 15 is divided by 30, the result is 25. What is the value of the number?

(A)   60
(B)   90
(C)   735
(D)   750
(E)   765

7. Hadley is trying to decide on two cell phone plans. Plan A charges $15 per month plus 5 cents per minute. Plan B charges $20 per month plus 3 cents per minute. If Hadley expects to use 250 minutes per month, which plan should she choose?

(A)   Plan A
(B)   Plan B
(C)   Either plan, they cost the same

8. Mr. Corn keeps two pencils for every student in his class plus a spare box of 12 pencils. If Mr. Corn keeps a total of 50 pencils, how many students are in his class?

(A)   19
(B)   25
(C)   38
(D)   50
(E)   100

Solutions to word problems (unit 6.4)

1. (A)

	Rate	Time	Distance
Mary	32	0.75	24

Mary would drive at 32 mph for 0.75 hours. Her roundtrip distance is 32(.75)=24 miles. So her Grandma lives 12 miles away.

2. (D)

	Rate	Time	Distance
Alan	200	5	1000
Bob	x	1000/x	1000
TOTAL			2000

$$5 + \frac{1000}{x} < 9$$

$$\frac{1000}{x} < 4, \ 1000 < 4x, \ 250 < x$$

3. (B)

	Rate	Time	Distance
First train	40	3	120
Second train	x	3	
TOTAL			270

Construct a table and fill in what is given. We can deduce that the second train has traveled 270-120=150 miles. Then solve 3x=150 or x=50 mph.

4. (D)

	Water	Juice	Total
Before	27	3	30
After	27+x	3	30+x

After adding water, the solution must be 3% juice. So

$$\frac{3}{30+x} = 0.03, \ 3 = 0.9 + 0.03x, \ 2.1 = 0.03x, \ 70 = x$$

.

5. (E)

	Total Solution	x Strength	=Pesticide
25% solution	x	.25	.25x
50% solution	20-x	.50	10-.5x
Desired	20	.30	6

Construct a table based on the equation: the total amount of solution multiplied by its strength equals the amount of pesticide. Fill in the bottom row, for the desired 20 liters of 30% solution. Mr. Corn needs 6 liters of pesticide. Let x be the amount of 25% solution to be purchased, and complete the table.

$$.25x + (10 - .5x) = 6, \ -.25x = -4, \ x = 16.$$

Mr. Corn should buy 16 liters of 25% solution and 4 liters of 50% solution.

6. (E)

$$\frac{x-15}{30} = 25, \ x - 15 = 750, \ x = 765$$

7. (C)

Plan A: $15 + (.05)(250) = 27.5$

Plan B: $20 + (.03)(250) = 27.5$

8. (A)

$$x = \frac{50 - 12}{2} = \frac{38}{2} = 19$$

6.5 Trigonometry for Right Triangles

The ACT® and SAT® subject tests have a few trigonometry problems. Many of them are easy if you know the basic information that is reviewed here. It is not necessary to be a trigonometry wizard to do well on the test.

This unit contains the trigonometry usually taught in Geometry class. It is derived from the properties of right triangles. The main idea is captured in the infamous mnemonic, SOHCAHTOA. Take a look at this diagram:

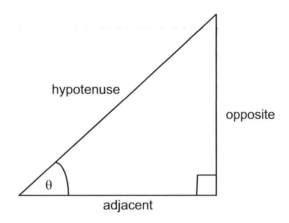

Notice that we have a right triangle, and we want to find the trigonometric ratios for one of its angles, labeled θ in the diagram. The ratios are:

S = $\sin\theta$ is equal to

O=   opposite over

H=   hypotenuse.

C= $\cos\theta$ is equal to

A=   adjacent over

H=   hypotenuse.

T= $\tan\theta$ is equal to

O=   opposite over

A=   adjacent.

From the SOHCAHTOA definitions, we can see that

$$\frac{\sin\theta}{\cos\theta} = \frac{\dfrac{opp}{hyp}}{\dfrac{adj}{hyp}} = \frac{opp}{adj} = \tan\theta$$

This is an important identity. The other really important identity is

$$\sin^2\theta + \cos^2\theta = 1$$

You are also expected to know the three reciprocal functions shown below.

$$\frac{1}{\sin \theta} = \csc \theta$$

$$\frac{1}{\cos \theta} = \sec \theta$$

$$\frac{1}{\tan \theta} = \cot \theta$$

<u>Calculator Tip:</u> Although the sine, cosine and tangent functions are on the graphing calculator, the reciprocal functions are not. They may be found getting a trigonometric value and then taking its inverse. For example, the $\csc 25°$ would be found by the keystrokes *SIN-25-)-enter-* x^{-1} *-enter.*

There are special angles that you are expected to know the exact values of their trigonometric functions (the approximate values can be found on your graphing calculator, using the SIN, COS and TAN keys). Fortunately these can be derived easily from the special right triangles that were covered earlier in section 4.2.

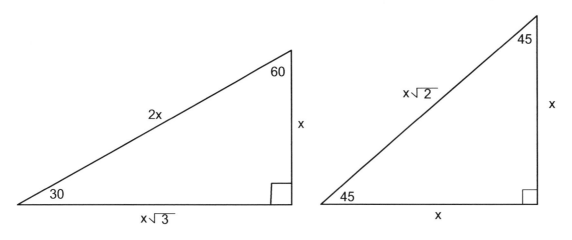

	$\sin \theta$	$\cos \theta$	$\tan \theta$
0	0	1	0
30	$\dfrac{x}{2x} = \dfrac{1}{2}$	$\dfrac{x\sqrt{3}}{2x} = \dfrac{\sqrt{3}}{2}$	$\dfrac{x}{x\sqrt{3}} = \dfrac{1}{\sqrt{3}} = \dfrac{\sqrt{3}}{3}$
45	$\dfrac{x}{x\sqrt{2}} = \dfrac{1}{\sqrt{2}} = \dfrac{\sqrt{2}}{2}$	$\dfrac{x}{x\sqrt{2}} = \dfrac{1}{\sqrt{2}} = \dfrac{\sqrt{2}}{2}$	$\dfrac{x}{x} = 1$
60	$\dfrac{x\sqrt{3}}{2x} = \dfrac{\sqrt{3}}{2}$	$\dfrac{x}{2x} = \dfrac{1}{2}$	$\dfrac{x\sqrt{3}}{x} = \sqrt{3}$
90	1	0	Undefined

Problems on trigonometry for right triangles (unit 6.5)

Use the figure below to solve problems 1-3.

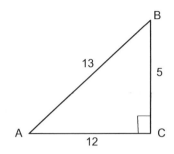

1. For the right triangle above, the $\sec A$ is:

   (A) $12/5$
   (B) $13/5$
   (C) $12/13$
   (D) $13/12$
   (E) $5/13$

2. For the triangle above, $\sin A + \cos B$ equals

   (A) $10/13$
   (B) 1
   (C) $17/13$
   (D) $24/13$
   (E) $30/13$

3. The following are equal to $5/12$ EXCEPT:

   (A) $\tan A$
   (B) $\cos B$
   (C) $\cot(90 - A)$
   (D) $1/\cot A$
   (E) $\cot B$

---

4. If the $\sin \theta = 5/7$ then the $\cot \theta$ equals:

   (A) $5/12$
   (B) $7/12$
   (C) $13/12$
   (D) $7/5$
   (E) $2\sqrt{6}/5$

5. The expression $\dfrac{\sin^2 \theta - \sin^4 \theta}{\cos^4 \theta}$ simplifies to:

   (A) $\sin^2 \theta$
   (B) $\cos^2 \theta$
   (C) $\tan^2 \theta$
   (D) $\tan^4 \theta$
   (E) $2\sin \theta \cos \theta$

6. The $(\cos 30°)(\sin 45°)$ is equal to:

   (A) $\dfrac{\sqrt{5}}{2}$
   (B) $\dfrac{\sqrt{5}}{4}$
   (C) $\dfrac{\sqrt{6}}{2}$
   (D) $\dfrac{\sqrt{6}}{4}$
   (E) $\dfrac{\sqrt{2}}{4}$

7. If the ratio of the angles in a triangle is 3:2:1 then the sine of the smallest angle is:

   (A) $1/2$
   (B) $\sqrt{2}/4$
   (C) $\dfrac{\sqrt{3}}{2}$
   (D) 1
   (E) $\dfrac{\sqrt{3}}{3}$

Solutions to problems on trigonometry for right triangles (unit 6.5)

1 (D)

$$\cos A = \frac{12}{13}$$

$$\sec A = \frac{1}{\cos A} = \frac{13}{12}$$

2. (A)

$$\sin A + \cos B = \frac{5}{13} + \frac{5}{13} = \frac{10}{13}$$

3. (B)

$$\cos B = \frac{5}{13}$$

4. (E)

If a right triangle has a hypotenuse of 7 and one of its legs is 5, then the length of the other leg is:

$$\sqrt{7^2 - 5^2} = \sqrt{49 - 25} = \sqrt{24} = 2\sqrt{6}$$

$$\cot \theta = \frac{2\sqrt{6}}{5}$$

5. (C)

$$\frac{\sin^2 \theta - \sin^4 \theta}{\cos^4 \theta} = \left(\frac{\sin^2 \theta}{\cos^2 \theta} \right) \frac{(1 - \sin^2 \theta)}{\cos^2 \theta}$$

$$= \tan^2 \theta \left(\frac{\cos^2 \theta}{\cos^2 \theta} \right) = \tan^2 \theta$$

6. (D)

$$(\cos 30°)(\sin 45°) = \frac{\sqrt{3}}{2} \cdot \frac{\sqrt{2}}{2} = \frac{\sqrt{6}}{4}$$

7. (A)

This is a 30-60-90 triangle. It can be found using the approach to mixture problems from unit 3.6:

$$3x + 2x + x = 180, \ 6x = 180, \ x = 30$$

$$\sin 30 = \frac{1}{2}$$

6.6 Trigonometry for all triangles

The trigonometry in the previous unit is usually taught in Geometry class and is usually applied in the context of right triangles. Later, in pre-calculus or analysis, you learn that the trigonometric functions apply to angles universally. The $\sin 30°$ is $1/2$ whether or not that thirty degree angle lies in a right triangle or some other kind of triangle. Don't worry if you have not taken pre-calculus or analysis – what you need to know is covered here.

Radian Measure

In addition to measuring angles in degrees, it is necessary to know how to measure angles in radians. To convert between radians and degrees by hand, just remember that π radians is equal to 180 degrees. With this knowledge, you can set up a ratio to do any conversion

$$\frac{\pi}{180} = \frac{\text{radians}}{\text{degrees}} .$$

Suppose we want to convert 25 degrees to radians. We plug-in, cross-multiply and solve for radians:

$$\frac{\pi}{180} = \frac{r}{25} , \ 180r = 25\pi , \ r = \frac{25\pi}{180} = 0.436$$

If we wanted to convert 2 radians to degrees:

$$\frac{\pi}{180} = \frac{2}{d} , \ \pi d = 360 , \ d = \frac{360}{\pi} = 114.6$$

Calculator Tip: Conversions may also be done on the graphing calculator. To convert 25 degrees to radians, set the mode of the calculator to radians. Next enter 25 followed by 2nd-ANGLE-1. This gives 25 degrees. Hit the enter key. This gives you the answer in radians. To convert 2 radians to degrees, set the mode of the calculator to degrees. Next enter 2 followed by 2nd-ANGLE-2. This gives radians. Hit the enter key. This gives you the answer in degrees. When converting angles on the calculator, make sure the mode is set to the target (degrees or radians).

Any triangle

Previously, you learned the definition of trigonometry functions in the context of the right triangle. Also you know that $a^2 + b^2 = c^2$, but only when a and b are legs of a right triangle and when c is the hypotenuse of a right triangle. This section extends those ideas to any triangle, so this material is much more useful (in the real world, most triangles are probably not right triangles).

Consider the general triangle shown below. Notice that it is not a right triangle, or any special triangle.

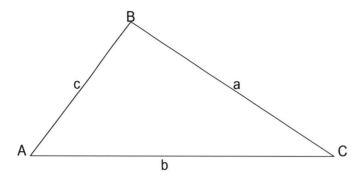

The vertices (angles) of the triangle are denoted by capital letters and the legs of the triangle are denoted by lower case letters.

There are two "laws" that are needed about triangles in general, and also may be applied to right triangles. The first is the law of sines,

$$\frac{\sin A}{a} = \frac{\sin B}{b} = \frac{\sin C}{c}$$

In words, the law of sines says that the ratio of the sine of an angle to the length of its opposite side is the same for all of the angles in any triangle.

The other is the law of cosines:

$$a^2 = b^2 + c^2 - 2bc \cos A$$

$$b^2 = a^2 + c^2 - 2ac \cos B$$

$$c^2 = a^2 + b^2 - 2ab \cos C$$

Each of the equations above is equivalent. The last equation should remind you of the Pythagorean Theorem. If angle C is a right angle, cosC is zero, and the law of cosines becomes the same as the Pythagorean Theorem.

The law of sines is most often applied in AAS, ASA and SSA situations. You are given some information and expected to derive the rest using the law of sines. For example, with AAS suppose you are given that A=25, B=40 and a=10. To find b

$$\frac{\sin 25}{10} = \frac{\sin 40}{b} \ , \ b = \frac{10 \sin 40}{\sin 25} = \frac{10(0.6428)}{0.4226} = 15.21$$

The law of cosines is most often applied in SAS and SSS situations. For example, with SAS suppose you are given that b=10, c=15 and A=30. To find a:

$$a^2 = 10^2 + 15^2 - 2(10)(15)\cos 30 = 100 + 225 - 300\left(\frac{\sqrt{3}}{2}\right) = 65.2$$

Changes to amplitude and period

	Amplitude	Period	Phase Shift	Vertical Shift
$y = a \sin b(x-h) + k$	$\|a\|$	$\dfrac{2\pi}{\|b\|}$	h	k
$y = a \cos b(x-h) + k$	$\|a\|$	$\dfrac{2\pi}{\|b\|}$	h	k
$y = a \tan b(x-h) + k$	undefined	$\dfrac{\pi}{\|b\|}$	h	k

The table above summarizes the effect of translations (sliding a graph horizontally or vertically) and scale changes (multiplying either variable by a constant) on the graphs of the trigonometric functions.

Sliding the graph horizontally by h units is called a phase shift. Sliding the graph vertically by k units is called a vertical shift.

Multiplying the y-variable by a constant causes the amplitude of the graph to change. Recall that the amplitude is ½ of the difference between the maximum and minimum values of the function. Multiplying the x-variable by a constant causes the period to change. The period is the length of a full repeat of the function.

The functions $\sin x$ and $\cos x$ have periods of 2π and amplitudes of 1. The function $\tan x$ has a period of π and an undefined amplitude (the tangent ranges from $-\infty$ to $+\infty$).

Problems on trigonometry for all triangles (unit 6.6)

1. What is the radian measure of an angle that is 150 degrees?

   (A) $-\pi/6$

   (B) $\pi/6$

   (C) $\pi/5$

   (D) $5\pi/6$

   (E) $6\pi/5$

2. What is the degree measure of an angle that is $\dfrac{7\pi}{6}$ radians?

   (A)   4

   (B)   154

   (C)   210

   (D)   240

   (E)   1260

3. In the triangle below, find the value of x:

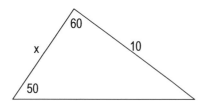

   (A)   8.2 units

   (B)   8.8 units

   (C)   10.8 units

   (D)   11.3 units

   (E)   12.3 units

4. In the triangle below, find the value of x:

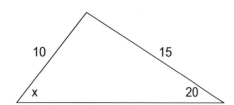

   (A)   0.2 degrees

   (B)   0.5 degrees

   (C)   22.7 degrees

   (D)   30.9 degrees

   (E)   129.1 degrees

5. In the triangle below, find the value of x:

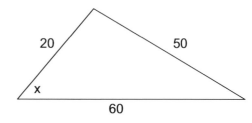

   (A)   0.6 degrees

   (B)   18.2 degrees

   (C)   51.3 degrees

   (D)   88.6 degrees

   (E)   110.5 degrees

6. Compared to the original equation, $y = \cos x$, the amplitude and period of the new equation, $y = \cos(x-2)+2$, are:

   (A)   both doubled

   (B)   both halved

   (C)   amplitude doubled, period halved

   (D)   amplitude halved, period doubled

   (E)   both unchanged

7. Find the amplitude and period of the following equation: $y = 2\sin(3x-9)+7$.

   (A)   amplitude=3, period=4π

   (B)   amplitude=2, period=$2\pi/3$

   (C)   amplitude=1/2, period=$2\pi/3$

   (D)   amplitude=1/2, period=π

   (E)   amplitude=2, period=6π

Solutions to problems on trigonometry for all triangles (unit 6.6)

1. (D)

$$\frac{\pi}{180} = \frac{r}{150} \ , \ r = \frac{150\pi}{180} = \frac{5\pi}{6}$$

2. (C)

$$\frac{\pi}{180} = \frac{\frac{7\pi}{6}}{d} \ , \ \pi d = \frac{1260\pi}{6} \ , d = 210$$

3. (E)

The third angle must be 70 degrees:

$$180 - (50 + 60) = 70$$

$$\frac{\sin 50}{10} = \frac{\sin 70}{x} \ , \ x = \frac{10\sin 70}{\sin 50} = 12.267$$

4. (D)

$$\frac{\sin 20}{10} = \frac{\sin x}{15} \ , \ \sin x = \frac{15\sin 20}{10} = 0.513, x = 30.9$$

5. (C)

$$50^2 = 20^2 + 60^2 - 2(20)(60)\cos X$$
$$\cos X = 0.625, X = 51.3$$

6. (E)

This equation has been translated, and therefore the amplitude and period are unchanged. The curve has been shifted right by 2 units and up by 2 units.

7. (B)

$$y = 2\sin(3x - 9) + 7 = 2\sin 3(x - 3) + 7$$
$$a = 2, \ b = 3$$

amplitude = 2, period = $2\pi / 3$

Part 2: How to Take the Math ACT®

BEFORE DOING ANYTHING ELSE, BUY A COPY OF THE THIRD EDITION OF THE REAL ACT® PREP GUIDE. You can find it at any book store or online retailer. The ISBN for the book is 978-0768934403 (the version with the CD) or 978-0768934328 (the version without the CD). In my opinion the CD is not useful and you can save a few dollars by buying the version without it.

If you have more than five weeks to prepare for the test:

Step 1. Use Part 1 of this book and do as many sections of math review as possible.

You should concentrate on the math topics where your knowledge is weakest and/or concentrate on the math topics that appear most often (see Appendix 1 for a list of these). For each math topic, read the lesson, do the homework problems, and study the solutions to the problems that you got wrong or that you could not solve. When you have five weeks to go before the test, begin step 2.

If you have five weeks or fewer to prepare for the test:

Step 2. Understand the base strategy for taking the test.

There are 60 problems on the math ACT® and you have 60 minutes in which to complete them. The base strategy is to read and solve problems until the first 59 minutes have elapsed. During the last minute of the test, bubble in any problems that you do not get to. That is the base strategy and it is where you should start. After you get some experience with the test, you can consider variations of the base strategy.

Step 3. Establish your target score.

 You should have some idea of the target score that you want to get on the test. This could be from an ACT® that you took before, an SAT® that you took before, or your PSAT® score. Another way to set your target score is to base it on your math grades in school. If you are an A-student in math, try for a 31 or higher (this is an SAT® score of 700). If you are a B-student, try for a 26 or higher (this is an SAT® score of 600). If you are a C-student, try for a 21 (this is an SAT® score of 500). Do not worry about the precision of your target, you can adjust this as you work through the practice test cycle described below.

Step 4. Find your pace.

For many students, the key to achieving your target score will be finding the right pace. During the 60 minutes allowed, if you read too many problems you will make too many mistakes. If you read too few problems you will not have answered enough to reach your goal. It is a matter of speed versus accuracy.

The table below gives you a rough guide to finding the right pace using the base strategy. Please keep in mind that these numbers are approximate.

Guide to Finding Your Pace

If your target is:	and your error rate* is:	you could stop reading at:	and randomly bubble:
31 (SAT 700)	5%	50	51-60
31 (SAT 700)	10%	55	56-60
26 (SAT 600)	5%	40	41-60
26 (SAT 600)	10%	45	46-60
26 (SAT 600)	15%	48	49-60
26 (SAT 600)	20%	52	53-60
21 (SAT 500)	5%	28	29-60
21 (SAT 500)	10%	30	31-60
21 (SAT 500)	15%	32	33-60
21 (SAT 500)	20%	34	35-60
21 (SAT 500)	25%	36	37-60
21 (SAT 500)	30%	40	41-60
21 (SAT 500)	35%	45	46-60
21 (SAT 500)	40%	50	51-60

*Your error rate is the number of incorrect problems among those problems that you read divided by the number of problems that you have read.

Step 5. Complete the practice-taking cycle as many times as possible.

You should complete as many of the practice tests as possible, using The Real ACT® Prep Guide. If you manage to complete all five of these tests, a sixth practice test can be found on the ACT web site. The link to the practice test is http://www.actstudent.org/testprep/ . When you are on that web page, download the booklet called Preparing for the ACT. You will find that it contains a lot of useful information and a practice test.

The details of the practice-taking cycle are as follows:

Step 5a. Review the general techniques that apply to most math topics.

A list of these techniques may be found in Appendix 3.

Step 5b. Complete a practice test following the base strategy or one of the variations of the base strategy.

Tear out an answer sheet (there is an answer sheet before each practice test). Make sure you have a watch or clock to time yourself and make sure you will not be interrupted for the next 60 minutes.

The base strategy for the test is to read and solve problems until the first 59 minutes have elapsed. During the last minute of the test, randomly bubble in any problems that you do not get to.

Follow this procedure for reading a problem:

1. Read the next problem carefully.
2. Try to solve the problem using the math you learned in school or one of the general techniques found in Appendix 3.
3. If you are unable to solve the problem:
    (a) Try to eliminate one or more of the answer choices.
    (b) Randomly bubble-in a remaining answer choice.

REMEMBER TO ALWAYS BUBBLE-IN AN ANSWER CHOICE!

Step 5c. <u>Grade your practice test.</u>

First, you need to correct the test. Answers for each test are at the back of the book. Answers to the first math test are on page 875 of <u>The Real ACT® Prep Guide</u>.

Next, calculate your score. It is best to use the practice test tracking sheet in Appendix 4. Enter the date you took the test, which test was taken, the number of correct answers, and the number of incorrect answers (these two should sum to 60 problems). Put down the question number of the last problem you were able to read . Next calculate your error rate. The raw score (it ranges from 0-60) is the number of problems that were answered correctly. Using the conversion table for your practice test, convert your raw score to a scaled score (it ranges from 1-36). The conversion table for the first practice test is on page 878 of <u>The Real ACT® Prep Guide</u>.

Step 5d. <u>Review the problems that were incorrect.</u>

Review the problems that you answered incorrectly and also review the problems where a lucky guess just happened to be the correct answer. For each of these problems you should use Appendix 2 to figure out what math topic was being tested. Based on that you could go back to Part 1 of this book to review that math topic by reading the lesson, completing the homework problems, and studying the solutions. You could also use Appendix 1 to find other problems in <u>The Real ACT® Prep Guide</u> that test the same math topic.

Step 5e. <u>Consider modifying your pace or modifying the base strategy.</u>

The decision about pace should be based on your tracking sheet and the Guide to Finding Your Pace table above. Believe it or not, slowing down is often better than speeding up. When you slow down your error rate should be lower. Or you could try reading more problems (speeding up) to see what happens to your error rate. Finding your pace is an iterative trial-and-error process that takes several practice tests.

After a few practice tests, you may want to modify the base strategy. Common modifications are:

- Do not read every problem in the first 59 minutes. Instead you could quickly bubble-in any problem that is obviously outside your ability or any problem that would take too long to answer. At the end of 59 minutes, randomly bubble any problems at the end that you could not get to.

- Read problems for fewer than 59 minutes, then scan the remaining problems for ones that are easy to answer. This modification may sound easy but it is difficult to do because as you approach the end of the test your attention is divided between the current problem that you are supposed to be reading and the problems that lie at the end of the test. Also it is difficult to identify the easy problems among those that remain.

Repeat steps 5a through 5e as many times as possible. As stated earlier, if you use all five practice tests in <u>The Real ACT® Prep Guide</u>, you can download and print a sixth official practice test from http://www.actstudent.org/testprep/ .

Appendix 1: Index of most popular math topics (in order of popularity)

Math Topic	Popular Sub-topics	Sample Problems	
4.6 Slopes, distance and midpoint	Slopes of lines Distance formula Midpoint formula Coordinate graphing Equation of a line	168/17 169/22 171/31 172/35 174/45 307/16 308/19 308/21 311/33 453/15 453/17 455/24	456/28 459/38 591/17 593/26 596/38 596/39 736/17 739/31 742/42 745/54 747/59
4.2 Triangles	Similar triangles Similar shapes Special right triangles Pythagorean theorem	168/20 169/25 173/37 173/39 305/7 306/14 310/31 315/48 316/50 316/52 450/4	457/30 459/41 588/1 591/15 592/20 594/28 598/44 598/45 739/30 741/38
6.4 Word Problems	Translating words into algebraic expressions Translating words into algebraic equations or inequalities	164/3 173/36 304/2 304/4 305/5 306/11 306/9 309/27 450/3 451/6 459/40	588/2 588/4 589/7 590/13 591/18 592/19 594/30 733/6 736/21 740/37
3.1 Solving equations and inequalities	Solving equations Solving inequalities Number lines	165/8 169/23 171/30 172/32 172/34 176/51 306/12 307/18 451/7	454/20 454/21 457/32 457/33 458/36 589/9 732/1 737/25

Math Topic	Popular Sub-topics	Sample Problems	
4.4 Polygons	Area Perimeter Volume How many little fit into big	165/6 172/33 173/38 174/41 176/52 305/6 313/38 315/47	316/51 589/6 590/14 593/24 599/47 735/13 736/18 740/35
6.6 Trigonometry for all triangles	Angles in various quadrants Basic identities Period and amplitude Radian measure	177/54 179/60 312/35 318/55 458/37 462/49	464/53 465/58 601/53 603/58 745/53 746/58
4.3 Circles	Area Circumference Circle graph	175/46 175/47 176/53 310/30 318/57 460/43	463/51 595/34 598/46 602/57 735/15
6.5 Trigonometry for right triangles	SOHCAHTOA	175/46 175/47 176/53 310/30 318/57	460/43 463/51 595/34 598/46 735/15
3.6 Ratios	Solving equations Direct variation Mixture problems	168/19 304/1 304/3 307/15 309/25	456/25 463/52 589/8 734/12 736/20
2.6 Averages	Sum Count Average	164/4 167/14 450/1 452/11 465/59	595/35 600/51 734/10 742/40 744/50
4.1 Angles and lines	Parallel lines Supplementary angles	173/40 307/17 314/43 451/8 458/35	590/10 734/8 737/23 743/44 743/45

Math Topic	Popular Sub-topics	Sample Problems	
5.6 Functions	Graphs and tables Evaluating a function Funny functions	177/56 309/23 317/54 462/48 590/11	591/16 593/25 732/3 747/60
4.5 Solids	Volume Surface area How many little fit into big	170/27 306/13 459/39 460/42 460/45	465/57 597/43 603/60 740/36 745/55
2.1 Integers, primes and digits	Even/odd integers Positive/negative integers Prime numbers	314/44 599/48 603/59 733/5	734/11 737/26 742/41 744/47
2.2 Fractions	Common denominator Multiplying and dividing	164/1 174/42 451/9 455/23	595/33 738/29 739/34
3.5 FOILing and factoring	FOIL Factor a quadratic	313/41 318/56 452/12 590/12	592/23 593/27 596/36
3.4 Distributing and common factor	Distribute Find common factor	165/7 174/43 452/10 592/21	733/7 735/14 737/25
6.1 Counting and probability	Combinations Permutations Factorials	166/12 168/18 309/24	452/13 589/5 738/27
3.3 Solving pairs of equations	Substitution Elimination Graphing	178/59 312/36 592/22	734/9 737/24 744/49
5.1 Sequences	Arithmetic sequence Geometric sequence Sums	165/9 312/37 317/53	594/32 737/22 739/32
2.5 Percentages	Percentage increase/decrease	174/44 319/60 465/60	600/50 600/52

Math Topic	Popular Sub-topics	Sample Problems	
5.2 Absolute value	Equalities Inequalities	309/26 315/49 456/27	464/54 601/55
5.3 Exponents	Multiplication Division Powers	164/2 453/18 457/31	732/2 745/52
5.7 Logarithms	Laws of logs	319/59 456/29	599/49 746/56
5.9 Complex numbers and rational numbers	Powers of i Rational numbers	175/48 597/40	597/41 601/55
5.5 Translations and reflections	Translations Reflections Rotations	178/58 454/19	744/48 746/57
2.4 Order of operations and scientific notation	Order of operations Scientific notation	313/39 460/44	736/19

Appendix 2: Index of problems and math topics

PRACTICE TEST 1					
Page/Problem	Math Topic	Page/Problem	Math Topic	Page/Problem	Math Topic
164/1	2.2	169/21	---	174/41	4.4
164/2	5.3	169/22	4.6	174/42	2.2
164/3	6.4	169/23	3.1	174/43	3.4
164/4	2.6	169/24	6.5	174/44	2.5
165/5	---	169/25	4.2	174/45	4.6
165/6	4.4	170/26	---	175/46	4.3
165/7	3.4	170/27	4.5	175/47	4.3
165/8	3.1	170/28	6.5	175/48	5.9
165/9	5.1	171/29	---	175/49	---
166/10	---	171/30	3.1	176/50	6.2
166/11	---	171/31	4.6	176/51	3.1
166/12	6.1	172/32	3.1	176/52	4.4
166/13	5.8	172/33	4.4	176/53	4.3
167/14	2.6	172/34	3.1	177/54	6.6
167/15	---	172/35	4.6	177/55	---
167/16	---	173/36	6.4	177/56	5.6
168/17	4.6	173/37	4.2	178/57	---
168/18	6.1	173/38	4.4	178/58	5.5
168/19	3.6	173/39	4.1	178/59	3.3
168/20	4.2	173/40	4.1	179/60	6.6

PRACTICE TEST 2					
Page/Problem	Math Topic	Page/Problem	Math Topic	Page/Problem	Math Topic
304/1	3.6	308/21	4.6	313/41	3.5
304/2	6.4	308/22	---	314/42	5.8
304/3	3.6	309/23	5.6	314/43	4.1
304/4	6.4	309/24	6.1	314/44	2.1
305/5	6.4	309/25	3.6	314/45	6.5
305/6	4.4	309/26	5.2	315/46	---
305/7	4.2	309/27	6.4	315/47	4.4
305/8	---	310/28	---	315/48	4.2
306/9	6.4	310/29	6.3	315/49	5.2
306/10	---	310/30	4.3	316/50	4.2
306/11	6.4	310/31	4.2	316/51	4.2
306/12	3.1	311/32	---	316/52	4.2
306/13	4.5	311/33	4.6	317/53	5.1
306/14	4.2	311/34	---	317/54	5.6
307/15	3.6	312/35	6.6	318/55	6.6
307/16	4.6	312/36	3.3	318/56	3.5
307/17	4.1	312/37	5.1	318/57	4.3
307/18	3.1	313/38	4.4	319/58	---
308/19	4.6	313/39	2.4	319/59	5.7
308/20	6.5	313/40	---	319/60	2.5

PRACTICE TEST 3					
Page/Problem	Math Topic	Page/Problem	Math Topic	Page/Problem	Math Topic
450/1	2.6	454/21	3.1	459/41	4.2
450/2	---	455/22	5.8	460/42	4.5
450/3	6.4	455/23	2.2	460/43	4.3
450/4	4.2	455/24	4.6	460/44	2.4
451/5	---	456/25	3.6	460/45	4.5
451/6	6.4	456/26	3.1	461/46	6.5
451/7	3.1	456/27	5.2	461/47	---
451/8	4.1	456/28	4.6	462/48	5.6
451/9	2.2	456/29	5.7	462/49	6.6
452/10	3.4	457/30	4.2	462/50	---
452/11	2.6	457/31	5.3	463/51	4.3
452/12	3.5	457/32	3.1	463/52	3.6
452/13	6.1	457/33	3.1	464/53	6.6
452/14	3.2	458/34	---	464/54	5.2
453/15	4.6	458/35	4.1	464/55	5.4
453/16	2.3	458/36	3.1	464/56	---
453/17	4.6	458/37	6.6	465/57	4.5
453/18	5.3	459/38	4.6	465/58	6.6
454/19	5.5	459/39	4.5	465/59	2.6
454/20	3.1	459/40	6.4	465/60	2.5

PRACTICE TEST 4					
Page/Problem	Math Topic	Page/Problem	Math Topic	Page/Problem	Math Topic
588/1	4.2	592/21	3.4	597/41	5.9
588/2	6.4	592/22	3.3	597/42	5.4
588/3	---	592/23	3.5	597/43	4.5
588/4	6.4	593/24	4.4	598/44	4.2
589/5	6.1	593/25	5.6	598/45	4.2
589/6	4.4	593/26	4.6	598/46	4.3
589/7	6.4	593/27	3.5	599/47	4.4
589/8	3.6	594/28	4.2	599/48	2.1
589/9	3.1	594/29	6.3	599/49	5.7
590/10	4.1	594/30	6.4	600/50	2.5
590/11	5.6	594/31	---	600/51	2.6
590/12	3.5	594/32	5.1	600/52	2.5
590/13	6.4	595/33	2.2	601/53	6.6
590/14	4.4	595/34	4.3	601/54	6.5
591/15	4.2	595/35	2.6	601/55	5.2
591/16	5.6	596/36	3.5	602/56	---
591/17	4.6	596/37	6.5	602/57	4.3
591/18	6.4	596/38	4.6	603/58	6.6
592/19	6.4	596/39	4.6	603/59	2.1
592/20	4.2	597/40	5.9	603/60	4.5

PRACTICE TEST 5					
Page/Problem	Math Topic	Page/Problem	Math Topic	Page/Problem	Math Topic
732/1	3.1	736/21	6.4	742/41	2.1
732/2	5.3	737/22	5.1	742/42	4.6
732/3	5.6	737/23	4.1	742/43	6.5
733/4	---	737/24	3.3	743/44	4.1
733/5	2.1	737/25	3.1	743/45	4.1
733/6	6.4	737/26	2.1	743/46	6.5
733/7	3.4	738/27	6.1	744/47	2.1
734/8	4.1	738/28	6.3	744/48	5.5
734/9	3.3	738/29	2.2	744/49	3.3
734/10	2.6	739/30	4.2	744/50	2.6
734/11	2.1	739/31	4.6	745/51	---
734/12	3.6	739/32	5.1	745/52	5.3
735/13	4.4	739/33	4.2	745/53	6.6
735/14	3.4	739/34	2.2	745/54	4.6
735/15	4.3	740/35	4.4	745/55	4.5
735/16	---	740/36	4.5	746/56	5.7
736/17	4.6	740/37	6.4	746/57	5.5
736/18	4.4	741/38	4.2	746/58	6.6
736/19	2.4	741/39	---	747/59	4.6
736/20	3.6	742/40	2.6	747/60	5.6

Appendix 3: General techniques that apply to many math topics

In Part 1 of this book you can learn the math that you need to solve problems. That is really the best way to approach the ACT®. However when you are taking the test and you do not know how to solve the problem using the math that you learned in school, one or more of these general techniques may be applicable.

1. <u>Educated Guessing</u>

This technique applies to problems that you have read and understood to some degree, but cannot solve. In that situation you should try to eliminate as many answer choices as possible before randomly bubbling-in and answer. If you have no idea of what the problem is about, do not waste time eliminating an answer choice, just randomly bubble something in.

As stated before and will be stated again, the best approach is the direct solution. Read the problem carefully, calculate the solution using the math you learned in school, and match your answer with an answer choice.

EXAMPLE PROBLEM	AN EDUCATED GUESS
If a math class consists of 21 students total and there are five more boys than girls, how many girls are there in the class? (A) 5 (B) 8 (C) 11 (D) 13 (E) 16	Even if you cannot solve this problem directly, you can certainly eliminate some answer choices. We are told that there are more boys than girls in the class. That means that more than half of the students are boys. If there are 21 students total, then at least 11 of them must be boys and fewer than 11 of them must be girls. You can eliminate answer choices (C), (D) and (E).

Some problems from <u>The Real ACT Prep Guide</u> where educated guessing could be used:

Page 164, problem 2	Page 453, problem 15
Even if you forgot your laws of exponents, you can still multiply. Just multiply $3 \cdot 2 \cdot 4 = 24$. Eliminate answer choices (F) and (G), then guess. The answer is (H).	Even if you forgot how to calculate the midpoint, it must be between -5 and 17. Eliminate (A) and (E), then guess. The answer is (B).
Page 166, problem 12	Page 457, problem 31
Even if you forgot how to do probability, it is clear that less than half the marbles in the bag are white, so the probability of choosing a marble that is not white must be greater than one-half. Eliminate (J) and guess. The answer is (K).	Use your calculator to find that $(-2)^4 = 16$. Eliminate (A), (B), and (C), then take a guess. The answer is (E).

Page 174, problem 41	Page 590, problem 10
Add the sides that are marked. Their sum is 4+6+4+10+6+26=56. So the perimeter must be greater than 56. Eliminate answer choices (A), (B), and (C), then guess. The answer is (E).	Even though diagrams are not drawn to scale, it is rather obvious that angle BCE is larger than 90 degrees. Eliminate answer choice (F) and guess. The answer is (J).
Page 176, problem 52	**Page 593, problem 24**
Drawing and then counting all of the diagonals could be messy and drive you crazy. But there are clearly more than eight diagonals total. There are five diagonals just from one vertex. Eliminate (F) and guess. The answer is (H).	Even if you cannot figure out all of the details, you know that the area has to be smaller than 15x25 =375 square feet. Eliminate answer choices (J) and (K) and guess. The answer is (H).
Page 306, problem 11	**Page 50, problem 50**
If one hamburger and one soft drink cost $2.10, it is safe to assume that the soft drink cost less than $1.00 (sugar water costs less than ground meat). Eliminate (D) and (E), then guess. The answer is (C).	The average (mean) of four numbers is 32. If you remove the smallest number from consideration, the average (mean) of the remaining three numbers must be greater than 32. Eliminate answer choices (F) and (G) and guess. The answer is (J).

2. Backsolving

Every math problem on the ACT® is multiple choice. Many students prefer multiple choice problems because the answer is right there. It is among the five answer choices and "all you have to do" is find it. One way to find it is to backsolve.

As stated before, the best approach is the direct solution. Read the problem carefully, calculate the solution, and match your answer with an answer choice. If you are not able to calculate the solution, then backsolving is an option.

To backsolve a problem, simply plug each of the answer choices into the original problem and see which one works. Many times the answer choices are ordered from smallest to largest (or largest to smallest). If that is the case, try the middle answer choice first. If it is not correct, go up or down from there.

Some problems are structured so that they cannot be backsolved, so this technique cannot be applied throughout the test. Also, backsolving takes time.

EXAMPLE PROBLEM	SOLVE BY BACKSOLVING
What value of x satisfies the equation $2\|x-3\|=8$? (A) -7 (B) -1 (C) 0 (D) 1 (E) 2	Plug in answer choices. (A) $2\|-7-3\|=2\cdot10=20$ **(B)** $2\|-1-3\|=2\cdot4=8$ (C) $2\|0-3\|=2\cdot3=6$ (D) $2\|1-3\|=2\cdot2=4$ (E) $2\|2-3\|=2\cdot1=2$

Some problems from <u>The Real ACT Prep Guide</u> where backsolving could be used:

Page 165, problem 8	Page 456, problem 26
(F) $4\left(\dfrac{7}{5}\right)+3=\dfrac{28}{5}+3=\dfrac{43}{5}$ $9\left(\dfrac{7}{5}\right)-4=\dfrac{63}{5}-4=\dfrac{43}{5}$ There is an equality, so (F) is the answer. (G) $4\left(\dfrac{5}{7}\right)+3=\dfrac{20}{7}+3=\dfrac{41}{7}$ $9\left(\dfrac{5}{7}\right)-4=\dfrac{45}{7}-4=\dfrac{17}{7}$ (H) $4\left(\dfrac{7}{13}\right)+3=\dfrac{28}{13}+3=\dfrac{67}{13}$ $9\left(\dfrac{7}{13}\right)-4=\dfrac{63}{13}-4=\dfrac{11}{13}$ (J) $4\left(\dfrac{1}{5}\right)+3=\dfrac{4}{5}+3=\dfrac{19}{5}$ $9\left(\dfrac{1}{5}\right)-4=\dfrac{9}{5}-4=-\dfrac{11}{5}$ (K) $4\left(\dfrac{-1}{5}\right)+3=\dfrac{-4}{5}+3=\dfrac{11}{5}$ $9\left(\dfrac{-1}{5}\right)-4=\dfrac{-9}{5}-4=-\dfrac{29}{5}$	(F) $\dfrac{7-11}{9-11}=\dfrac{-4}{-2}=2$ (G) $\dfrac{7-5}{9-5}=\dfrac{2}{4}=\dfrac{1}{2}$ (H) $\dfrac{7-2.5}{9-2.5}=\dfrac{4.5}{6.5}=0.7$ (J) $\dfrac{7-1\frac{2}{3}}{9-1\frac{2}{3}}=\dfrac{\frac{16}{3}}{\frac{22}{3}}=\dfrac{16}{22}=\dfrac{8}{11}$ (K) $\dfrac{7+5}{9+5}=\dfrac{12}{14}=\dfrac{6}{7}$ (G) resolves to one-half so it is the answer.
Page 453, problem 18	Page 597, problem 42
First, find that $8^3=512$. (F) $\left(2^2\right)(4)=16$ (G) $\left(2^3\right)(4)=32$ (H) $\left(2^4\right)(4)=64$ (J) $\left(2^{4.5}\right)(4)=90.51$ (K) $\left(2^7\right)(4)=512$ (K) matches 512 so it is the answer.	(F) $(1-3)^2+2=4+2=6$ (G) $(2-3)^2+2=1+2=3$ (H) $(3-3)^2+2=0+2=2$ (J) $(4-3)^2+2=1+2=3$ (K) $(5-3)^2+2=4+2=6$ (H) yields the smallest value so it is the answer.

3. Substitution

Substitution can be widely used, especially instead of using algebra. In fact, unless you are an A-student in math, I strongly suggest solving problems using substitution whenever possible. The A-students can go ahead and use algebra. A good example appears below.

EXAMPLE PROBLEM	SOLVE BY SUBSTITUTION
A store clerk was asked to markup the price of a pair of shoes by 20%. Instead the clerk marked the price down by 20%. By what percentage does the price now have to be increased in order to be correct? (A) 20% (B) 30% (C) 33% (D) 40% (E) 50% I	Assume the original price was $100. It was erroneously marked down to $80 when it should have been marked up to $120. Therefore the wrong $80 price must be increased by $40 to obtain the correct price of $120. This is a 50% increase over the wrong price. The answer is (E).
	SOLVE USING ALGEBRA
	Assume the original price was x dollars. It was erroneously marked down to .8x dollars when it should have been marked up to 1.2x dollars. Therefore it must be increased by 1.2x -.8x=.4x dollars. The increase of .4x dollars is 50% over the wrong price of .8x dollars. The answer is (E).

Some problems from The Real ACT Prep Guide where substitution could be used:

Page 169, problem 21	Page 465, problem 57
Let $x=1, y=2, z=3$. Then $\dfrac{x}{y}=\dfrac{1}{2}$ which is what we will look for. Substitute into each of the answer choices. (A) $\dfrac{x \cdot z}{y \cdot z}=\dfrac{1 \cdot 3}{2 \cdot 3}=\dfrac{3}{6}=\dfrac{1}{2}$ (A) is correct because it resolves to one-half. (B) $\dfrac{x \cdot x}{y \cdot y}=\dfrac{1 \cdot 1}{2 \cdot 2}=\dfrac{1}{4}$ (C) $\dfrac{y \cdot x}{x \cdot y}=\dfrac{2 \cdot 1}{1 \cdot 2}=\dfrac{2}{2}=1$ (D) $\dfrac{x-z}{y-z}=\dfrac{1-3}{2-3}=\dfrac{-2}{-1}=2$ (E) $\dfrac{x+z}{y+z}=\dfrac{1+3}{2+3}=\dfrac{4}{5}$	Let the edge of the smaller cube be one unit. Then the volume of the smaller cube is $s^3=1^3=1$. The edge of the larger cube must be twice as long, so it must be two units. The volume of the larger cube is $s^3=2^3=8$. The ratio of the volume of the larger cube to the volume of the smaller cube is $\dfrac{8}{1}=8$. **(D)**

Page 319, problem 60	Page 596, problem 36
Let the original 1990 distance be 100 feet. Then the 1991 distance would be 10% more, or 110 feet. Next, the 1992 distance would be 20% more than 110 feet, or 132 feet. The percentage increase from 1990 to 1992: $$\frac{132-100}{100}=32\% \qquad \text{(F)}$$	$x>1$ so we set $x=2$. Evaluate $$\frac{(2^2+16+7)(2-3)}{(2^2+8-21)(2+1)}=\frac{27(-1)}{(-9)(3)}=\frac{-27}{-27}=1$$ (F) is the only answer choice that evaluates to 1. (G) $9/7$ (H) $\dfrac{2-3}{2+3}=\dfrac{-1}{5}$ (J) $\dfrac{2(1-3)}{1+1}=\dfrac{-4}{2}=-2$ (K) $\dfrac{4(2-3)}{2+1}=\dfrac{-4}{3}$
Page 464, problem 56	**Page 742, problem 41**
Choose values of a, b, and c so that: $a=2b+3c-5$. Let $b=1, c=2$. Then $a=3$. The new value of b becomes 0 and the new value of c becomes 4. Now $a=2(0)+3(4)-5=7$. The value of a increased from 3 to 7, which is an increase of 4. (F)	x can be any positive integer so we set $x=1$. Therefore $8x+13x=8+13=21$. The number 21 is divisible by 8 and by 21 so we have narrowed the choices to (B) and (D). Next try $x=2$. Therefore $8x+13x=16+26=42$. 42 is not divisible by 8 so the correct answer is (D).

4. Use your graphing calculator

This may come as a surprise to you, but on the ACT® most students use their extremely powerful graphing calculator to do simple arithmetic if they use it at all. The graphing calculator can be a very valuable tool if used with a little creativity, as shown below.

Note that the TI-89 and TI-92 calculators are not allowed on the ACT®, nor are versions of the TI-Nspire calculator with the Computer Algebra System (CAS).

EXAMPLE PROBLEM	SOLVE WITH THE GRAPHING CALCULATOR
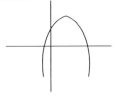 Above is the graph of the function $y = ax^2 + bx + c$, where a<0, b>0 and c>-0. Which of the graphs below could be the graph of the function $y = -ax^2 + bx + c$? (A)  (B) 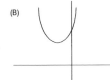 (C) 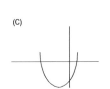 (D) (E) Cannot be determined	The A-student might notice that the only difference between the two equations is the sign of the lead coefficient. So the new equation must open up and its y-intercept must remain the same. The only graph with those characteristics is (B). However many students have difficulty with parabolas. So for them it is far better to use substitution and the graphing calculator. Try values of a, b, and c in your graphing calculator until you have a graph that looks like the one on top. Let's say for example that you end up with $y = -x^2 + 3x + 5$ Enter this and check that it looks like the graph on top. Next put $y = x^2 + 3x + 5$ into your calculator and notice that it looks most like graph (B).

Some problems from <u>The Real ACT Prep Guide</u> where the graphing calculator could be used:

Page 169, problem 23	Page 317, problem 54
Enter $x^2 - 36x$ into the Y= equation editor of the calculator and see where the graph crosses the x-axis. You have to adjust the window to see that the graph crosses at x=0 and x=36, or use the calc-zero function. (B)	Enter the first equation into the calculator – the other two equations are clearly lines. The graph of $x^2 - 2$ is a parabola opening up, so eliminate (F), and (G). The parabola does not go through the origin, eliminate (H). (J) is not the graph of a function (look at 0<x<1 where it fails the vertical line test). The answer is (K).
Page 178, problem 57	Page 318, problem 55
Enter $(2x^2 + x)/x$ into the Y= equation editor of the calculator and hit the graph key. You can immediately see it is a line, so eliminate (D) and (E). The y-intercept is above the origin, so eliminate (B). The x-intercept is greater than -1, so eliminate (C). The answer is (A).	With the calculator in radian mode, find that $\cos^{-1}(-0.385) = 1.97$. The value of 1.97 is between $\pi/2$ and $2\pi/3$. (D)
Page 179, problem 60	Page 463, problem 50
The author wants you to use the difference formula from trigonometry, but it is not necessary. With your calculator in radian mode, find that $$\sin\left(\frac{\pi}{12}\right) = 0.2588.$$ Use your calculator to convert each of the answer choices to decimal. The answer that matches 0.2588 is (K).	It will take a while, but you could plug three equations into the calculator for each of the answer choices. Answer choice (F) will give you that pattern that matches the diagram.
Page 308, problem 19	Page 601, problem 55
Enter each of the answer choices into the Y= equation editor of the calculator and hit the graph key. All of them are lines except answer (E).	Eliminate answer choice (A) because it is rational. In the Y= equation editor, enter abs(x^2-12)-4 into the first line and press the graph key (the absolute value function is found at math-num-abs). With the graph displayed, press 2nd-calc-value. In the X= enter the value of each of the other answer choices. The only one that produces a Y=0 is (C).

5. <u>Draw a picture</u>

Many of the word problems can be solved easily if you read the problem carefully and draw a picture that matches the words in the problem. Sometimes students forget to draw a picture or try to solve the problem in their heads because they think that drawing will use up too much time. Although it may feel like it uses a lot of time, it really does not, and it will reduce the likelihood of making a very silly mistake that you will regret.

EXAMPLE PROBLEM	SOLVE BY DRWING A PICTURE
Sally drives south at the rate of 30 mph and at the same time Willy drives west at the rate of 60 mph. If Sally and Willy started at the same place at the same time, how far apart will they be after two hours? (A) 104 miles (B) 134 miles (C) 180 miles (D) 10,800 miles (E) 18,000 miles	After two hours Sally will have driven 60 miles and Willy will have driven 120 miles, so the picture looks like this: Willy — 120 miles — Start, 60 miles, x miles, Sally It is now easy to see that we are interested in the hypotenuse of the right triangle. $$60^2 + 120^2 = x^2$$ $$18,000 = x^2$$ $$134 = x$$ (B)

Some problems from The Real ACT Prep Guide where drawing a picture will help:

Page 165, problem 6	Page 457, problem 32
A picture isn't really necessary but it helps avoid silly mistakes. The perimeter is 150+200+150+200=700. **(J)**	A picture clarifies the sequence of points in this word problem. We make them equidistant because the problem does not specify distances. With the picture in hand, it is clear that the answer is CD<BC. **(K)**

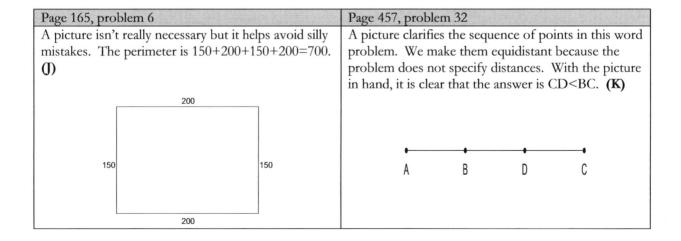

Page 173, problem 37	Page 603, problem 58
A quick sketch makes it easy to see that this is simple Pythagorean Theorem. $10^2 + x^2 = 30^2$, $x = 28.3$. **(C)** 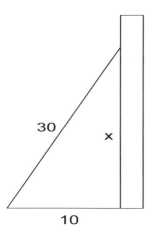	A picture will enable you to get this problem correct, including the signs (which can be tricky), by placing it in the proper quadrant.. From knowing that tangent is opposite over adjacent, we can draw this diagram. From Pythagorean Theorem we find that the hypotenuse is 35. So the sine is opposite over hypotenuse, or 7/35 (K). 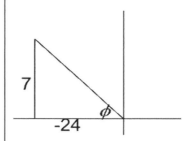
Page 307, problem 16	Page 737, problem 23
A picture not only clarifies this one, it can actually give you the answer. y=4. **(H)** 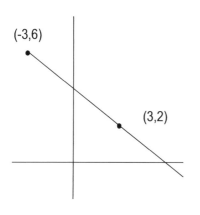	A diagram will help avoid a silly mistake on this very easy problem. With a diagram it is easy to see that angle CBD must equal 180-38=142 degrees. 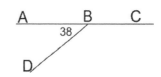

6. Make an Organized List

Some of the problems on the test are called reasoning problems because to solve them you have to weave your way through a maze of possible solutions. This type of problem cannot be solved using math alone, and the solution is a matter of common sense, or reasoning.

The way to approach this type of problem is to make an organized list. Often the list takes the form of a table.

EXAMPLE PROBLEM	SOLVE BY MAKING A LIST
If the sum of two distinct prime numbers is odd, the value of one of them must be: (A) 0 (B) 1 (C) 2 (D) 3 (E) 4	Construct a table of prime number and their sums, then look for a pattern. |	2	3	5	7
---	---	---	---	---
2	----	5	7	9
3	5	----	8	10
5	7	8	----	12
7	9	10	12	----	 Notice the cells of the table which are odd. The only odds appear in the row or column involving 2. The other cells are all even. Therefore the answer is (C). GUESS: This is a great problem for guessing because 0, 1 and 4 are not prime numbers. If you knew this, you could have guessed either (C) or (D).

Some problems from <u>The Real ACT Prep Guide</u> where making an organized list will help:

Page 175, problem 49	Page 314, problem 44
In order to see what is happening, make a list: 	row	dots	cumulative total
---	---	---
1	1	1
2	3	4
3	5	9
4	7	16
5	9	25 | The "trick" is to realize that what is required is the cumulative total, i.e., the number of dots in <u>all</u> of the first n rows. It is easy to see that that number is the square of the rows. (D)	Remember that two is the only even prime number. So we only have to check odd numbers: | n	prime?
31	Yes
33	No, 3
35	No, 5
37	Yes
39	No, 3
41	Yes
43	Yes
45	No, 5
47	Yes
49	No, 7 | There are five prime numbers on the list. (G)

Page 313, problem 40	Page 603, problem 59
This is organized trial and error. Try squares of different numbers to determine the answer.	You can go crazy with all the possible answers, but making a table really helps. There is no point in going beyond 4 for w because 64 is a perfect square and a perfect cube. Only two values of x will do the job (B).

Page 313, problem 40:

n	n^2
31	961
32	1,024
99	9,801
100	10,000

You can see that to obtain a perfect square with four digits, the square root must have two digits. (G)

Page 603, problem 59:

w	z	2^w	x	x^z	
1	4	2	2	$2^4 = 16$	No
2	3	4	4	$4^3 = 64$	Yes
3	2	8	8	$8^2 = 64$	Yes
4	1	16	16	$16^1 = 16$	No

Appendix 4: Practice test tracking sheet

Date	Test	Correct	Wrong	Last Problem Read	Error Rate*	Scaled Score
	Red 1					
	Red 2					
	Red 3					
	Red 4					
	Red 5					

$$*\text{Error Rate} = \frac{\text{number of incorrect problems among problems read}}{\text{number of problems that were read}}$$

Made in the USA
San Bernardino, CA
17 June 2017